HOMES FOR OUR TIME 2

Philip Jodidio

HOMES FOR OUR TIME 2

Contemporary Houses around the World

Zeitgenössische Häuser aus aller Welt

Maisons contemporaines autour du monde

TASCHEN

CONTENTS

CONTENTS

THE WATERS AROUND YOU HAVE GROWN

I walk up to my door and hate to turn the key
Emptiness is all that waits inside for me
That's how it is when the one you love is gone
That's how it is when your house is not a home

The lyrics of Roger Miller's 1970 song "When a house is not a home" capture something essential about the idea of "home." Modernity in architecture and design can be cold and empty, or it can reflect a real sense of connection to place, to the natural world, and, of course, to love. Then too, there is what the architect or the designer can provide in the way of spaces, volumes, and materials, and there is that whole material and immaterial world of the residents who call a place home. It is too long ago to remember when dandy critics made a killing identifying the next trend in architecture, the Post and surely the past. Internet and world-straddling information have not only opened entire areas of the world to knowledge about what happens elsewhere, the reverse is true as well. Long the fiefdom of the European and American movers and shakers of contemporary architecture, the real truth is that invention and change is everywhere, and there is and probably never will be again any dominant style. The point of this volume, which strives to be about homes, is precisely that there are as many ways to design a residence as there are architects. Of course there is newness in the ubiquity of computer-assisted design and construction, but there is also a much deeper and more fundamental awareness of what exists and what can be done to preserve rather than ravage the earth. The private homes featured here range in size (and cost) from the very modest to the extravagant. Clearly an independent structure designed by an architect for a single family is a luxury and an exception no matter what its size, as compared to the living conditions of the vast majority. A beautiful home is a kind of dream, a shelter too from many of the world's problems, much closer to heaven than to the hell of refugees, for example. But we will set aside the obvious to concentrate on these "homes for our time," which may not be for everyone, but they are at least an invitation to dream.

Bonfire of the Vanities

The broadening appeal of architecture, which is to say the increased availability of information all over the world via Internet, may have had some impact on the degree of notoriety of individual architects. In this book, for example, only two of the 61 architects selected are Pritzker Prize winners. Frank O. Gehry is present, and that is more of a reminiscence and an update than a choice for reasons of pure innovation. Gehry's original house in Santa Monica (1978) was in some sense at the very beginning of his career, showing how asphalt surfaces and chain-link fence were potentially elements in a new artistic palette. Today, at more than 95 years of age, Frank Gehry is not a pace setter, but that is natural. Instead, here, he is symbolic in the more general sense of the fading of the uber-architect, of the starchitect if one prefers. The former First Lady of the United States famously wore a jacket with the words "I really don't care, do you?" scrawled on its back. If there is no more dominant style, can there really be dominant architects? Or do we not care so much anymore about their personalities, their foibles, their vestimentary signatures—that Frank Lloyd Wright hat, those Corbu glasses? One architectural office in this volume, Frankie Pappas, has gone so far as to erase individual identities. "Imagine," they say, that "we could create a fictional persona—a collective pseudonym—that allowed us to put aside our egotisms, our blusters, our vanities, and find a group of people whose similar ideals and different talents create beautiful solutions for a remarkable new world." Nor, surely, is it an accident that their House of the Big Arch (Waterberg, South Africa, 2019, see page 232) was built without cutting any existing trees, adapting to the terrain using sophisticated design methods and creating a structure just 3.3 meters wide precisely to preserve the site. There are multiple new attitudes emerging in contemporary architecture—this example, a rejection of "stardom," a concern for the environment, a continually evolving use of technology to achieve today's goals—these are part of the trends that are sweeping the world of architecture.

We will admit that other young architects still dream of the pantheon of the stars, but perhaps that time is just gone. Talent fortunately still exists and hopefully there are numerous new faces in this volume that will age gracefully and in the fullness of creativity—*famoso ma non troppo*. A well-known Brazilian architect (not in this book) once explained to the author that three generations of Brazilian architects had been sacrificed to the glory of Oscar Niemeyer. Niemeyer was still active beyond his 100th birthday. He continued to draw enormous curving lines on a broad white board in his Copacabana offices, lines that became buildings, making concrete "The Curves of Time." And if the cult of genius seems to have lost its luster, perhaps there will be place for more talents to rise, and for new ideas to make their way.

Barclay & Crousse, Casa Huayoccari, Huayoccari, Cusco, Peru, 2016–18.

Previous double page: *Eduardo Cadaval, The Theater, Barcelona, Spain, 2019–20.*

Page 2: *Ensamble Studio, Ca'n Terra, Menorca, Spain, 2018–20.*

Individually Yours

Again, it is clear, these are houses for the privileged, for those who have found a beautiful site on the Pacific coast of Chile or even a tiny precious plot in Setagaya (Tokyo) where they can build the house of their dreams. That is really the point of such a book though—to select what is exceptional, rare, even impossibly beautiful. And houses of course allow for clients and architects with the will, the means, and the imagination to create new forms, to allow the typology of the individual residence to evolve, even in the face of (and sometimes because of) the looming catastrophes wrought by the economy, the climate, and the latest virus. The culture of waste that dominated so much of modern industry, including that of construction, is under increasing pressure to save energy and precious materials. And yet, this powerful constriction arrives precisely when technology, placed at the service of design but also of materials, offers an exploding palette of new possibilities. Identical pieces that had to be manufactured in their thousands in order to reach the necessary economies of scale can now be turned out as individual, unique elements conceived and formed by computer-driven tools. Where beauty is present here, it is quite often that of natural settings, with the architecture frequently playing a role of what the French call the *écrin*, the frame or the jewel box.

Luciano Lerner Basso, Fortunata House, Caxias do Sul, Brazil, 2019–20.

Who Run the World? Girls (girls)

This book contains projects that were selected for their beauty, their innovative approach, their geographical spread, but not because of who did them. If there are only two Pritzker Prize winners, that is because the most famous (and often elderly) architects concentrate on larger buildings. No special effort was made, for example, to seek out female architects, yet in this book, readers will find the work of Sandra Barclay (Barclay & Crousse), Cecilia Rueda and María Díaz (Barozzi Veiga), Lina Bellovičová, Bergendy Cooke, Débora Mesa (Ensamble Studio), Stacey Farrell, Dagmar Stepanova (Formafatal), Michelle McFarlane (McFarlane Biggar), Lisa Bovell (Mcleod Bovell), Jing Liu (SO–IL), Débora Mendes (Tetro), Suzuko Yamada, and Cazú Zegers. Sometimes partnered with men, these architects have made their own mark in an environment that has a long history of placing men in the primary roles. Surely the enduring influence of Zaha Hadid has something to do with this, but the trend has an even broader base. The National Architecture Accrediting Board (NAAB) in the United States reported in 2019 that the gender breakdown of enrolled students was 51% male and 49% female. This makes the future of architecture clear; there has been a substantive and significant shift toward gender balance. Beyoncé sang it in her 2011 hit, "Run the World (Girls)" even if architects were not her main subject of preoccupation...
The same cannot be said for racial equality, but examples such as that of David Adjaye who was born in Dar es Salaam, Tanzania, did weigh in the balance of the future of the profession. His Mole House (London, 2013–18, see page 58) is a remake of a detached Victorian house which was occupied for 40 years by a person known as the Hackney Mole Man. In this unusual setting, the architect, and the client, the artist Sue Webber, decided to retain as much of the original character of the house as possible, using reclaimed London bricks where new elements were needed. Examples of well-known architects who continue to design private houses are fairly numerous—the case of Tadao Ando comes to mind—but Adjaye's investment of time and energy in a relatively small project is of interest. Modernism was all about sweeping away the old and building the shining new city of grids. Redoing existing structures, rebuilding them, and updating has become an increasingly important part of contemporary house (and other) design. This is, of course, another excellent way to reduce the waste of resources, and sources of pollution related to entirely new construction.
Again, the geographical spread of houses published here is also a measure of the very profound changes in architecture that are underway. China, Vietnam, Sri Lanka, South Africa, India, and other locations not often present in past broad-subject books about architecture are represented here; again, not because the author was looking for a touch of exoticism. These places are the new mainstream, the hope of architecture. The significance of these changes cannot be overestimated, there is a revolution underway, as is, of course, the case in other areas because of the ubiquity of Internet and computer-driven design and construction technology.
Nor are women and architects from different horizons satisfied to play secondary roles or to continue to simply imitate the models established in London or Los Angeles. The Daita2019 residence by Suzuko Yamada (Tokyo, 2019, see page 444) might be an example of this trend. Not yet 40 years old, Yamada wanted to create a new kind of living space for families. She says: "I wondered if it would be possible to create a house where bare life is softly enveloped by layers of wire and objects that create a variety of depths, and where the sunlight and the gazes of people passing by on the street are kept at a distance."
Residential design has long begun to eschew the strict typological formats of the past where a house always had a separate living room, dining room, and kitchen. Open spaces, and variable functions, have been gaining ground in residential architecture for many years. *The Un-Private*

House, an exhibition held in 1999 at New York's Museum of Modern Art, already called attention to a new generation of homes: "There have been fundamental changes in all of the aspects that constitute the private house," said the exhibition curator, Terry Riley. "Changes in the family, changes in the relationship between the house and work. For several centuries, the way one defined the private house was by the absence of work. There have been changes in the notion of domesticity. Changes in the notion of privacy itself."

Guillermo Acuña Arquitectos Asociados (GAAA), Isla Lebe, Rilan, Chiloé, Chile, 2016–20.

Gorillas in the Mist

Yamada has taken this evolving vision of domesticity even further. In her Daita2019 house, there are timbers, "steel, single-pipe posts and beams, and braces; there are also stair risers and handrails, window sash frames, furniture, curtains, books, clothes, and other miscellaneous items, potted trees and plants, bicycles, shovels, and a vast amount of books, videotapes, and DVDs." Somehow, she built without placing walls between the garden and the interiors, creating a structure that appears to fly in the face of any sense of architectural beauty, while still obtaining what so often lacks in contemporary buildings—the very essence of daily life. Yamada's ideas generate a home that looks as though it is surrounded by temporary scaffolding, perhaps sublimating the idea of *mono no aware*—the Japanese awareness of impermanence, and the transience of things—but also privileging a kind of personal or family comfort expressed beyond the canons of contemporary architecture. Yamada worked in the office Sou Fujimoto (2007–11) before creating her own firm. When asked in 2018 if he consciously sought to bring nature into his architecture, Fujimoto replied: "Yes, not just nature, but creating spaces where people can feel as if they're in a forest or can feel the openness to the sky. I'm always looking to strike a balance between nature and architecture, including the more metaphysical, and deeper meanings." It is interesting that Yamada references her own experience with gorillas in the forest of Rwanda to explain the design of Daita2019, but her very urban design goes even further along the path of seeking deeper meanings for the presence of nature, in the openness and ultimate flexibility of her design.

Another unexpected architect who has designed a house published here is Palinda Kannangara from Sri Lanka. His Frame Holiday Structure (Imaduwa, Sri Lanka, 2018, see page 286) was built with steel scaffolding, exposed brick, and timber floors for a budget of $40 000. Because the site was prone to frequent flooding and also because of budgetary constraints, Kannangara found that scaffolding offered an ideal solution, also because the structure can be easily dismounted and moved if necessary. Local climate allows the building to have few walls, and those were made with lightweight impermeable SuperFlex. Even furnishings were made with leftover site materials and other reclaimed elements.

Goodbye Dandies,
Hello the Rest of the World

At a certain point in time, for example after World War II, there was a very broadly based international effort to build rapidly and cheaply, to create the housing and other architecture required to get nations moving again. The grid-patterns of Modernism were well suited to fast design and construction. And yet, what was at its worst a cookie-cutter style was eventually rejected in favor of a kind of nostalgia dubbed Postmodernism for want of a better name. Much industrial Modernism generated a sameness or boredom that the Postmodern crew, cheered on by the likes of Charles Jencks, sought to paper over with superficial "traditional" forms. Inside, Postmodern buildings were pretty much like their more avowedly geometric forebears. Beneath those surface ornaments there was surely a longing for the longevity, nay the permanence, of the architecture of the past. Let us seek to make architecture the only real lasting artform, where

Baumraum, Green Dwelling, near Hannover, Germany, 2018–19.

appearance shimmers as brightly as the Emerald City. So where does the scaffolding of Yamada and Kannangara come in? In an architecture that is no longer dominated by Western ideals, but which lives and breathes in its time. Yamada does (even if unconsciously) call on the deeper Japanese sense of time and impermanence while still focusing on the here-and-now. Kannangara puts his talent as an architect to use in fashioning something that is both cheap and practical, fundamentally adapted to its location and its circumstances and not seeking to resuscitate some shining ideal. Neither of these homes indulges in the kind of voracious consumption of materials and expense that other projects in this book (which shall remain unnamed) accept. And yet the reader should rest assured, even the largest homes today, with few exceptions, are becoming ecologically aware. Floods and tornadoes have a way of being very convincing influencers.

The times, they are a-changin'

So, do we really care what the latest style is? I don't, do you? Instead, may we look within and beyond to see how responsible architect and client have been, saving trees, reducing energy consumption, making the most of what they have instead of pretending that there is more than there is. One residence in this book, the Loom House (Miller Hull, Bainbridge Island, Washington, 2019, see page 346) has been described as "the most ecologically ambitious home renovation on the planet," calling on salvaged materials and strictly controlled energy usage at all levels of the project. And yet the stone and wood beauty of this house, imparted too by its view on the waters near Seattle would make no owner feel that they had sacrificed architectural quality to achieve ecological sainthood. Architect and client did what they felt was becoming necessary, not because it is fashionable, but because, as Bob Dylan sang it in 1964:

Come gather 'round people
Wherever you roam
And admit that the waters
Around you have grown
And accept it that soon
You'll be drenched to the bone
If your time to you is worth savin'
Then you better start swimmin' or
you'll sink like a stone
For the times they are a-changin'

In a sense, houses deal with all levels of architecture, from that of responsibility and inventiveness to that of simple practicality. What does your house do to the world, how innovative is it, what can you do with your house, and what can't you do? Clearly clients and architects often have divergent goals; the best houses emerge when these forces converge rather than part ways. Much of the effort that goes into creating a carbon-neutral structure is purely invisible, for example. A bit of platinum and gold (LEED) goes a long way for the reputation of some architects but perhaps not as far for the owners of the house. It comes down for them to a case of conscience, save something for the future, or burn it all now. Sadly, the latter attitude has long prevailed and still raises its ugly head far too often. The difference unfortunately is now being made by unprecedented levels of natural catastrophe. What happens to LaLa Land when the water runs out and the whole thing slides into the sea? A bit exaggerated for the moment, but you get the idea. Act, and act now, this is becoming the mantra of many, and this awareness is having a huge influence on houses and their future design.

Stonehenge by the Sea

The dynamics of architecture are surely as complex as those of the underlying societies that produce remarkable homes, or less attractive ones. The (hopefully) impartial selection that went into this book certainly shows that Latin America produces some of the most stunning contemporary houses. Guillermo Acuña's Isla Lebe house, for example (Bilan, 2020, see page 50), makes use

McFarlane Biggar, Bowen Island House, Bowen Island, British Columbia, Canada, 2016–19.

of existing wooden structures in southern Chile, painting them red like the local chilco *(Fuchsia magellanica)*. One might think that a 315-square-meter house on what is nearly a private island just off the coast of Chile would cost a fortune and impinge on its natural surroundings. Here, that is not the case. Casa Huayoccari (Huayoccari, Cusco, Peru, 2018, see page 80) built by Barclay & Crousse at an altitude of nearly 3000 meters above sea level takes a harder, clearly more mountainous approach, blending into the setting with purposely angled openings and a concrete mass that preserves heat in the cool nights.
Luciano Lerner Basso's Fortunata House (Caxias do Sul, Brazil, 2020, see page 96) was built around a tree from an endangered species and sits on *pilotis* perched above the forest floor. Efficient cross ventilation, reuse of rainwater, natural lighting, and an ecological heating system are part of this scheme which makes use of reinforced concrete because of its low maintenance requirements. The images of this house show how well a modern structure can fit into a sloped, forest environment. The way in which it is built around a Brazilian pine *(Araucaria angustifolia)* also gives an indication of just how far and how fast concern for nature has traveled across the world of contemporary architecture.
The House for a Ceramist (The Guanacastes, (Orotina, Costa Rica, 2019, see page 152) by Victor Cañas, who was born in 1947, demonstrates that (slightly) older architects have also come into the fold where protection of the environment is concerned. The precise location of the residence and its design were determined in good part by the presence of mature Guancaste *(Enterolobium cyclocarpum)* trees. The house had to be lifted 80 centimeters off the ground to protect the roots of the trees. Cross ventilation and photovoltaic panels are also part of a largely passive energy strategy.
The Ochoquebradas House (Los Vilos, Chile, 2018, see page 192) was designed by Alejandro Aravena's group ELEMENTAL as part of a larger scheme that includes houses imagined by eight architects from Japan, Kengo Kuma and Sou Fujimoto, and eight from Chile, including Felipe Assadi, Guillermo Acuña, and Aravena. The ELEMENTAL scheme evokes powerful and one might say even archaic forces, dubbed "a certain primitiveness" by the architects. The $500 000 house is made up of three volumes: a horizontal one containing the basics for a couple, that slightly cantilevers over the cliff; a vertical block containing the other spaces requested by the organizer of the project, as well as a rooftop terrace; and between these two blocks "a slightly leaning and hollowed one containing a fire; not a chimney (which is already something civilized), but a fire (which is one of the most revolutionary yet oldest achievements of man)." The look here is decidedly elemental (as it were). ELEMENTAL states: "We chose to move backward toward the archaic, not as a nostalgic escape but as a natural filter against the clichés. In an era where the hunger for novelty is threatening architecture to become immediately obsolete, we looked for timelessness." A seashore kind of Stonehenge for the modern age it would seem.
The comments of ELEMENTAL also make clear that not every region, nor every architect is confronted with the same levels of awareness or evolution vis-à-vis the challenges of the dynamics of the contemporary world. Citing the danger that architecture might become "immediately obsolete," ELEMENTAL seeks the authenticity of the truly ancient, an interesting play on today's situation. But then it must be recognized that the houses in this volume and the architects who conceived them represent just a tiny fraction of what is and can be built in the world. Inventiveness and timeliness are the preserve of the very few, those who surely will influence what is to come. Alejandro Aravena is the second Pritzker Prize winner in this book—influential not only because of his close and frequent work with the Pritzker Jury, but very clearly for his work on trying to bring contemporary housing solutions to the disfavored. The Pritzker Jury

Above and page 19: *Elemental, Ochoquebradas House, Los Vilos, Chile, 2017–18.*

citation stated: "What really sets Aravena apart is his commitment to social housing. Since 2000 and the founding of ELEMENTAL, he and his collaborators have consistently realized works with clear social goals... they have built more than 2500 units using imaginative, flexible and direct architectural solutions for low-cost social housing."

A Debt to Reality, to Poverty, and Need

So here is another element of the equation—private houses are by no means the cutting edge of architectural engagement with the real world. They do remain a place of experimentation and invention, in part because of the often close relationship between architect and client, but also because a smaller scale implies a lower degree of risk. ELEMENTAL may have designed a surprising private house on the coast in an "archaic" mode, but they are also clearly involved in the task of making architecture more relevant to the modern world. Artists may invent the world to come, but the very real and concrete domain of architecture would seem to have some debt to reality, to poverty, and need. Architects such as Shigeru Ban (another Pritzker winner) have invested great energy and effort into causes such as emergency disaster housing even as they build private houses, but many of their colleagues remain focused on earnings and notoriety, more easily gained with a spectacular house for two than in a field of ruins. The concept of the social responsibility of contemporary architecture might well have flagged even as conceptual ideals such as "progress" in any cultural field waned. Obviously the industrial and repetitive image of Modernism came in good part with its renewed influence in America even as the world emerged from war and destruction. Like the ideals of the early Russian Constructivists, who hoped to fashion a new world for the many with technical functionality, Gropius and the Bauhaus also had a social conscience. Saying that modern architects "sold out" might be a bit too harsh, but clearly Gropius, Mies, and the others laid the seeds of aesthetically and financially driven paradigms that dominated first America and then much of the developed world after World War II. No, almost without exception the houses in this volume were not designed to better the lot of the many, but instead to please clients, but also to become progressively more responsible considering the planetary crises. What used to be an option for the ecologically minded minority has moved front and center. If legislation does not impose stricter standards, then common sense will.

The Sixth-Largest Continent (Europe)

The emergence of architects from "new" parts of the world has, of course, not specifically reduced the production of American, European, or Japanese architects. Rather, they may be getting less publicity because of the discovery of new faces and forms, not a bad thing really. Two new houses in Germany show the ideas and challenges that face the design and construction of individual houses. Andreas Wenning, who studied first as a cabinetmaker and then became an architect, has long made a specialty of designing tree houses. His expertise in that area led one client in Hanover to ask him to create not only a small tree house, but also an entire new residence (the Green Dwelling, near Hanover, Germany, 2019, see page 104). A major concern for the clients was the ecological quality of the construction and the building services. "The desire to use wood as an essential building material in this respect," says Wenning, "was very much to our liking." The tree houses of Wenning and his company baumraum are not only made of wood, but clearly the architect has a broad knowledge of its use as a building material. Building in trees without harming them is obviously an intimate approach to the natural world that much contemporary architecture has eschewed. Aside from the ubiquitous use of wood for this house, the architect also created an extensive green roof and used gas-condensing boilers, underfloor heating

and controlled ventilation as part of an overall green scheme.
A second German scheme is the home of the architect Carlos Zwick (House by the Lake, Potsdam, 2020, see page 464). Local regulations required that any new construction should be set 50 meters back from the shore of Lake Jungfern. Zwick took this rule as a basis for a careful scheme that damaged no existing trees on the site and required construction without a tower crane. Lifting the house off the ground on steel supports he managed to satisfy municipal authorities at the same time as he preserved the site. In an interesting reference, Zwick says that his inspiration for the House by the Lake is the Farnsworth House by Mies van der Rohe (Plano, Illinois, USA, 1951). Farnsworth is a one-room weekend retreat with an area of 206 square meters. It is lifted 1.6 meters above the site, which is prone to flooding. Its white color and slight elevation above the ground, together with full-height glazing, give the impression of an ethereal, perhaps temporary presence in the landscape. The House by the Lake, on the other hand, has a substantial usable floor area of 610 square meters. Floating twice as high above the ground (three meters) as its Miesian counterpart, the residence of Zwick is clad in narrow vertical strips of larch, instead of the expressed steel slabs that define the roof and floor of Farnsworth. The 40 diagonal posts that support the house are surely more present than the *pilotis* of Mies, and this structure has two connected rectangular elements as opposed to the four-sided orthodoxy of the older master. The net result might be seen as a contemporary version of Modernism, replacing white steel with graying wood, lifting the house up even higher (in part for administrative reasons) and still keeping the strict rectilinear language of the influential (originally German) school.

An Ode to Adaptive Reuse
The case of Adjaye's Mole House has already been cited, but it is far from being the only contemporary example of a house made over on the basis of an older residence. The London architects Carmody Groarke repurposed a Victorian-era brick warehouse for their House and Studio (Lambeth, London, 2018, see page 158). Brick façades remain the rule, but the interiors of the house are in concrete from floor to ceiling and the interior design would please even the most minimalist architecture fan. In a sense this design does practice a kind of interior *tabula rasa*, while maintaining an exterior presence that is in keeping with its neighborhood.
Another London-based architect went even further in the preservation of what seemed like a complete ruin. Working with a Grade 2-listed Victorian house and the remains of a 17th-century parchment factory, which is a scheduled monument, Will Gamble fashioned The Parchment Works (Northamptonshire, UK, 2018, see page 238). Rather than seeking to demolish the ruin, Gamble inserted two new elements in Corten steel, reclaimed brick, and oak. An existing cattle shed had its structural beams and stone walls exposed and a concrete plinth added to become another element of the composition. Built for a cost of 295 000 euros, the 200-square-meter residence, whose design was approved by Historic England, has been hailed as one of the most innovative contemporary houses in England.
Art has long glorified ruins, real and imagined, such as those seen in the paintings of Claude Lorrain (1600–82), or the prints of Piranesi (1720–78). Some artists went so far as to imagine future ruins, as was the case in Hubert Robert's *Imaginary View of the Grande Galerie in the Louvre in Ruins* (1796, Louvre Museum). All of these artistic versions of ruins seem to have in common a sense of nostalgia for the grandeur of the past, even if it came to imagining the present in ruins. The adaptive reuse of architecture has an even longer and richer history that can be traced back at least to the Romans. Temples suddenly became churches beginning with the rule of Theodosius in AD 379. The Pantheon became a Christian church dedicated to Santa Maria ad Martyres in AD 609. Closer to our time, the environmental impact of adaptive reuse has been carefully studied; from landfills overflowing with construction waste to the manufacture of new buildings, architecture in its various (new) forms is a voracious consumer of increasingly rare materials, and a major source of pollution. In a 2015 paper, Dr. Stephen Muench of the University of Washington wrote: "One individual reuse project cannot make a huge impact on carbon emissions, but when it is scaled to a whole city or country the impacts are huge. In Portland, for example, if the buildings that would be demolished and rebuilt were, instead, reused over the next ten years there would be a reduction of 231 000 metric tons of carbon dioxide emitted

5% of the country's total carbon dioxide reduction target over the next decade." This digression shows that finding contemporary houses that are built in ruins or that reuse existing structures is yet another sign of the times. It is a safe bet that there will be more cases like this and all over *the world.
The variety of houses in this book can only validate the words of the song that start this text. Often beautiful, they can be homes only if they are inhabited by love, so these are (hopefully) Homes for Our Time.

You say you want a revolution
The Beatles song continues with the lyrics:
You say you got a real solution
Well, you know
We'd all love to see the plan

And what if there is no plan, but it's still a revolution? There has long been discussion about the benefits of "green" architecture, just as issues such as gender or racial equality have been mulled over for years. So now, it's time. The world is experiencing millennial storms every year, the glaciers are melting, there is a mass extinction like no other before that is underway. Yes, of course, the houses in this book seems very attractive and calm. So perhaps the revolution is happening elsewhere, deeper into designs that take into account at least some of the factors that have made architecture the perennial poster boy of ecological irresponsibility. And if women at last can enroll in their numbers in schools of architecture around the world, that revolution too is happening without an announced plan handed down from some higher authority. Racial equality is slower to advance perhaps, but the signs of change are overwhelming. And if the rest of the world is suddenly "visible" thanks to Internet, if information circulates more freely, that too is a revolution that did not follow a preordained scheme. The world of technology makes everything from design to manufacturing more readily accessible in uniquely formed (bespoke!) materials and construction elements. And instead of costing more and being limited to the happy few, this technology actually costs less and makes unique buildings just as easy to realize as cookie-cutter grids. The ultimate diktat, that of the straight line, is also slowly melting into history,

on economies of scale. But this will surely never mean that an architect cannot make a square or rectangular building; most of the houses in this book are a take on that paradigm: it means only (and here is the revolution) that choice exists. The revolution in contemporary architecture, most quickly and fully expressed in private houses, is an epochal event, not because any theoretician (or worse an architecture critic) ever formulated its ideas. Instead, it is the combined force of climate, history, and technology that is bending the forms and methods of architecture. Climate (change) is the undeniable, ultimate force that is already making its exigencies known.

And admit that the waters
Around you have grown
And accept it that soon
You'll be drenched to the bone

History is expressed in the realization that a small number of elderly white men cannot hold on to power forever, and through the evolving economies and cultures of so many countries across the world. Women are (at last) present and despite the Taliban, there is no looking back. Technology is the unheralded enabler of massive change. In his 2004 book of the same name, Bruce Mau wrote: "Massive Change is not about the world of design, it's about the design of the world." The revolution is not imminent, it is immanent, and it is here.

ELEMENTAL, Ochoquebradas House, Los Vilos,

DAS WASSER UM EUCH IST GESTIEGEN

"I walk up to my door and hate to turn the key Emptiness is all that waits inside for me That's how it is when the one you love is gone That's how it is when your house is not a home"

(Ich gehe auf meine Tür zu und hasse es,
den Schlüssel umzudrehen
Leere ist alles, was mich im Inneren erwartet
So ist es, wenn die Liebste fort ist
So ist es, wenn dein Haus kein Zuhause ist)

Der Text von Roger Millers Song „When a house is not a home" (1970) verrät etwas Grundlegendes über das Wesen eines „Zuhauses". Modernität in Architektur und Design kann kalt und leer sein, sie kann aber auch ein echtes Gefühl der Verbundenheit mit einem Ort, mit der Natur und natürlich mit der Liebe widerspiegeln. Es gibt das, was der Architekt oder Designer in Form von Raum, Volumen und Materialien zur Verfügung stellen kann, und dann gibt es noch die ganze materielle und immaterielle Welt der Bewohner, die einen Ort ihr Zuhause nennen. Zu lange ist es her, um sich jener dandyhaften Kritiker zu erinnern, die sich einst eine goldene Nase damit verdienten, die nächsten Architekturtrends zu bestimmen, die kommenden sowie zweifellos auch die vergangenen. Das Internet und die weltumspannenden Informationen eröffneten nicht nur ganzen Weltregionen das Wissen über das, was anderswo geschieht – auch das Gegenteil ist der Fall. Lange Zeit eine Domäne europäischer und amerikanischer Macher der zeitgenössischen Architektur, ist es in Wirklichkeit so: Erfindungen und Veränderungen finden überall statt, ein vorherrschender Stil existiert nicht mehr, und aller Voraussicht nach wird es einen solchen auch nie wieder geben. Die Pointe dieses Bandes, der sich dem Zuhause verschrieben hat, besteht gerade darin, dass es so viele Möglichkeiten gibt, ein Haus zu gestalten, wie es Architekten gibt. Natürlich ist die Allgegenwart von computergestütztem Design und Bau etwas Neues, aber es gibt auch ein viel tieferes und grundlegenderes Bewusstsein für das, was existiert und was getan werden kann, um die Erde zu bewahren, anstatt sie zu verwüsten. Die hier vorgestellten Privathäuser reichen in ihrer Größe (und ihren Kosten) von sehr bescheiden bis hin zu extravagant. Ein von einem Architekten entworfenes Gebäude für eine einzelne Familie ist natürlich ein Luxus und eine Ausnahme, unabhängig von seiner Größe, verglichen mit den Lebensbedingungen der großen Mehrheit. Ein schönes Haus ist eine Art Traum, auch ein Schutz vor vielen Problemen der Welt, viel näher am Himmel als zum Beispiel an der Hölle, die Flüchtlinge täglich erleben. Aber wir wollen das Offensichtliche beiseitelassen und uns auf diese „Häuser für unsere Zeit" konzentrieren, die vielleicht nicht jedermanns Sache sind, aber zumindest zum Träumen einladen.

Lagerfeuer der Eitelkeiten

Die wachsende Attraktivität der Architektur, d. h. die zunehmende weltweite Verfügbarkeit von Informationen mittels des Internets, mag sich auf den Bekanntheitsgrad einzelner Architekten ausgewirkt haben. In diesem Buch sind nur zwei der 61 ausgewählten Architekten Pritzker-Preisträger. Frank O. Gehry ist einer von ihnen, und das eher als Reminiszenz und Update als aus Gründen reiner Innovation. Gehrys Haus in Santa Monica in seiner ursprünglichen Gestalt von 1978 stand in gewisser Weise am Anfang seiner Karriere und bewies, dass Asphaltflächen und Maschendrahtzaun potenzielle Elemente einer neuen künstlerischen Palette sind. Heute ist Frank Gehry kein Trendsetter mehr, aber das ist im Alter von mehr als 95 Jahren nur natürlich und verständlich. Stattdessen steht er hier symbolisch im allgemeineren Sinne für das Verblassen des Über-Architekten, des Starchitekten, wenn man so will. Die ehemalige First Lady der Vereinigten Staaten trug bekanntlich eine Jacke mit den auf den Rücken gekritzelten Worten „I really don't care, do you?" (Ist mir echt egal, und dir?). Wenn es keinen dominanten Stil mehr gibt, kann es dann überhaupt noch dominante Architekten geben? Oder sind uns ihre Persönlichkeiten, ihre Marotten, ihre Markenzeichen – der Frank-Lloyd-Wright-Hut, die Corbu-Brille – mehr oder weniger egal? Ein Architekturbüro, das in diesem Band vorgestellt wird, Frankie Pappas, ging sogar so weit, individuelle Identitäten auszulöschen. „Stellen Sie sich vor", sagen sie, „wir könnten eine fiktive Persona erschaffen – ein kollektives Pseudonym –, das uns erlaubt, unsere Egoismen, unser ganzes Getöse und unsere Eitelkeiten beiseitezulassen und eine Gruppe von Menschen zu finden, deren vergleichbare Ideale und unterschiedliche Talente wunderbare Lösungen für eine bemerkenswerte neue Welt schaffen würden." Sicherlich ist es auch kein Zufall, dass ihr House of the Big Arch (Waterberg, Südafrika, 2019, siehe Seite 232) gebaut wurde, ohne dass Bäume gefällt werden mussten. Sie passten sich dem Gelände mit ausgeklügelten Designmethoden an und schufen ein Gebäude von nur 3,3 Meter Breite, um den Standort in seiner bestehenden Form zu erhalten. In der zeitgenössischen Architektur zeichnen sich zahlreiche neue Haltungen ab: die Ablehnung von „Starallüren", die Sorge um die Umwelt, der sich ständig weiterentwickelnde Einsatz von Technologien zur Erreichung der heutigen

Frank O. Gehry, Santa Monica House, Santa Monica, California, USA, 2014–17.

Ziele – all dies gehört zu den Trends, welche die Welt der Architektur erobern. Zugegeben, manch junge Architekten träumen immer noch vom Pantheon der Stars, aber vielleicht ist diese Zeit einfach vorbei. Zum Glück gibt es noch Talente, und hoffentlich finden sich in diesem Band zahlreiche neue Gesichter, die in Würde und begleitet von blühender Kreativität altern werden – *famoso ma non troppo.* Ein bekannter brasilianischer Architekt (nicht in diesem Buch vertreten) erklärte dem Autor einst, dass drei Generationen brasilianischer Architekten dem Ruhm Oscar Niemeyers geopfert worden seien. Auch nach seinem 100. Geburtstag war Oscar Niemeyer immer noch aktiv. In seinem Büro an der Copacabana zeichnete er weiterhin riesige geschwungene Linien auf ein breites Whiteboard, Linien, die zu Gebäuden wurden und die „Kurven der Zeit" Wirklichkeit werden ließen. Und sollte der Geniekult seinen Glanz verloren haben, bietet sich vielleicht Raum für weitere Talente und neue Ideen, die sich ihren Weg bahnen.

Ganz eigen – Ihr Eigen

Nochmals sei betont, dass es sich hier um Häuser für Privilegierte handelt, für jene, die ein wunderschönes Grundstück an der Pazifikküste Chiles oder sogar ein winziges, kostbares Grundstück in Setagaya (Tokio) gefunden haben, auf dem sie das Haus ihrer Träume bauen können. Aber das ist ja gerade der Sinn eines solchen Buches: das Außergewöhnliche, das Seltene, ja das unmöglich Schöne auszuwählen. Und natürlich bieten Häuser ihren Bauherren und Architekten die Möglichkeit, mit Willen, Mitteln und Vorstellungskraft neue Formen zu schaffen, die Typologie

Suzuko Yamada, Daita2019, Tokyo, Japan, 2018–19.

des individuellen Wohnens weiterzuentwickeln, sogar angesichts (und manchmal gerade wegen) der Katastrophen, die uns durch die Wirtschaft, das Klima und das neueste Virus bedrohen. Die Kultur der Verschwendung, die so viele Bereiche der modernen Industrie, einschließlich des Bauwesens, beherrscht, steht zunehmend unter dem Druck, Energie und wertvolle Materialien zu sparen. Doch diese starke Einschränkung tritt genau dann ein, wenn die Technologie im Dienste des Designs, aber auch der Materialien auf eine rasch wachsende Palette neuer Möglichkeiten zurückgreifen kann. Identische Bauteile, die früher zu Tausenden hergestellt werden mussten, um die erforderlichen wirtschaftlichen Mengenvorteile zu erzielen, können heute als individuelle, einzigartige Elemente hergestellt werden, von computergesteuerten Werkzeugen konzipiert und geformt. Wo sich hier Schönheit zeigt, ist es oft die umgebende Landschaft, die sich ihrer rühmen kann, und die Architektur spielt dann häufig die Rolle dessen, was die Franzosen *écrin* – das Schmuckkästchen – nennen.

Who Run the World? Girls (girls)

Dieser Bildband enthält Projekte, die aufgrund ihrer Schönheit, ihres innovativen Ansatzes und ihrer Repräsentation geografischer Vielfalt ausgewählt wurden, nicht aber aufgrund der Person, die sie erschuf. Die Tatsache, dass nur zwei Pritzker-Preisträger vertreten sind, gründet darin, dass sich die berühmtesten Architekten (meist fortgeschrittenen Alters) auf größere Gebäude konzentrieren. Zwar wurden keine besonderen Anstrengungen unternommen, um beispielsweise Architekt*innen* zu finden, doch lernt der Leser in diesem Buch die Arbeiten von Sandra Barclay (Barclay & Crousse), Cecilia Rueda und María Díaz (Barozzi Veiga) kennen sowie von Lina Bellovičová, Bergendy Cooke, Débora Mesa (Ensamble Studio), Stacey Farrell, Dagmar Stepanova (Formafatal), Michelle McFarlane (McFarlane Biggar), Lisa Bovell (Mcleod Bovell), Jing Liu (SO – IL), Débora Mendes (Tetro), Suzuko Yamada und Cazú Zegers. Sie alle arbeiten zuweilen mit Männern zusammen, haben sich aber in einem lange Zeit von Männern dominierten Umfeld einen eigenen Namen gemacht. Sicherlich hat der anhaltende Einfluss von Zaha Hadid etwas damit zu tun, aber der Trend stützt sich auf eine noch breitere Basis. Das National Architecture Accrediting Board (NAAB) in den USA meldete 2019 eine Geschlechterverteilung der eingeschriebenen Studenten von 51 (männlich) zu 49 Prozent (weiblich). Damit ist die Zukunft der Architektur klar. Eine wesentliche und signifikante Verschiebung in Richtung Geschlechtergleichgewicht hat stattgefunden. Beyoncé erkannte dies 2011 in ihrem Hit „Run the World (Girls)“ – auch wenn es sicherlich keine Architekten waren, die sie zu diesem Thema inspiriert hatten ...

Ähnliches lässt sich nicht über die Gleichstellung ethnischer Herkünfte sagen, aber Beispiele wie jenes von David Adjaye aus Daressalam, Tansania, waren für die Zukunft des Berufsstandes von Bedeutung. Sein Mole House (London, 2013–18, siehe Seite 58) ist ein Nachbau eines freistehenden viktorianischen Hauses, das 40 Jahre lang vom sog. Hackney Mole Man bewohnt wurde. In der ungewöhnlichen Umgebung entschieden sich Architekt und Bauherrin, die Künstlerin Sue Webber, für die weitestgehende Erhaltung des ursprünglichen Charakters des Hauses und setzten dort, wo neue Elemente benötigt wurden, wiederverwendete Londoner Ziegel ein. Beispiele bekannter Architekten, die auch weiterhin Privathäuser entwerfen, gibt es viele – denken wir nur an Tadao Ando –, aber die Intensität, mit der Adjaye Zeit und Energie in ein relativ kleines Projekt investierte, weckt Interesse. In der Moderne ging es darum, das Alte hinwegzufegen und eine strahlend neue Stadt nach Rastern zu bauen. Die Umgestaltung bestehender Strukturen, ihr Wiederaufbau und ihre Aktualisierung sind zu einem immer wichtigeren Bestandteil des zeitgenössischen Designs von (unter anderem) Wohnhäusern geworden. Dies ist natürlich ein weiterer großartiger Weg, Ressourcenverschwendung und Umweltverschmutzung durch einen kompletten Neubau zu reduzieren. Auch die geografische Verteilung der hier vorgestellten Häuser ist ein Indikator für die derzeitigen tiefgreifenden Veränderungen in der Architektur. Sie finden in diesem Buch China, Vietnam, Sri Lanka, Südafrika, Indien und andere Orte vertreten, die in früheren Architekturbüchern nur selten auftauchten – allerdings nicht, weil der Autor einen Hauch von Exotik anstrebte. Vielmehr stellen diese Orte den neuen Mainstream dar, die Hoffnung der Architektur. Die Bedeutung dieser Veränderungen kann gar nicht hoch genug eingeschätzt werden, es ist eine Revolution im Gange, wie sie natürlich auch in anderen Bereichen aufgrund der Allgegenwart des Internets und der computergesteuerten Design- und Bautechnologie stattfindet. Auch geben sich Frauen und Architekten verschiedenster Herkunft nicht damit zufrieden, eine Nebenrolle zu spielen oder einfach die in London oder Los Angeles etablierten Modelle zu imitieren. Das Daita2019-Wohnhaus von Suzuko Yamada (Tokio, 2019, siehe Seite 444) steht beispielhaft für diesen Trend. Noch keine 40 Jahre alt wollte Yamada eine neue Art von Lebensraum für Familien schaffen. „Ich fragte mich, ob es möglich wäre, ein Haus zu schaffen, in dem das unverhüllte Leben sanft von Schichten aus Draht und Objekten ummantelt wird, die eine Vielzahl von Tiefen schaffen, und in dem das Sonnenlicht und die Blicke der Menschen, die auf der Straße vorübergehen, auf Abstand gehalten werden", erklärt Yamada. Wohndesign hat längst begonnen, sich von jenen strengen typologischen Formaten der Vergangenheit zu lösen, die für ein Haus stets ein separates Wohnzimmer, ein Esszimmer und eine Küche vorsahen. Offene Räume und variable Funktionen befinden sich in der Wohnarchitektur seit vielen Jahren auf dem Vormarsch. Die Ausstellung *The Un-Private House* (1999) des New Yorker Museum of Modern Art verwies bereits auf eine neue Generation von Wohnhäusern: „Sämtliche Aspekte, die das Privathaus ausmachen, unterlagen grundlegenden Veränderungen", stellt der Kurator der Ausstellung, Terry Riley, fest. „Veränderungen des Familienbildes, Veränderungen in der Beziehung zwischen dem Haus und der Arbeit. Mehrere Jahrhunderte lang definierten wir das Privathaus durch die Abwesenheit von Arbeit. Die Vorstellung von Häuslichkeit ist nun eine andere. Der Begriff des Privaten selbst hat sich verändert."

Palinda Kannangara, Frame Holiday Structure, Imaduwa, Sri Lanka, 2018.

Gorillas im Nebel

Yamada hat diese sich entwickelnde Vision von Häuslichkeit noch weitergedacht und umgesetzt. Ihr Haus Daita2019 vereint Holz, „Stahl, Einrohrpfosten, Balken und Verstrebungen. Es gibt auch Treppenstufen und Handläufe, Fensterrahmen, Möbel, Vorhänge, Bücher, Kleidung und diverse andere Gegenstände, Topfbäume und -pflanzen, Fahrräder, Schaufeln und eine Unmenge an Büchern, Videokassetten und DVDs." Irgendwie schaffte sie es, auf Wände zwischen Garten und Innenräumen zu verzichten, und errichtete so eine Struktur, die jedem Sinn für architektonische Schönheit zu widersprechen scheint und dennoch das umfasst, was zeitgenössischen Gebäuden so oft fehlt – die Essenz des Alltags. Yamadas Ideen lassen ein Haus entstehen, das wirkt, als sei es von einem provisorischen Gerüst umgeben, und so vielleicht die Idee des *mono no aware* – des japanischen Bewusstseins von Unbeständigkeit und Vergänglichkeit der Dinge – sublimiert. Sie privilegiert aber auch eine Art persönlichen oder familiären Komforts, der jenseits des Kanons der zeitgenössischen Architektur zum Ausdruck kommt. Yamada arbeitete für das Architekturbüro Sou Fujimoto (2007–11), bevor sie ihr eigenes Büro gründete. Auf die Frage im Jahr 2018, ob er bewusst versuche, Natur in seine Architektur einfließen zu lassen, antwortete Fujimoto: „Ja, nicht nur die Natur, sondern ich versuche auch, Räume zu schaffen, in denen die Menschen das Gefühl haben, sich in einem Wald zu befinden, oder in denen sie die Offenheit des Himmels spüren. Ich versuche stets, ein Gleichgewicht zwischen Natur und Architektur herzustellen und dabei die eher metaphysischen und tieferen Bedeutungen mit einzuschließen."

Lina Bellovičová, House LO, Chriby, Czech Republic, 2019–20.

Interessant ist, dass Yamada ihre Erfahrungen mit Gorillas im ruandischen Wald zur Erklärung des Daita2019-Designs anführt, doch mit seiner Offenheit und ultimativen Flexibilität begibt sich ihr sehr urbanes Design noch weiter auf die Suche nach tieferen Bedeutungen für die Präsenz der Natur.

Ein weiterer unerwarteter Architekt eines hier vorgestellten Hauses ist Palinda Kannangara aus Sri Lanka. Seine Frame Holiday Structure (Imaduwa, Sri Lanka, 2018, siehe Seite 286) mit Stahlgerüst, Sichtziegeln und Holzböden wurde für 40 000 Dollar errichtet. Aufgrund der Anfälligkeit des Standorts für Überschwemmungen und des begrenzten Budgets erachtete Kannangara ein Gerüst als ideale Lösung, auch da die Struktur bei Bedarf leicht demontiert und versetzt werden kann. Bedingt durch das lokale Klima, verfügt das Gebäude nur über wenige Wände, die wiederum aus leichtem, undurchlässigem SuperFlex bestehen. Sogar die Möbel wurden aus übrig gebliebenen Baustellenmaterialien und anderen wiederverwerteten Elementen hergestellt.

Lebt wohl, Dandys – hallo, Rest der Welt

Zu einer gewissen Zeit, beispielsweise nach dem Zweiten Weltkrieg, herrschte international das Bestreben vor, schnell und billig zu bauen, um Wohnraum und andere Infrastrukturen zu schaffen, die erforderlich waren, um die Nationen wieder in Gang zu bringen. Dabei eigneten sich die Rastermuster der Moderne für schnelles Entwerfen. Und doch wurde das, was im schlimmsten Fall schablonenhaft geriet, schließlich zugunsten einer Art Nostalgie abgelehnt, die man in Ermangelung eines besseren Namens als „Postmoderne" bezeichnete. Ein Großteil der industriellen Moderne erzeugte Gleichförmigkeit oder Langeweile, was die Postmodernen, angefeuert von Leuten wie Charles Jencks, mit oberflächlichen „traditionellen" Formen zu übertünchen versuchten. In ihrem Inneren ähnelten die postmodernen Gebäude wesentlich ihren erklärtermaßen geometrischen Vorgängern. Hinter diesen Oberflächenornamenten verbarg sich sicherlich eine Sehnsucht nach der Langlebigkeit, ja gar der Beständigkeit der Architektur der Vergangenheit. Versuchen wir also, die Architektur zur einzigen wirklich dauerhaften Kunstform zu machen, deren Erscheinungsbild so glänzend strahlt wie die Smaragdenstadt im Lande Oz. Wie passen also die Gerüste von Yamada und Kannangara in dieses Bild? In eine Architektur, die nicht mehr von westlichen Idealen beherrscht wird, sondern die in ihrer Zeit lebt und atmet. Yamada beruft sich (wenn auch unbewusst) auf den profunden Sinn der Japaner für Zeit und Vergänglichkeit und konzentriert sich dennoch auf das Hier und Jetzt. Kannangara setzt sein architektonisches Talent ein, um etwas zu schaffen, das sowohl günstig als auch praktisch ist, das stark an seinen Standort und seine Situation angepasst ist und nicht versucht, irgendein strahlendes Ideal wiederzubeleben. Keines dieser Häuser frönt jenem unersättlichen Material- und Kostenverbrauch, denen sich andere Projekte in diesem Buch (die ungenannt bleiben sollen) hingeben. Und doch kann der Leser sicher sein, dass selbst die größten Häuser heute, von wenigen Ausnahmen abgesehen, von einem ökologischen Bewusstsein geprägt sind. Überschwemmungen und Tornados können sehr überzeugende Einflussnehmer sein.

The times, they are a-changin'

Interessiert es uns also wirklich, was der letzte Schrei ist? Mich nicht, Sie etwa? Schauen wir stattdessen genauer hin, um zu prüfen, wie verantwortungsbewusst Architekt und Bauherr agierten, wie sie keine Bäume abholzten, den Energieverbrauch reduzierten und das Beste aus dem Vorgegebenen herausholten, anstatt so zu tun, als gäbe es mehr, als tatsächlich vorhanden ist. Ein Haus in diesem Buch, das Loom House (Miller Hull, Bainbridge Island, Washington, USA, 2019, siehe Seite 346), wurde als „die ökologisch ehrgeizigste Wohnhausrenovierung der Welt" bezeichnet, bei der auf allen Projektebenen wiederverwerteter Baustoff verwendet und der Energieverbrauch streng kontrolliert wurde. Und doch würde die Schönheit dieses Stein- und Holzhauses, die auch durch die Aussicht auf einen See nahe Seattle noch verstärkt wird, keinem Eigentümer das Gefühl verleihen, er habe architektonische Qualität geopfert, um ökologische Heiligkeit zu erlangen. Architekt und Bauherr taten vielmehr das, was sie für notwendig hielten, nicht weil die Mode es ihnen diktierte, sondern – wie Bob Dylan es 1964 ausdrückte – weil:

Come gather 'round people
Wherever you roam
And admit that the waters
Around you have grown
And accept it that soon
You'll be drenched to the bone
If your time to you is worth savin'
Then you better start swimmin'
or you'll sink like a stone
For the times they are a-changin'

(Kommt zusammen, Leute
Wo immer ihr umherstreift
Und gebt zu, dass das Wasser
Um euch gestiegen ist
Und akzeptiert, dass ihr bald
Bis auf die Knochen durchnässt sein werdet
Wenn euch eure Zeit etwas wert ist
Dann fangt besser an zu schwimmen,
oder ihr werdet wie ein Stein untergehen
Denn die Zeiten, sie ändern sich)

In gewissem Sinne geht es bei Häusern um alle Ebenen der Architektur, von der Verantwortung und dem Erfindungsreichtum bis hin zur einfachen Zweckmäßigkeit. Was leistet ein Haus für die Welt, wie innovativ ist es, was kann es und was nicht? Es liegt auf der Hand, dass Bauherren und Architekten oft unterschiedliche Ziele vor Augen haben; die besten Häuser entstehen, wenn diese Kräfte zusammenfließen, anstatt getrennt zu verlaufen. So ist beispielsweise der Aufwand für ein kohlenstoffneutrales Gebäude größtenteils gar nicht sichtbar. Eine Platin- und Goldzertifizierung (LEED) trägt zwar ihr Scherflein zum guten Ruf manch eines Architekten bei, aber für die Hauseigentümer bedeutet sie viel mehr. Für sie ist es eine Gewissensfrage, ob sie etwas für die Zukunft bewahren oder verbrannte Erde hinterlassen. Leider herrschte letztere Haltung lange Zeit vor und ist noch heute viel zu oft präsent. Den entscheidenden Unterschied machen jetzt leider Naturkatastrophen von bislang ungekanntem

Carlos Zwick, House by the Lake, Potsdam, Germany, 2016–20.

Ausmaß. Was passiert mit LaLa Land, wenn das Wasser abläuft und das Ganze ins Meer rutscht? Das wirkt jetzt ein bisschen übertrieben, aber Sie wissen, was ich meine. Wir müssen handeln, und zwar jetzt! Dies entwickelt sich zum Mantra vieler, und dieses Bewusstsein wirkt sich stark auf den Bau und die künftige Gestaltung von Häusern aus.

Stonehenge am Meer

Die Dynamik der Architektur ist sicherlich ebenso komplex wie jene der ihr zugrunde liegenden Gesellschaften mit ihren jeweiligen bemerkenswerten oder weniger ansprechenden Wohnhäusern. Die (hoffentlich) unparteiische Auswahl für dieses Buch zeigt, dass Lateinamerika einige der beeindruckendsten zeitgenössischen Häuser hervorbringt. Das Haus Isla Lebe von Guillermo Acuña im Süden Chile zum Beispiel (Rilan, 2020, siehe Seite 50) nutzt bestehende Holzstrukturen, angestrichen in dem Rot der einheimischen Fuchsia (*Fuchsia magellanica*). Man könnte meinen, ein 315 Quadratmeter großes Haus auf einer fast privaten Insel vor der chilenischen Küste koste ein Vermögen und wirke sich negativ auf die natürliche Umgebung aus. Das ist hier nicht der Fall. Die Casa Huayoccari (Huayoccari, Cusco, Peru, 2018, siehe Seite 80), von Barclay & Crousse auf fast 3000 Metern über dem Meeresspiegel errichtet, verfolgt einen härteren, deutlich bergigeren Ansatz und fügt sich mit bewusst schrägen Öffnungen sowie einer Betonmasse, die in den kühlen Nächten die Wärme speichert, in die Umgebung ein.
Luciano Lerner Bassos Fortunata House (Caxias do Sul, Brasilien, 2020, siehe Seite 96) wurde um einen Baum einer gefährdeten Art herum auf Pilotis errichtet und thront auf diese

Weise über dem Waldboden. Effiziente Querlüftung, Wiederverwendung von Regenwasser, natürliche Beleuchtung und ein ökologisches Heizsystem sind Teil des Konzepts, das aufgrund des geringen Wartungsbedarfs auf Stahlbeton zurückgreift. Die Bilder dieses Hauses zeigen, wie gut sich ein modernes Bauwerk in eine leicht abschüssige Waldumgebung einfügen kann. Die Art und Weise, wie es um eine Brasilkiefer (*Araucaria angustifolia*) herum gebaut wurde, zeigt auch, wie weit und schnell sich die Sorge um die Natur in der Welt der zeitgenössischen Architektur verbreitet hat. Das House for a Ceramist (The Guanacastes) (Orotina, Costa Rica, 2019, siehe Seite 152) von Victor Cañas, geboren 1947, beweist, dass sich auch (etwas) ältere Architekten für den Umweltschutz engagieren. Die genaue Lage des Hauses und sein Design wurden zu einem guten Teil durch den Bestand ausgewachsener Guancaste-Bäume (*Enterolobium cyclocarpum*) bestimmt. Um die Baumwurzeln zu schützen, musste das Haus 80 Zentimeter vom Boden abgehoben werden. Querlüftung und Fotovoltaikanlagen sind ebenfalls Teil des weitgehend passiven Energiekonzepts.

Das Ochoquebradas House (Los Vilos, Chile, 2018, siehe Seite 192) wurde von Alejandro Aravenas Gruppe ELEMENTAL im Rahmen eines umfassenderen Projekts mit Häusern von jeweils acht Architekten aus Japan, unter anderem Kengo Kuma und Sou Fujimoto, und Chile, darunter Felipe Assadi, Guillermo Acuña und Aravena, entworfen. Das ELEMENTAL-Konzept evoziert kraftvolle, ja gar archaische Kräfte, die von den Architekten als „eine gewisse Primitivität" bezeichnet werden. Das 500 000 Dollar teure Haus besteht aus drei Blöcken: einem horizontalen, der die Grundinfrastruktur für zwei Personen enthält und leicht über die Klippe hinausragt; einem vertikalen Block mit den weiteren vom Projektorganisator vorgegebenen Räumen sowie einer Dachterrasse; und zwischen diesen beiden Strukturen findet sich „ein leicht geneigter und ausgehöhlter Block mit einer Feuerstelle, kein Schornstein (der bereits etwas Zivilisiertes darstellt), sondern ein Ort für ein Feuer (das eine der revolutionärsten und zugleich ältesten Errungenschaften des Menschen ist)". Es sieht (sozusagen) entschieden elementar aus. ELEMENTAL erklärt: „Wir wollten uns auf das Archaische zurückbesinnen, nicht als nostalgische Flucht, sondern als natürlichen Filter gegen Klischees. In einer Zeit, in der der Hunger nach Neuem die Architektur sofort zu veralten droht, suchten wir nach Zeitlosigkeit." Eine Art Stonehenge am Meer für das moderne Zeitalter, so scheint es. ELEMENTALs Erläuterungen verdeutlichen zudem, dass nicht jede Region und nicht jeder Architekt den Herausforderungen der Dynamik der heutigen Welt mit dem gleichen Maß an Bewusstsein oder Entwicklung begegnet. Unter Verweis auf die Gefahr für die Architektur, „sofort zu veralten", strebt ELEMENTAL die Authentizität des wirklich Alten an, ein interessanter Umgang mit der heutigen Situation. Allerdings müssen wir uns darüber im Klaren sein, dass die Häuser in diesem Band und ihre Architekten nur einen winzigen Ausschnitt dessen zeigen, was in der Welt gebaut wird und gebaut werden kann. Erfindungsreichtum und Aktualität sind jenen Wenigen vorbehalten, die das Kommende mit Sicherheit beeinflussen werden. Alejandro Aravena ist der zweite Pritzker-Preisträger in diesem Buch – von großem Einfluss nicht nur aufgrund seiner engen und häufigen Zusammenarbeit mit der Pritzker-Jury, sondern vor allem wegen seiner Bemühungen um zeitgemäße Wohnlösungen für benachteiligte Menschen. In der Begründung der Pritzker-Jury heißt es: „Was Aravena wirklich auszeichnet, ist sein Engagement für den sozialen Wohnungsbau. Seit dem Jahr 2000 und der Gründung von ELEMENTAL haben er und seine Mitarbeiter immer wieder Werke mit klaren sozialen Zielen realisiert ... Sie haben mehr als 2500 Einheiten gebaut und dabei fantasievolle, flexible und unmittelbare architektonische Lösungen für den preisgünstigen sozialen Wohnungsbau eingesetzt."

Der Realität, der Armut und der Not verpflichtet

Dies ist also ein weiteres Element der Gleichung: Privathäuser bilden keineswegs die Spitze der architektonischen Auseinandersetzung mit der realen Welt. Sie sind nach wie vor ein Ort des Experimentierens und Erfindens, was zum Teil an der oft engen Beziehung zwischen Architekt und Bauherren liegt, aber auch daran, dass ein kleinerer Maßstab ein geringeres Risiko mit sich bringt. ELEMENTAL mag zwar ein erstaunliches Privathaus an der Küste in „archaischem" Stil entworfen haben, aber die Gruppe widmet sich auch klar der Aufgabe, Architektur in der modernen Welt mehr Relevanz zu verleihen. Künstler mögen die Welt von morgen erfinden, aber der sehr reale und konkrete Bereich der Architektur scheint der

Realität, der Armut und der Not verpflichtet zu sein. Architekten wie Shigeru Ban (ein weiterer Pritzker-Preisträger) investierten viel Energie und Mühe in Projekte wie den Bau von Notunterkünften in Katastrophenfällen, auch wenn sie daneben Privathäuser entwerfen, doch viele ihrer Kollegen konzentrieren sich nach wie vor auf den Verdienst und Bekanntheitsgrad, die mit einem spektakulären Zwei-Personen-Haus leichter erreichbar sind als auf einem Trümmerfeld. Das Konzept der sozialen Verantwortung zeitgenössischer Architektur könnte durchaus ebenso verblasst sein, wie auch konzeptionelle Ideale wie der „Fortschritt" in allen anderen kulturellen Bereichen immer schwächer werden. Das industrielle und repetitive Image der Moderne kam offensichtlich zu einem guten Teil durch ihren Einfluss in Amerika zustande, als die Welt gerade Krieg und Zerstörung hinter sich gelassen hatte. Ebenso wie die frühen russischen Konstruktivisten, die hofften, mit technischer Funktionalität eine neue Welt für viele zu schaffen, hatten auch Gropius und das Bauhaus ein soziales Gewissen. Zu behaupten, die modernen Architekten hätten „ihre Ideale verraten", klänge vielleicht ein wenig zu hart, aber Gropius, Mies und die anderen legten eindeutig den Grundstein für jene ästhetisch und finanziell motivierten Paradigmen, die nach dem Zweiten Weltkrieg zunächst Amerika und dann weite Teile der entwickelten Welt dominierten. Nein, die Häuser in diesem Band wurden zwar fast ausnahmslos nicht mit dem Zweck entworfen, das Los der vielen zu verbessern, sondern um den Kunden zu gefallen, aber auch, um angesichts der planetarischen Krisen mehr Verantwortung zu übernehmen. Was früher eine Option für die ökologisch denkende Minderheit war, ist in den Vordergrund gerückt. Wenn die Gesetzgebung keine strengeren Standards vorschreibt, dann wird es der gesunde Menschenverstand tun.

Der sechstgrößte Kontinent (Europa)

Die wachsende Präsenz von Architekten aus „neuen" Teilen der Welt verringerte natürlich nicht das Schaffensvolumen amerikanischer, europäischer oder japanischer Architekten. Vielmehr scheint es, als würden diese durch die Entdeckung neuer Gesichter und Formen weniger prominent wahrgenommen – was an sich im Grunde nicht schlecht ist. Zwei neue Häuser in Deutschland zeigen, mit welchen Ideen und Herausforderungen der Entwurf und Bau von Privathäusern verbunden ist. Andreas Wenning,

Will Gamble, The Parchment Works, Northamptonshire, UK, 2017–18.

der vom Tischler zum Architekten wurde, konzentriert sich seit Langem auf die Gestaltung von Baumhäusern. Sein Fachwissen auf diesem Gebiet veranlasste einen Kunden in Hannover, ihn zu bitten, nicht nur ein kleines Baumhaus, sondern ein komplettes neues Wohnhaus zu entwerfen (Green Dwelling, in der Nähe von Hannover, Deutschland, 2019, siehe Seite 104). Ein wichtiges Anliegen des Bauherrn war die ökologische Qualität der Konstruktion und der Haustechnik. „Der Wunsch, hier Holz als wesentlichen Baustoff einzusetzen, kam uns sehr entgegen", so Wenning. Auch wenn seine Baumhäuser (baumraum) nicht nur aus Holz bestehen, verfügt der Architekt offensichtlich über ein umfassendes Wissen über die Verwendung von Holz als Baumaterial. In Bäumen zu bauen, ohne sie zu beschädigen, ist eine sichtlich intime Annäherung an die Natur, die von der zeitgenössischen Architektur zumeist gemieden wurde. Abgesehen von der allgegenwärtigen Verwendung von Holz für dieses Wohnhaus legte der Architekt ein umfangreiches Gründach an und integrierte u. a. einen Gas-Brennwertkessel, eine Fußbodenheizung und kontrollierte Belüftung in ein grünes Gesamtkonzept.

Ein zweites deutsches Projekt ist das Haus des Architekten Carlos Zwick (Haus am See, Potsdam, Deutschland, 2020, siehe Seite 464). Die örtlichen Vorschriften verlangen, dass alle Neubauten einen Abstand von 50 Metern vom Ufer des Jungfernsees einhalten müssen. Zwick legte diese Forderung einem sorgfältigen Plan zugrunde, der keine bestehenden Bäume beschädigte und einen Bau ohne Turmkran ermöglichte. Indem er das Haus vom Boden abhob und auf Stahlstützen setzte, gelang es ihn, die städtischen Behörden zufriedenzustellen und gleichzeitig den Grundstückszustand zu bewahren. Als Inspiration für sein Haus am See verweist Zwick interessanterweise auf Farnsworth House von Mies van der Rohe (Plano, Illinois, USA, 1951). Farnsworth ist ein Ein-Zimmer-Wochenendhaus mit einer Fläche von 206 Quadratmetern. Es wurde 1,6 Meter über das überschwemmungsgefährdete Gelände angehoben. Seine weiße Farbe und die erhöhte Lage über dem Boden in Verbindung mit der raumhohen Verglasung vermitteln den Eindruck einer ätherischen, vielleicht nur vorübergehenden Präsenz inmitten der Landschaft. Das Haus am See hingegen verfügt über eine beachtliche Nutzfläche von 610 Quadratmetern. Das von Zwick entworfene Wohnhaus schwebt doppelt so hoch über dem Boden (drei Meter) wie sein Mies'sches Gegenstück und ist mit schmalen vertikalen Lärchenholzstreifen verkleidet anstatt mit sichtbaren Stahlplatten, die Dach und Boden von Farnsworth prägen. Die 40 diagonalen Stützpfosten sind sicherlich präsenter als die Pilotis von Mies, und zudem weist diese Struktur zwei miteinander verbundene rechteckige Elemente auf im Gegensatz zu der vierseitigen Orthodoxie des älteren Meisters. Das Endergebnis könnte als eine zeitgenössische Version der Moderne betrachtet werden, mit grauem Holz statt weißem Stahl, einer größeren Erhebung über dem Boden (teilweise administrativen Gründen geschuldet) und dennoch verfasst in jener strengen geradlinigen Sprache der einflussreichen (ursprünglich deutschen) Schule.

Eine Ode an die Umnutzung

Das Mole House von Adjaye fand bereits Erwähnung, ist aber bei Weitem nicht das einzige aktuelle Beispiel für ein Gebäude, das sich der vorgegebenen Strukturen eines älteren Wohnhauses bedient. Für sein House and Studio entschied sich das Londoner Architekturbüro Carmody Groarke für die Umnutzung eines Backsteinlagerhaus aus viktorianischer Zeit (Lambeth, London, 2018, siehe Seite 158). Die für die Zeit und Gegend gängigen Backsteinfassaden blieben erhalten, die Innenräume aber sind vom Boden bis zur Decke aus Beton, und die Inneneinrichtung lässt selbst die Herzen der minimalistischsten Architekturfans höherschlagen. In gewisser Weise praktiziert dieses Design eine Art innere Tabula rasa, während es gleichzeitig eine äußere Präsenz im Einklang mit seiner Nachbarschaft beibehält. Ein anderer in London ansässiger Architekt ging mit der Erhaltung einer scheinbar vollständigen Ruine sogar noch weiter. Aus einem denkmalgeschützten viktorianischen Haus und den Überresten einer denkmalgeschützten Pergamentfabrik aus dem 17. Jahrhundert schuf Will Gamble The Parchment Works (Northamptonshire, Großbritannien, 2018, siehe Seite 238). Anstatt die Ruine abzureißen, fügte Gamble zwei neue Elemente aus Cortenstahl, wiederverwendeten Ziegelsteinen und Eiche ein. Er legte die tragenden Balken und Steinwände eines Viehstalls frei und fügte einen Betonsockel hinzu, der ein weiteres Element der Komposition darstellt. Das 200 Quadratmeter große Haus, von Historic England genehmigt, kostete 295 000 Euro und wurde als eines der innovativsten Häuser Großbritanniens der jüngsten Zeit gefeiert.

Die Kunst verherrlicht seit jeher reale und imaginäre Ruinen, wie sie in den Gemälden Claude Lorrains (1600–82) oder in Piranesis Grafiken (1720–78) zu sehen sind. Einige Künstler gingen sogar so weit, sich künftige Ruinen vorzustellen, wie in Hubert Roberts *Imaginäre Ansicht der Großen Galerie des Louvre als Ruine* (1796, Louvre). All diese künstlerischen Ruinenversionen scheint ein Gefühl der Nostalgie für die Erhabenheit der Vergangenheit zu einen, das zuweilen sogar darauf hinauslief, sich die Gegenwart in Ruinen vorzustellen. Die Umnutzung von Architektur hat eine noch längere und ereignisreichere Geschichte, die mindestens bis in die Römerzeit zurückverfolgt werden kann. Mit der Herrschaft von Theodosius im Jahr 379 n. Chr. wurden aus Tempeln plötzlich Kirchen. Das Pantheon verwandelte sich 609 n. Chr. in eine christliche, Santa Maria ad Martyres geweihte Kirche. Vor einiger Zeit wurden die Umweltauswirkungen von Umnutzungen sorgfältig untersucht. Von den mit Bauabfällen überfüllten Mülldeponien bis hin zur Herstellung neuer Gebäude ist die Architektur in ihren verschiedenen (neuen) Formen ein unersättlicher Verbraucher immer seltenerer Materialien und ein wesentlicher Verursacher von Umweltverschmutzung. 2015 schrieb Dr. Stephen Muench von der University of Washington: „Ein einzelnes Umnutzungsprojekt kann keine großen Auswirkungen auf die Kohlendioxidemissionen haben, aber übertragen wir den Gedanken auf eine ganze Stadt oder ein ganzes Land, sind die Auswirkungen enorm. Würden beispielsweise in Portland die Gebäude, die abgerissen und neu errichtet werden müssten für die nächsten zehn Jahre umgenutzt, so führte dies zu einer Verringerung der Kohlendioxidemissionen um 231 000 Tonnen. Dies entspricht etwa 15 Prozent des gesamten CO2-Reduktionsziels des Landes für die nächsten zehn Jahre." Dieser Exkurs zeigt, dass es ein weiteres Zeichen der Zeit ist, moderne Häuser ausfindig zu machen, die aus und mit Ruinen gebaut wurden oder die bestehende Strukturen wiederverwenden. Es darf als sicher gelten, dass es mehr und mehr Fälle wie die hier vorgestellten überall auf der Welt geben wird. Die Vielfalt der Häuser in diesem Buch kann die Worte des Songs, mit denen dieser Text begann, nur bestätigen. Oft sind sie wunderschön, aber sie können nur dann ein Zuhause sein, wenn Liebe in ihnen wohnt und sie so (hoffentlich) unserer Zeit ein Zuhause geben.

You say you want a revolution
Im Beatles-Song heißt es weiter:

You say you got a real solution
Well, you know
We'd all love to see the plan

(Ihr sagt, ihr habt eine echte Lösung
Nun, wisst ihr
Wir alle würden den Plan gerne sehen)

Und was, wenn es keinen Plan, aber trotzdem eine Revolution gibt? Die Vorteile „grüner" Architektur stehen seit Langem zur Diskussion, wie auch über Themen wie Gleichberechtigung der Geschlechter oder Ethnien seit Jahren diskutiert wird. Jetzt also ist es an der Zeit. Jedes Jahr erlebt die Welt Jahrtausendstürme, die Gletscher schmelzen, ein unvergleichliches Massenaussterben ist im Gange. Ja, natürlich, die Häuser in diesem Buch wirken sehr verlockend und in sich ruhend. Vielleicht findet die Revolution also woanders statt, nämlich in den Entwürfen, die zumindest einige jener Faktoren berücksichtigen, welche die Architektur zum immerwährenden Aushängeschild für ökologische Verantwortungslosigkeit gemacht haben. Und wenn Frauen endlich in großer Zahl an Architekturschulen in der ganzen Welt studieren können, so findet auch diese Revolution ohne einen angekündigten, von einer höheren Instanz erlassenen Plan statt. Die Gleichstellung aller Menschen schreitet vielleicht langsamer voran, aber die Zeichen des Wandels sind überwältigend. Und wenn der Rest der Welt dank des Internets plötzlich „sichtbar" ist, wenn Informationen freier zirkulieren, dann ist auch das eine Revolution, die keinem vorherbestimmten Schema folgt. Vom Entwurf bis zur Herstellung ist dank der Welt der Technologie mit einzigartig geformten (maßgeschneiderten!) Materialien und Bauelementen alles leichter zugänglich. Und anstatt mehr zu kosten und wenigen Glücklichen vorbehalten zu sein, kostet diese Technologie sogar weniger, und einzigartige Gebäude sind genauso leicht realisierbar wie Raster von der Stange. Das ultimative Diktat, jenes der geraden Linie, ist bald Geschichte, da geradliniges Denken stark auf Skaleneffekten beruhte.
Aber dies bedeutet sicher nicht, dass ein Architekt kein quadratisches oder rechteckiges Gebäude mehr bauen darf; die meisten Häuser in diesem Buch repräsentieren eine Variante dieses Paradigmas: Es bedeutet lediglich (und hierin besteht die Revolution), dass wir die Wahl haben. Die Revolution in der zeitgenössischen Architektur, die in Privathäusern am schnellsten und umfassendsten zum Ausdruck kommt, ist ein epochales Ereignis. Nicht weil jemals irgendein Theoretiker (oder schlimmer noch: ein Architekturkritiker) seine Ideen formuliert hätte. Vielmehr ist es die kombinierte Kraft von Klima, Geschichte und Technologie, welche die Formen und Methoden der Architektur verbiegt. Das Klima (bzw. der Klimawandel) ist die unbestreitbare, ultimative Kraft, die bereits jetzt ihre Erfordernisse kundtut.

And admit that the waters
Around you have grown
And accept it that soon
You'll be drenched to the bone

Die Geschichte drückt sich in der Erkenntnis aus, dass eine kleine Zahl alter weißer Männer nicht ewig an der Macht bleiben kann, und dies dank der Entwicklung der Wirtschaft und der Kulturen so vieler Länder der Welt. Frauen sind (endlich) präsent, und ungeachtet der Taliban gibt es keinen Weg zurück. Die Technologie ist der unangekündigte Wegbereiter eines massiven Wandels. In seinem gleichnamigen Buch von 2004 schrieb Bruce Mau: „Bei massivem Wandel geht es nicht um die Welt der Gestaltung, sondern um die Gestaltung der Welt." Die Revolution steht nicht unmittelbar bevor, sie ist immanent, und sie ist hier.

Pages 30–31: *DECA Architecture, Hourglass Corral, Milos, Cyclades, Greece, 2017–20.*

Philip Jodidio

LES EAUX AUTOUR DE VOUS ONT MONTÉ

I walk up to my door and hate to turn the key
Emptiness is all that waits inside for me
That's how it is when the one you love is gone
That's how it is when your house is not a home

(Je marche vers ma porte et je déteste
tourner la clé
Le vide est tout ce qui m'attend à l'intérieur
C'est comme ça quand la personne
aimée est partie
C'est comme ça quand ta maison n'est
pas une maison)

Les paroles de la chanson de Roger Miller en 1970 *When a house is not a home* transmettent quelque chose de véritablement essentiel sur le concept de maison. La modernité dans l'architecture et le design peut s'avérer froide et vide, elle peut aussi révéler un véritable sentiment du rapport au lieu, à la nature et, bien sûr, à l'amour. Sans oublier ce que l'architecte ou le designer peut apporter en matière d'espaces, de volumes et de matériaux, ainsi que ce tout matériel et immatériel de ceux qui trouvent quelque part leur chez-soi. Tout le monde a oublié, tant cela fait longtemps que les critiques dandys ont, en leur temps, frappé les esprits en identifiant la prochaine tendance de l'architecture, celle à venir et sans aucun doute celle passée. Si Internet et la diffusion mondiale de l'information ont permis à des régions entières de la Terre de savoir ce qui se passe ailleurs, l'inverse est aussi vrai. Aujourd'hui, après avoir longtemps été l'apanage des représentants européens et américains les plus influents de l'architecture contemporaine, l'inventivité et l'innovation sont partout, il n'y a plus et il n'y aura sans doute plus jamais de style dominant. C'est aussi l'argument avancé dans ce livre, qui se veut consacré aux maisons : il existe autant de manières de concevoir une habitation que d'architectes. Bien sûr, la généralisation de la conception et de la construction assistées par ordinateur est source de nouveauté, mais une conscience beaucoup plus profonde et plus fondamentale est née de ce qui existe et de ce qui peut être fait pour préserver plutôt que pour détruire la planète. Les maisons individuelles présentées ici ont des tailles (et des coûts) qui vont de la plus modeste à la plus extraordinaire. Il va de soi qu'une structure indépendante conçue par un architecte pour une famille représente un luxe et une exception, quelle que soit sa taille par rapport aux conditions d'habitat de l'immense majorité. Une belle maison est comme un rêve, un refuge aussi pour échapper à de nombreux problèmes du monde, souvent bien plus proche du ciel que de l'enfer que connaissent, par exemple, les réfugiés. Mais laissons l'évidence de côté pour nous concentrer sur ces « maisons pour notre temps » qui, si elles ne sont peut-être pas celles de tout le monde, restent tout au moins une invitation à rêver.

Le Bûcher des vanités
L'attrait croissant de l'architecture – on pourrait aussi parler d'accès amplifié à l'information dans le monde entier grâce à Internet – a sans doute joué un rôle dans la notoriété de certains architectes. Seuls deux des 61 architectes présentés ici, à titre d'exemple, ont gagné le prix Pritzker. Et si Frank O. Gehry est représenté, c'est un choix qui relève plus de la réminiscence et de la revalorisation que de la pure innovation. Sa première maison à Santa Monica (1978) marque pour ainsi dire le tout début de sa carrière en démontrant le potentiel des surfaces en asphalte et des clôtures à mailles de chaîne pour une palette d'artiste. Aujourd'hui, à plus de 95 ans, Frank Gehry ne donne plus le ton, et c'est bien naturel, mais il est le symbole au sens plus général du déclin de l'« uber-architecte », ou du « starchitecte ». L'ancienne première dame des États-Unis a, de même, défrayé la chronique en portant une veste avec griffonné dans le dos « really don't care, do you? » (« Je m'en fiche complètement, et vous ? »). Car s'il n'y a plus de style dominant, peut-il vraiment y avoir des architectes dominants ? Ou alors nous ne nous intéressons plus autant à leurs personnalités, leurs manies, leurs accessoires fétiches – comme le chapeau de Frank Lloyd Wright ou les lunettes du Corbusier ? L'un des cabinets d'architecture présentés ici, Frankie Pappas, a été jusqu'à gommer les identités personnelles. « Imaginez, disent-ils, pouvoir créer une personne fictive – un pseudonyme collectif – qui nous permette de mettre de côté nos égocentrismes, nos rodomontades et nos vanités pour trouver un groupe de gens dont les idéaux semblables et les talents divers sont à l'origine de solutions belles pour un monde nouveau et remarquable. » Ce n'est certainement pas non plus un hasard si leur Maison à la grande arche (House of the Big Arch, Waterberg, Afrique du Sud, 2019, voir page 232) a été construite sans couper aucun arbre et adaptée au site à l'aide de méthodes de conception avancées afin de créer une structure dont la largeur n'excède pas 3,3 mètres, précisément pour préserver le site. De nombreuses nouvelles attitudes émergent ainsi dans l'architecture contemporaine et s'inscrivent parmi les tendances qui traversent ce domaine, tels l'exemple cité, le rejet de la « célébrité », le souci de l'environnement, l'utilisation en évolution constante de la technologie pour atteindre les objectifs d'aujourd'hui.

SO–IL, Duravcevic-Ben Ari House, Long Island, New York, USA, 2016–19.

On admettra que d'autres jeunes architectes rêvent encore du panthéon des stars, mais peut-être que cette époque est tout simplement révolue ? Cependant, le talent existe encore, heureusement, et on peut espérer que nombre des nouveaux visages présentés dans les pages qui suivent vieilliront dans la grâce et la plénitude de la créativité — *famoso ma non troppo*. Un architecte brésilien de renom (absent de ce livre) a expliqué une fois à l'auteur que trois générations d'architectes brésiliens avaient été sacrifiées à la gloire d'Oscar Niemeyer. Ce dernier est resté actif jusqu'au-delà de son 100e anniversaire, continuant à tracer d'immenses lignes courbes sur un grand tableau blanc dans son bureau de Copacabana, des lignes qui deviendront des bâtiments, donnant forme aux « courbes du temps ». Si le culte du génie semble avoir perdu de son lustre, cela laissera peut-être la place à l'émergence de nouveaux talents et à l'avancée de nouvelles idées.

Individuellement vôtre
Une fois encore, il est bien clair que ces maisons sont destinées aux privilégiés, à ceux qui ont découvert un site admirable sur la côte pacifique du Chili, ou seulement une parcelle minuscule, mais précieuse, à Setagaya (Tokyo) où construire la maison de leurs rêves. Mais c'est précisément ce que veut ce livre, donner à voir l'exceptionnel, le plus rare, la beauté même impossible. Et les maisons sont naturellement l'opportunité – pour les clients et les architectes qui possèdent la volonté, les moyens et l'imagination – de créer de nouvelles formes, de permettre à la typologie de la résidence personnelle d'évoluer, malgré

les catastrophes qui menacent et que nous préparent l'économie, le climat et le dernier virus (et parfois à cause d'elles). La culture du jetable qui a tant dominé l'industrie moderne, y compris celle de la construction, est aujourd'hui soumise à une pression croissante pour économiser l'énergie et les précieux matériaux. Mais cette contrainte forte arrive précisément au moment où la technologie, mise au service de la conception, mais aussi des matériaux, ouvre un éventail véritablement sensationnel de nouvelles possibilités. Des éléments identiques qui devaient être fabriqués par milliers pour atteindre les économies d'échelle requises peuvent désormais s'avérer des pièces uniques personnalisées, conçues et formées par des outils commandés par ordinateur. Lorsque la beauté est présente ici, c'est souvent celle des décors naturels, tandis que l'architecture joue souvent un rôle d'écrin.

Who Run the World? Girls (girls)

Ce livre présente des projets qui ont été choisis pour leur beauté, leur approche innovante, leur répartition géographique, et non pas pour leur auteur. Si l'on n'y trouve que deux lauréats du prix Pritzker, c'est parce que les architectes les plus célèbres (souvent plus âgés) préfèrent les bâtiments de plus grandes dimensions. De même, aucun effort particulier n'a été fait pour trouver, par exemple, des femmes architectes, et pourtant les lecteurs y verront le travail de Sandra Barclay (Barclay & Crousse), Cecilia Rueda et María Díaz (Barozzi Veiga), Lina Bellovičová, Bergendy Cooke, Débora Mesa (Ensamble Studio), Stacey Farrell, Dagmar Stepanova (Formafatal), Michelle McFarlane (McFarlane Biggar), Lisa Bovell (McLeod Bovell), Jing Liu (SO-IL), Débora Mendes (Tetro), Suzuko Yamada et Cazú Zegers. Parfois avec des partenaires masculins, elles se sont illustrées dans un milieu connu pour sa longue histoire d'hommes occupant le devant de la scène. L'influence durable de Zaha Hadid l'explique certainement en partie, mais c'est une tendance qui repose sur une base plus large. Le National Architectural Accrediting Board (NAAB, Conseil national d'accréditation en architecture) des États-Unis a, par exemple, fait état en 2019 d'une répartition entre les sexes de 51 % d'hommes et 49 % de femmes parmi les étudiants en architecture. L'avenir de la discipline est donc clairement tracé : un tournant significatif et décisif s'est opéré entre les sexes. Beyoncé l'a chanté dans son tube de 2011, *Run the World (Girls)* – même si les architectes n'étaient pas son sujet de préoccupation principal...

On ne peut pas en dire autant de l'égalité raciale, mais les exemples comme celui de David Adjaye, né à Dar-es-Salam, en Tanzanie, ont pesé dans la balance pour l'avenir de la profession. Sa Mole House (Londres, 2013–18, voir page 58) est le *remake* d'une maison individuelle victorienne dont l'occupant pendant quarante ans était connu sous le nom d'« homme-taupe » (Mole Man). Dans ce cadre inhabituel, l'architecte et sa cliente, l'artiste Sue Webber, ont décidé de conserver le plus possible le caractère d'origine de la maison en utilisant notamment des briques londoniennes récupérées lorsque de nouveaux éléments étaient nécessaires. Si les exemples ne manquent pas d'architectes de renom qui créent encore des demeures individuelles – on pense notamment à Tadao Ando –, le temps et l'énergie investis par Adjaye dans ce projet relativement mineur attirent cependant l'attention. Si le modernisme ne pensait qu'à balayer l'ancien pour bâtir sa nouvelle cité quadrillée et brillante, la conception contemporaine de maisons (et d'autres objets) consiste aujourd'hui pour une part de plus en plus importante à reproduire des structures existantes, à les reconstruire et les mettre au goût du jour. C'est aussi, bien sûr, un autre moyen excellent de limiter le gaspillage des ressources et la pollution causée par les nouvelles constructions.

La répartition géographique des maisons publiées ici, elle aussi, est révélatrice des changements très profonds qui sont à l'œuvre dans l'architecture. La Chine, le Vietnam, le Sri Lanka, l'Afrique du Sud, l'Inde et d'autres pays qui étaient autrefois le plus souvent absents des livres d'architecture généralistes sont représentés ici et, là encore, sans que l'auteur ait spécifiquement cherché une touche d'exotisme. Ces lieux sont simplement la nouvelle tendance, l'espoir de l'architecture. L'importance de ces changements ne saurait être surestimée, c'est une révolution qui est en cours, la même que celle à laquelle on assiste dans d'autres secteurs du fait de l'omniprésence d'Internet, de la conception et des technologies de construction assistées par ordinateur.

Ni les femmes ni les architectes de différents horizons ne se satisfont cependant de jouer des rôles secondaires ou de continuer à simplement imiter les modèles imposés depuis Londres ou Los Angeles. La résidence Daita2019 de

Suzuko Yamada (Tokyo, 2019, voir page 444) est peut-être un exemple de cette tendance. Âgée de tout juste 37 ans au moment de la mise sous presse de ce livre, l'architecte a cherché à créer un environnement d'un genre nouveau pour la vie familiale qu'elle définit en ces termes : « Je me suis demandé s'il serait possible de créer une maison où la vie serait simplement enveloppée en douceur de plusieurs couches de fil de fer et d'objets qui donneraient naissance à des profondeurs variées et où les rayons du soleil et les regards des passants seraient tenus à distance. » Cela fait longtemps que les maisons cherchent à échapper aux formats typologiques stricts du passé qui imposaient un salon, une salle à manger et une cuisine séparés. Les espaces ouverts et les fonctions modulaires gagnent du terrain dans l'architecture résidentielle depuis des années déjà. C'est une exposition au Museum of Modern Art, « The Un-Private House », qui a attiré l'attention en 1999 sur une nouvelle génération de maisons : « Des changements fondamentaux se sont produits et ont touché tous les aspects de la maison individuelle », déclarait alors son commissaire Terry Riley. « La famille a changé, ainsi que la relation entre maison et travail. Il y a plusieurs siècles, la maison était définie par l'absence de travail. La notion de vie domestique elle aussi a changé. Et le concept de vie privée en soi. »

Gorilles dans la brume

Yamada a poussé encore plus loin cette vision évolutive de la vie domestique. Dans sa maison Daita2019, on trouve « du bois de charpente, des éléments en acier, des poteaux à tube unique et des poutres, et des attaches ; il y a aussi des contremarches et des rampes d'escalier, des cadres de fenêtres à guillotine, des meubles, des rideaux, des livres, des vêtements et d'autres objets divers, des arbres et des plantes en pots, des bicyclettes, des pelles et une grande quantité de livres, cassettes vidéo et DVD ». Elle est parvenue, on ne sait comment, à la construire sans aucun mur entre le jardin et l'intérieur, créant une structure qui donne l'impression de voler, défiant tout sens de la beauté architecturale, tout en captant ce qui manque si souvent aux bâtiments contemporains – l'essence même de la vie quotidienne. L'imagination de Yamada a créé une maison qui paraît comme entourée d'échafaudages provisoires, peut-être pour transcender le concept de *mono no aware* – le sentiment

McLeod Bovell, Blackcliff House, West Vancouver, British Columbia, Canada, 2016–19.

japonais de l'éphémère et de la nature fugitive des choses –, mais aussi pour privilégier un certain confort personnel ou familial qui s'exprime au-delà des canons de l'architecture contemporaine. Yamada a travaillé dans l'agence de Sou Fujimoto (2007–11) avant d'ouvrir la sienne. Lorsque la question lui a été posée en 2018 s'il cherchait délibérément à faire entrer la nature dans son architecture, ce dernier a répondu : « Oui, mais pas seulement la nature, je veux créer des espaces dans lesquels les gens se sentent comme dans une forêt ou perçoivent l'ouverture vers le ciel. Je cherche en permanence le juste milieu entre nature et architecture, y compris leurs significations plus métaphysiques et profondes. » On notera avec intérêt que Yamada, elle aussi, évoque sa rencontre avec des gorilles dans une forêt du Rwanda pour expliquer la conception de Daita2019, même si son design extrêmement urbain va beaucoup plus loin dans la quête d'un sens plus profond à la présence de la nature, dans l'ouverture et la flexibilité suprême du concept. Le Sri-Lankais Palinda Kannangara est un autre architecte surprenant dont l'une des maisons est publiée ici. Sa Frame Holiday Structure (Imaduwa, Sri Lanka, 2018, voir page 286) a été construite en échafaudages d'acier, briques apparentes et planchers pour un budget de 40 000 dollars. Comme le site est sujet à des inondations fréquentes, et aussi en raison de contraintes budgétaires, l'architecte a pensé que les échafaudages formaient une solution idéale, d'autant plus qu'ils permettent à l'ensemble d'être facilement démonté et déplacé au besoin. Le climat local permet de limiter le nombre de murs qui sont enduits de Superflex léger et imperméable. Même le mobilier est fait en matériaux de récupération ou trouvés sur place.

Adieu les dandys, bonjour le reste du monde

À certains moments de l'histoire, par exemple après la Seconde Guerre mondiale, on a assisté à un vaste effort international pour construire rapidement et bon marché afin de créer des logements et d'autres architectures nécessaires pour redonner une impulsion au monde. Les motifs quadrillés du modernisme convenaient parfaitement à cette rapidité de conception et de construction. Pourtant, ce style qui évoquait au pire un style au cordeau sera finalement rejeté au profit d'une nostalgie baptisée postmodernisme faute de mieux. Le modernisme industriel générait le plus souvent une uniformité ou une monotonie que les tenants du postmodernisme, encouragé par Charles Jencks et ses pareils, ont cherché à recouvrir superficiellement de formes « traditionnelles » – alors qu'à l'intérieur, les bâtiments postmodernes ressemblaient presque en tout point à leurs prédécesseurs plus ouvertement géométriques. Les ornements de surface dissimulaient certainement une nostalgie de la longévité, ou plutôt de la permanence de l'architecture d'antan, cherchant à faire de la discipline la seule forme d'art véritablement durable où l'apparence chatoie d'autant de feux que la Cité d'émeraude au pays d'Oz. Mais où placer les échafaudages de Yamada et Kannangara ? Dans une architecture qui n'est plus dominée par les idéaux de l'Occident, mais qui vit et respire avec son temps. Yamada fait appel (même si c'est inconsciemment) au sens japonais plus profond du temps et de l'éphémère, tout en continuant de privilégier le caractère immédiat des choses. Kannangara met son talent d'architecte à profit pour façonner une construction à la fois bon marché et pratique, parfaitement adaptée à son environnement et aux circonstances, qui ne cherche pas à ressusciter un quelconque idéal resplendissant. Aucune de ces maisons ne se laisse aller à la consommation effrénée de matériaux et d'argent dont d'autres projets présentés ici (qui resteront anonymes) s'accommodent. Mais le lecteur peut dormir sur ses deux oreilles : même les plus vastes maisons sont aujourd'hui de plus en plus écologiques, à peu d'exceptions près. Les inondations et les tornades ont leur manière bien à elles d'exercer une influence très convaincante.

The times, they are a-changin'

Mais nous soucions-nous vraiment du dernier style ? Moi pas, et vous ? Peut-être pouvons-nous plutôt nous tourner vers l'intérieur et voir plus loin, dans quelle mesure par exemple l'architecte et son client ont-ils fait preuve de responsabilité en épargnant des arbres et en diminuant la consommation d'énergie, sachant tirer le meilleur parti de ce qu'ils ont au lieu de prétendre avoir toujours plus. L'une des maisons présentées ici, la Loom House (Miller Hull, Bainbridge Island, Washington, États-Unis, 2019, voir page 346), qualifiée de « rénovation la plus écologiquement ambitieuse de notre planète », se distingue par ses matériaux de récupération et le contrôle strict de la consommation d'énergie à tous les niveaux du projet. Et pourtant, sa beauté de pierre et de bois – qu'elle doit aussi à la vue sur l'océan près de Seattle – ne saurait faire penser à aucun propriétaire que la qualité architecturale a été sacrifiée pour parvenir à la sainteté écologique. L'architecte et le client ont simplement fait ce qu'ils considéraient comme en train de devenir nécessaire, pas pour suivre la mode, mais parce que, comme Bob Dylan le chantait en 1964 :

Come gather 'round people
Wherever you roam
And admit that the waters
Around you have grown
And accept it that soon
You'll be drenched to the bone
If your time to you is worth savin'
Then you better start swimmin'
or you'll sink like a stone
For the times they are a-changin'

(Rassemblez-vous braves gens
D'où que vous veniez,
Et admettez que les eaux,
Autour de vous ont monté.
Acceptez que bientôt
Vous serez trempés jusqu'aux os,
Et si votre existence, mérite à vos yeux,
d'être sauvée,
Vous feriez bien de commencer à nager pour
ne pas couler comme une pierre,
Car les temps sont en train de changer)

On peut dire que les maisons synthétisent tous les niveaux de l'architecture, de la responsabilité et l'inventivité jusqu'à l'aspect simplement pratique. Mais qu'est-ce qu'une maison fait pour le monde, quel est son degré d'innovation, que permet-elle de faire, et que ne permet-elle pas ? Les clients et les architectes semblent avoir des avis souvent divergents ; les maisons les plus réussies voient le jour lorsque ces forces convergent plutôt que d'emprunter des voies séparées. Mais la plupart des efforts déployés pour créer une structure neutre en carbone, par exemple, restent simplement invisibles. Une touche de platine et d'or (LEED) contribue grandement à la réputation de certains architectes, mais il n'en va pas forcément de même pour les propriétaires de la maison. Ils se trouvent quant à eux confrontés à un véritable cas de conscience lorsqu'il faut choisir entre épargner pour plus tard ou dépenser tout sans attendre. Malheureusement, c'est cette dernière attitude qui a longtemps dominé et qui continue de se manifester beaucoup trop souvent dans toute sa laideur. Et c'est le nombre sans précédent de catastrophes naturelles qui fait aujourd'hui la différence. Que va-t-il advenir de La Land lorsqu'il n'y aura plus d'eau et que le pays glissera dans la mer ? C'est encore un peu excessif, mais cela donne une idée de la chose. Agir, et agir maintenant, est en train de devenir le leitmotiv de nombreuses personnes, et cette nouvelle conscience influe considérablement sur les maisons et leur future conception.

Stonehenge-sur-Mer

La dynamique de l'architecture est certainement aussi complexe que celle des sociétés dans lesquelles des maisons remarquables – ou d'autres moins intéressantes – sont réalisées. La sélection, que nous espérons impartiale, de ce livre montre sans doute que l'Amérique latine produit aujourd'hui bon nombre des demeures contemporaines les plus étonnantes. La maison de Guillermo Acuña sur l'île de Lebe, par exemple (Rilan, 2020, voir page 50), dans le Sud du Chili, utilise des structures en bois existantes, peintes dans un rouge rappelant les fleurs du fuchsia de Magellan (*Fuchsia magellanica*) qui pousse sur place. On pourrait penser qu'une maison de 315 mètres carrés sur une île presque privée au large de la côte du Chili coûte une fortune et affecte le décor naturel. Ce n'est pas le cas ici. La maison Huayoccari (Huayoccari, Cusco, Pérou, 2018, voir page 80) construite par Barclay & Crousse à presque 3000 mètres au-dessus du niveau de la mer adopte une approche plus dure et clairement plus montagnarde, se fondant dans

Mia Design Studio, Villa Tan Dinh, District 3, Ho Chi Minh City, Vietnam, 2020.

le paysage avec ses ouvertures délibérément anguleuses et une masse de béton pour conserver la chaleur pendant les nuits fraîches.

La maison Fortunata de Luciano Lerner Basso (Caxias do Sul, Brésil, 2020, voir page 96) a été construite autour d'un arbre d'une espèce menacée et perchée sur des pilotis au-dessus du sol forestier. Le concept comprend un système efficace de ventilation croisée, la réutilisation de l'eau de pluie, un éclairage naturel et un chauffage écologique. L'architecte a opté pour le béton armé à cause du peu d'entretien que ce matériau exige. Les photos montrent comment une structure moderne peut être intégrée à un versant forestier. Sa construction autour d'un pin du Paraná (*Araucaria angustifolia*) est aussi un indice de la mesure et de la vitesse à laquelle le respect de la nature a gagné l'architecture contemporaine dans le monde entier.
La Maison pour un céramiste (The Guanacastes, Orotina, Costa Rica, 2019, voir page 152) de Victor Cañas, né en 1947, montre, quant à elle, que les architectes (un peu) plus âgés suivent aussi le mouvement dès lors qu'il s'agit de protéger l'environnement. L'emplacement précis de la maison et sa conception ont été en grande partie déterminés par la présence de guanacastes (*Enterolobium cyclocarpum*) adultes. La construction a dû être surélevée à 80 centimètres au-dessus du sol pour protéger les racines des arbres. La stratégie énergétique, majoritairement passive, comprend une ventilation croisée et des panneaux photovoltaïques.
La maison Ochoquebradas (Los Vilos, Chili, 2018, voir page 192) a été conçue par le groupe

Adjaye Associates, Mole House, London, UK, 2013–18.

ELEMENTAL autour d'Alejandro Aravena et fait partie d'un ensemble plus important de maisons imaginées par huit architectes japonais, dont Kengo Kuma et Sou Fujimoto, et huit architectes chiliens parmi lesquels Felipe Assadi, Guillermo Acuña et Aravena. Le concept d'ELEMENTAL évoque des forces puissantes, d'aucuns diraient archaïques, qualifiées de « quelque peu primitives » par les architectes. La maison de 500 000 dollars compte trois volumes : un bloc horizontal qui contient le nécessaire pour un couple et s'avance légèrement en surplomb au-dessus de la falaise ; un bloc vertical avec les autres espaces exigés par l'organisateur du projet et un toit en terrasse et, entre les deux, un bloc « légèrement incliné et évidé où se trouve un feu – pas une cheminée (qui serait déjà un élément civilisé), mais un feu (qui est l'un des acquis les plus révolutionnaires, même si c'est aussi l'un des plus anciens, de l'être humain) ». L'expression de l'ensemble est résolument élémentaire (pour ainsi dire) et ELEMENTAL explique « avoir choisi de reculer vers l'archaïsme, non pour une évasion nostalgique, mais pour servir de filtre naturel contre les clichés. À notre époque où la faim de nouveauté menace l'architecture de devenir immédiatement obsolète, nous avons cherché l'intemporalité ». On pourrait y voir comme un Stonehenge en bord de mer de l'époque moderne.
Les commentaires d'ELEMENTAL montrent aussi que toutes les régions du monde et tous les architectes ne présentent pas le même degré de sensibilisation ou d'évolution face aux défis du monde contemporain et de sa dynamique. Citant le danger pour l'architecture de devenir « immédiatement obsolète », ELEMENTAL cherche l'authenticité du véritablement ancien, un pari intéressant sur la situation actuelle. Il faut cependant reconnaître aussi que les maisons de ce livre et les architectes qui les ont imaginées ne représentent qu'une minuscule fraction de ce qui est construit et de ce qui peut être construit dans le monde. L'inventivité et l'intemporalité sont le privilège d'un très petit nombre, ce sont eux qui exerceront sans doute la plus grande influence sur ceux à venir. Alejandro Aravena est le deuxième lauréat du prix Pritzker de ce livre – mais ce n'est pas uniquement à sa collaboration étroite et fréquente avec le jury du prix qu'il se doit d'être aussi influent, c'est aussi sans aucun doute pour son travail qui cherche à apporter des solutions d'habitat contemporain aux plus défavorisés. Selon le jury du prix Pritzker : « Ce qui place véritablement Aravena à part, c'est son engagement en faveur du logement social. Depuis 2000 et la fondation d'ELEMENTAL, lui et ses collaborateurs ont constamment réalisé des projets aux objectifs sociaux clairs… Ils ont construit plus de 2500 unités d'habitation à l'aide de solutions architecturales imaginatives, modulaires et directement applicables au logement social à bas prix. »

Ce que nous devons à la réalité, la pauvreté et le besoin

C'est un autre terme de l'équation qui apparaît ici : les maisons individuelles ne sont en aucun cas particulièrement représentatives de la rencontre entre l'architecture et le monde réel. Elles restent un lieu d'expérimentation et d'invention, en partie du fait de la relation souvent étroite entre l'architecte et son client, mais aussi parce qu'une échelle moindre comporte un risque moindre. Si ELEMENTAL a conçu sur un mode « archaïque » une étonnante maison individuelle sur la côte, il ne fait aucun doute que ses collaborateurs travaillent aussi beaucoup à rendre l'architecture plus pertinente par rapport au monde moderne. Les artistes inventent peut-être le monde de demain, mais le champ d'action très réel et concret de l'architecture pourrait résider dans ce qu'elle doit à la réalité, la pauvreté et le besoin. Certains architectes comme Shigeru Ban (un autre lauréat du prix Pritzker) ont déployé beaucoup d'énergie et d'efforts pour des causes telles que le logement d'urgence après une catastrophe, même s'ils construisent aussi des maisons individuelles, mais bon nombre de leurs collègues continuent de chercher avant tout la richesse et la célébrité – plus faciles à gagner avec une maison remarquable pour deux personnes que sur un champ de ruines. L'idée de la responsabilité sociale de l'architecture contemporaine pourrait bien décliner, alors même que des idéaux conceptuels comme celui de « progrès » sont eux aussi en perte de vitesse dans tous les domaines de la culture. Il est évident, de même, que l'image industrielle et répétitive du modernisme vient en grande partie de son regain d'influence en Amérique, alors que le monde sortait de la guerre et de la destruction. Comme les idéaux des premiers constructivistes russes, qui espéraient donner forme à un monde nouveau pour tous à l'aide de la fonctionnalité technique, Gropius et le Bauhaus avaient eux aussi une conscience sociale. C'est peut-être aller un peu fort que d'affirmer que les architectes modernes ont « vendu leur stock », mais Gropius, Mies van der Rohe et les autres ont clairement semé les germes de paradigmes esthétiques et financiers qui ont dominé, d'abord l'Amérique, puis une majeure partie des pays développés après la Seconde Guerre mondiale. Car non, sans presque aucune exception, les maisons présentées ici n'ont pas été construites pour améliorer le sort de tous, mais bien pour plaire à des clients individuels – et aussi pour faire preuve de plus en plus de responsabilité face aux crises qui secouent la planète. Ce qui n'était qu'une option pour la minorité sensible aux questions écologiques a gagné le devant de la scène. Si les législations n'imposent pas de normes plus strictes, le bon sens le fera.

Le sixième continent (l'Europe)

L'émergence d'architectes de « nouvelles » parties du monde n'a, bien sûr, pas réduit pour autant la production de leurs confrères américains, européens ou japonais. Mais avec la découverte de nouveaux visages et de nouvelles formes, ils ne bénéficient peut-être plus d'autant de publicité, ce qui n'est vraiment pas une mauvaise chose. Deux nouvelles maisons en Allemagne illustrent les idées et les défis auxquels sont confrontés les architectes pour la conception et la construction de maisons individuelles. Andreas Wenning, qui a d'abord appris l'ébénisterie avant de devenir architecte, a longtemps été spécialisé dans la conception de maisons dans les arbres. Son expertise dans ce domaine a incité l'un de ses clients à Hanovre à lui demander, en plus d'une petite maison dans les arbres, un nouveau logement entier (l'Habitat vert, Green Dwelling, près de Hanovre, Allemagne, 2019, voir page 104). La qualité écologique de la construction et des fonctions de la structure était une préoccupation majeure de son client. « Le désir d'utiliser du bois comme matériau de construction principal à cet égard, explique Wenning, était parfaitement à notre goût. » En effet, si ses maisons dans les arbres ne se limitent pas à l'utilisation du bois, l'architecte possède manifestement une grande expérience de ce matériau de construction. Mais construire dans les arbres sans les abîmer constitue de toute évidence une approche intimiste du milieu naturel que l'architecture contemporaine s'est le plus souvent abstenue de suivre. Outre l'omniprésence du bois, l'architecte a imaginé faire de cette maison un projet vert global avec un vaste toit végétalisé, des chaudières à gaz à condensation, un chauffage par le sol et un système de contrôle de la ventilation.
L'autre projet allemand est la Maison au bord du lac de l'architecte Carlos Zwick (Haus am See, Potsdam, l'Allemagne, 2020, voir page 464). Des règlementations locales exigeaient que toute nouvelle construction soit en retrait à 50 mètres des rives du lac Jungfern. Zwick s'en est inspiré et a basé sur cette règle son projet conçu avec soin, qui a été réalisé sans toucher aux arbres sur le terrain et construit sans grue. Il a surélevé la maison sur des poteaux en acier et a pu ainsi satisfaire les autorités tout en préservant le site. Dans un commentaire très intéressant, Zwick déclare qu'il a trouvé l'inspiration pour

Formafatal, Atelier Villa, Bahia Ballena, Playa Hermosa, Costa Rica, 2016–19.

sa Haus am See dans la Farnsworth House de Mies van der Rohe (Plano, Illinois, États-Unis, 1951) – une retraite pour le week-end à pièce unique d'une superficie de 206 mètres carrés, surélevée à 1,6 mètre au-dessus du terrain souvent inondé. Le blanc et la légère élévation, ainsi que le vitrage sur toute la hauteur de la maison, donnent l'impression d'une présence comme aérienne, presque éphémère, dans le paysage. La Haus am See, de son côté, possède une surface au sol utile considérable de 610 mètres carrés. Flottant deux fois plus haut au-dessus du sol (trois mètres) que son double américain, la résidence de Zwick a un revêtement de bandes verticales étroites de mélèze, sans les plaques en acier qui définissent le toit et le sol de Farnsworth. Les 40 poteaux en diagonale qui portent la maison sont certainement plus présents que les pilotis de Mies van der Rohe, tandis qu'elle est constituée de deux éléments rectangulaires raccordés l'un à l'autre qui contrastent avec la stricte orthodoxie à quatre côtés du vieux maître. Le résultat peut être vu comme une version contemporaine du modernisme où l'acier blanc est remplacé par du bois grisé, la maison élevée encore plus haut (en partie pour des raisons administratives) tout en conservant l'expression strictement rectiligne de l'école (d'origine allemande) qui l'a influencée.

Ode à la réutilisation par l'adaptation

L'exemple de la Mole House d'Adjaye a déjà été cité, mais c'est loin d'être la seule maison récente construite sur la base d'une autre plus ancienne. Les architectes londoniens Carmody Groarke ont notamment reconverti un entrepôt victorien en briques pour en faire leur maison et studio (Lambeth, Londres, 2018, voir page 158). Les façades en briques restent de rigueur, mais l'intérieur est en béton du sol au plafond et sa conception ne déplairait pas au plus minimaliste des amateurs d'architecture. Le concept procède pour ainsi dire à une *tabula rasa* intérieure, tout en maintenant une présence extérieure qui ne se démarque pas du reste du quartier.
Un autre architecte basé à Londres a été encore plus loin dans la conservation de ce qui semblait une ruine complète. En travaillant sur une maison victorienne classée niveau 2 et les vestiges d'une fabrique de parchemin du XVIIe siècle – monument d'importance nationale –, Will Gamble a créé The Parchment Works (Northamptonshire, Royaume-Uni, 2018, voir page 238). Au lieu de démolir les ruines, il y a inséré deux nouveaux éléments en acier Corten, briques récupérées et chêne. Il a rendu apparents les poutres porteuses et les murs de pierre d'une étable existante, tandis qu'un socle en béton y était rajouté pour en faire un autre élément de la composition. La résidence de 200 mètres carrés construite pour 295 000 euros a été approuvée par les monuments historiques anglais et saluée comme l'une des maisons récentes les plus innovantes d'Angleterre.
L'art a longtemps glorifié les ruines, qu'elles soient réelles ou imaginaires, comme celles que l'on voit dans les tableaux de Claude Lorrain (1600–1682) ou les gravures de Piranèse (1720–1778). Certains artistes ont même été jusqu'à imaginer de futures ruines, comme la *Vue imaginaire de la grande galerie du Louvre en ruines* (1796, musée du Louvre) de Hubert Robert (1733–1808). Ces visions artistiques des ruines semblent toutes avoir en commun une certaine nostalgie pour la grandeur du passé, même si elles nous faisaient imaginer le présent en ruines. La réutilisation après adaptation de l'architecture a derrière elle une histoire bien plus longue et plus riche, que l'on peut faire remonter au moins jusqu'à l'époque romaine. Les temples deviennent ainsi des églises avec l'avènement de Théodose en 379, le Panthéon est reconverti en une église chrétienne consacrée à Sainte-Marie et aux Martyrs en 609. Plus proche de nous, l'impact sur l'environnement de la réutilisation et de l'adaptation a fait l'objet d'études précises. Des décharges qui débordent de déchets de construction à la réalisation de nouveaux bâtiments, l'architecture sous ses différentes (nouvelles) formes consomme en masse des matériaux de plus en plus rares et est une source de pollution majeure. Stephen Muench de l'université de Washington a notamment écrit dans un article récent : « Un projet de réutilisation individuel ne peut guère à lui seul avoir un impact important sur les émissions de carbone, mais à l'échelle de toute une ville ou de tout un pays, l'impact est énorme. À Portland par exemple, si les bâtiments qui seront démolis et reconstruits étaient plutôt réutilisés pendant les dix prochaines années, cela reviendrait à 231 000 tonnes de dioxyde de carbone de moins rejeté dans l'atmosphère, soit 15 % environ de l'objectif total de réduction des émissions du pays pour la prochaine décennie. » Cette parenthèse montre à quel point c'est un autre signe des temps que de

voir des maisons contemporaines construites sur des ruines ou qui réutilisent des structures existantes. On peut parier sans risque que les exemples seront bientôt plus nombreux dans le monde entier.
La grande diversité des maisons présentées ici ne peut que confirmer la chanson qui ouvre ce texte. Souvent belles, elles ne seront véritablement des maisons que si l'amour les habite, telles sont (on l'espère) les maisons pour notre temps.

You say you want a revolution
La chanson des Beatles continue avec les paroles :

You say you got a real solution
Well, you know / We'd all love to see the plan

(Tu dis que tu as une bonne solution
Bon, tu sais / Nous aimerions tous voir le plan)

Et s'il n'y avait pas de plan, mais quand même une révolution ? On discute depuis longtemps des avantages de l'architecture « verte », tout comme des questions de l'égalité des sexes ou de l'égalité raciale qui sont tournées dans tous les sens depuis des années. Mais maintenant, il est temps. Le monde connaît chaque année de nouvelles tempêtes millénaires, les glaciers sont en train de fondre, une extinction de masse sans précédent est en train de se produire. Alors oui, bien sûr, les maisons présentées ici ont l'air séduisantes et très calmes. Peut-être que la révolution se déroule ailleurs, au plus profond de concepts qui prennent en compte au moins certains des facteurs qui ont fait de l'architecture la perpétuelle icône de l'irresponsabilité écologique. Mais si au moins les femmes peuvent s'inscrire en nombre dans les écoles d'architecture du monde entier, cette révolution aussi est en train de se produire sans qu'un plan annoncé ait été transmis par une quelconque autorité supérieure. Quant à l'égalité raciale, elle progresse peut-être plus lentement mais les signes du changement sont plus forts que tout. Et si le reste du monde est devenu d'un seul coup « visible » grâce à Internet, si l'information circule plus librement, c'est aussi une révolution qui ne suit pas un plan prédéterminé. L'univers de la technologie rend tout plus accessible, de la conception à la fabrication, dans des matériaux et éléments de construction spécifiquement formés (sur mesure !). Et au lieu de coûter davantage et d'être réservée à quelques rares privilégiés, cette technologie est en fin de compte moins coûteuse et permet de construire des bâtiments uniques aussi facilement qu'avec des quadrillages au cordeau. De même le dernier diktat, celui de la ligne droite, est lui aussi peu à peu relégué aux oubliettes de l'histoire, car la pensée rectiligne était avant tout basée sur les économies d'échelle. Cela ne veut pas dire pour autant qu'un architecte ne peut plus construire un bâtiment carré ou rectangulaire – la plupart des maisons présentées ici sont des variations de ce paradigme –, cela veut seulement dire (et c'est la véritable révolution) que le choix est possible. La révolution de l'architecture contemporaine, qui s'exprime plus rapidement et plus entièrement dans les maisons individuelles, est un évènement historique, mais pas parce qu'un théoricien (ou, pire, un critique d'architecture) en a formulé les idées : ce sont les forces combinées du climat, de l'histoire et de la technologie qui font plier les formes et les méthodes architecturales. Car le (changement du) climat est l'incontestable force ultime qui affirme d'ores et déjà ses exigences.

And admit that the waters
Around you have grown
And accept it that soon
You'll be drenched to the bone

L'histoire trouve une expression dans le constat qu'un petit nombre d'hommes mûrs blancs ne peut pas s'accrocher au pouvoir indéfiniment et dans l'évolution des économies et des cultures de tant de pays dans le monde. Les femmes sont (enfin) présentes et les talibans n'y changeront rien, tout retour en arrière est exclu. La technologie, enfin, est l'agent non annoncé d'un changement massif. Dans son livre du même titre datant de 2004, Bruce Mau écrivait : « Le changement le plus massif ne concerne pas le monde du design, mais le design du monde. » La révolution n'est pas imminente, elle est immanente, et elle est ici.

Pages 42–43: SO–IL, Duravcevic-Ben Ari House, Long Island, New York, USA, 2016–19.

93 DESIGN STUDIO

Mountain House of Lew
Chongqing, China, 2017–19
Area: 300 m^2

The name of the Mountain House of Lew is derived from the architect's own name, which is 刘九三 or Liu Jiusan, and is further anglicized as Lew Joeson.

The architect rebuilt his own family house at the request of his father. His father asked for something grand enough to receive as many as 30 people at the time of the area's Spring Festival with as many terraces as possible. The center of the design is the original courtyard of the previous residence whose Feng Shui pattern was not to be disturbed. A high single-slope roof preserves the experience of the courtyard and maximizes window area. A box protruding from the roof houses a multifunctional space with views of both the front and back of the house and provides a balcony facing the courtyard. A semi-open path connects the front and back in a circular route that the architect likens to classical Chinese gardens. The principal resident of the house is the grandmother of the architect who has her bedroom, kitchen and living area on the same level. The lowest point of the sloping roof covers a storage room which can also be used as a temporary sleeping area for family gathering. Three lower-level bedrooms are complemented by a box with a sloping roof that can be used as a meeting room or temporary fold-out bed area. Lew, the name of the house, is an Anglicization of Liu, the family name of the architect.

Der Architekt baute sein Elternhaus auf Wunsch seines Vaters um, dem ein Haus vorschwebte, groß genug, um zum regionalen Frühlingsfest bis zu 30 Personen zu beherbergen, und mit möglichst vielen Terrassen. Mittelpunkt des Entwurfs ist der ursprüngliche Innenhof des früheren Wohnhauses, dessen Feng-Shui-Muster nicht verändert werden sollte. Ein hohes Pultdach bewahrt den Charakter des Hofs und maximiert die Fensterfläche. Ein aus dem Dach herausragender Kasten birgt einen multifunktionalen Raum mit Blick auf Vorder- und Rückseite des Hauses und verfügt über einen Balkon mit Hofblick. Ein halboffener Weg verbindet die Vorder- und Rückseite in einem Rundweg, den der Architekt mit klassischen chinesischen Gärten vergleicht. Die Hauptbewohnerin des Hauses ist die Großmutter des Architekten, deren Schlafzimmer, Küche und Wohnbereich auf einer Ebene liegen. Der tiefste Punkt der Dachschräge deckt einen Abstellraum ab, der bei Familientreffen auch als temporärer Schlafbereich genutzt werden kann. Drei Schlafzimmer im Untergeschoss wurden durch je eine Box mit schrägem Dach ergänzt, die als Versammlungsraum oder vorübergehender Schlafplatz dienen kann. Der Name des Hauses – Lew – ist eine Anglisierung von Liu, dem Familiennamen des Architekten.

The ceilings and walls seen here are partially clad in bamboo.

L'architecte a reconstruit ici sa maison familiale à la demande de son père, qui la souhaitait assez grande pour recevoir jusqu'à 30 personnes pendant le festival du printemps de la région, et avec le plus de terrasses possibles. L'ensemble est centré sur la cour d'origine de la première habitation, dont la disposition feng shui ne devait pas être troublée. Un haut toit à pente unique préserve l'atmosphère de la cour pour une surface de fenêtres maximale. Un caisson dépasse du toit et abrite un espace polyvalent avec vue à la fois sur l'avant et l'arrière de la maison et un balcon face à la cour. Un passage semi-couvert relie l'avant et l'arrière sur un trajet circulaire que l'architecte compare aux jardins chinois classiques. La principale occupante de la maison est la grand-mère de l'architecte, elle possède sa chambre à coucher, sa cuisine et son salon sur un seul niveau. À son point le plus bas, le toit incliné recouvre une pièce de rangement qui peut aussi servir de chambre d'appoint lors des réunions de famille. Trois chambres au niveau inférieur sont complétées par un bloc au toit incliné qui peut offrir une salle de réunion ou un dortoir provisoire avec des lits pliants. Le nom de la maison – Lew – est une forme anglicisée de Liu, le nom de famille de l'architecte.

GUILLERMO ACUÑA ARQUITECTOS ASOCIADOS (GAAA)

Isla Lebe
Rilan, Chiloé, Chile, 2016–20
Area: 315 m²
Site area: 4.8 hectares
Collaboration: Luis Miranda (Carpenter/Builder)

'he structures are seen near the waters of the 3ay of Rilán on the image above. The converted ormer boathouse with its red-painted ground floor s visible on the right page.

'he Isla Lebe is part of the Chiloé archipelago ınd is located just 150 meters from the coast ɔf the bay of Rilan, in Southern Chile in the .os Lagos region. Its total area is 4.8 hectares, vith a length of 600 meters and a width of 30 meters. At low tide it is connected to the coast, meaning that the Isla Lebe is in a constant state of flux, a reality that the architect ıas used to inspire his designs for this place. Relatively austere wooden structures covered with larch shingles, alternating with large vertical panes of glass, have been built here over time, ncluding a boathouse, a guest house, and two 60-square-meter buildings connected by walkways. The ground level of the former boathouse s used for the kitchen and dining room and is painted bright red because of an indigenous lowering bush that grows on the island – called chilco (*Fuchsia magellanica*). The architect's living space is on the new upper level, and furnishings from the house were in part recovered from a local church that was destroyed in an earthquake. Guillermo Acuña explains, "An exterior staircase connects to a house that became two guesthouses. A terrace and walkways lead tc two houses that are identical (but one proportionally larger than the other), and continue through the site, which is being reforested, finally leading to the beach. The architecture changes and the landscape changes."

Die Isla Lebe gehört zum Archipel von Chiloé und liegt nur 150 Meter vor der Küste der Bucht von Rilan im Süden Chiles in der Region Los Lagos. Ihre Gesamtfläche beträgt 4,8 Hektar mit 600 Meter Länge und 80 Meter Breite. Bei Ebbe ist sie mit der Küste verbunden, sodass sich die Insel in ständiger Bewegung befindet, eine

arge glazed windows in the guesthouse dining room ffer views of the fjord, while high ceilings and wood urfaces contribute to a feeling of comfort within view f a broad natural expanse.

Tatsache, die den Architekten zu seinen Entwürfen für diesen Ort inspirierte. Hier wurden relativ karge Holzbauten mit einer Außenverkleidung aus Lärchenschindeln errichtet, die sich mit großen vertikalen Glasscheiben abwechseln. Unter diesen Gebäuden befinden sich ein Bootshaus, ein Gästehaus und zwei durch Stege miteinander verbundene 60 Quadratmeter große Bauten. Das Erdgeschoss des ehemaligen Bootshauses dient als Küche und Esszimmer und ist in Anlehnung an einen einheimischen, auf der Insel wachsenden Strauch namens Chilco (*Fuchsia magellanica*) leuchtend rot gestrichen. Der Wohnraum des Architekten befindet sich im neuen Obergeschoss, und die Einrichtungsgegenstände des Hauses wurden zum Teil aus einer örtlichen, bei einem Erdbeben zerstörten Kirche geborgen. „Eine Außentreppe führt zu einem Haus, aus dem zwei Gästehäuser entstanden", schildert Guillermo Acuña. „Über eine Terrasse und Gehwege erreicht man erst zwei identische Häuser (eines davon allerdings proportional größer als das andere) und dann durch das aufgeforstete Gelände hindurch den Strand. Die Architektur verändert sich und die Landschaft verändert sich."

Isla Lebe est l'une des îles de l'archipel de Chiloé, située à seulement 150 mètres de la côte dans la baie de Rilan – dans la province chilienne de Los Lagos, dans le sud du pays. Sa surface est de 4,8 hectares, elle est longue de 600 mètres et large de 80 mètres. Elle est rattachée au littoral à marée basse, ce qui donne une impression de flux et de reflux constants, un fait dont l'architecte s'est inspiré pour ses créations sur l'île. Des structures en bois relativement austères couvertes en bardeaux de mélèze qui alternent avec de grandes vitres verticales

An exterior view of house 3, where the kitchen-living room opens to the landscape over the garden and water.

y ont été construites, notamment un hangar à bateaux, une pension et deux bâtiments de 60 mètres carrés reliés les uns aux autres par des passages. Le rez-de-chaussée de l'ancien hangar à bateaux sert de cuisine et de salle à manger, il est peint dans un rouge vif qui rappelle les fleurs d'un buisson local qui pousse sur l'île, appelé chilco ou fuchsia de Magellan (*Fuchsia magellanica*). L'architecte a aménagé son lieu de vie au nouvel étage, meublé en partie avec des objets récupérés dans une église locale détruite par un tremblement de terre. Guillermo Acuña explique qu'« un escalier extérieur mène à une maison transformée en deux maisons d'hôtes. Une terrasse et des sentiers permettent de rejoindre deux autres maisons identiques (même si l'une est proportionnellement plus grande que l'autre) et se poursuivent sur tout le site reboisé avant d'arriver à la plage. L'architecture change et le paysage change avec elle ».

ADJAYE ASSOCIATES

Mole House
London, UK, 2013–18
Area: 256 m²
Collaboration: Yohannes Bereket, Isabel De Azevedo, Irena Stoeva

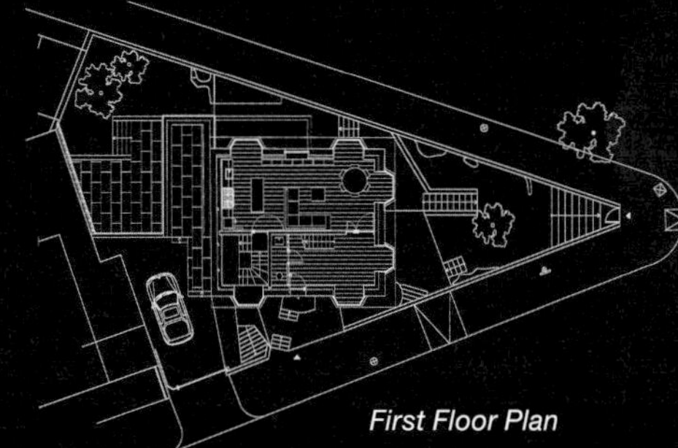

First Floor Plan

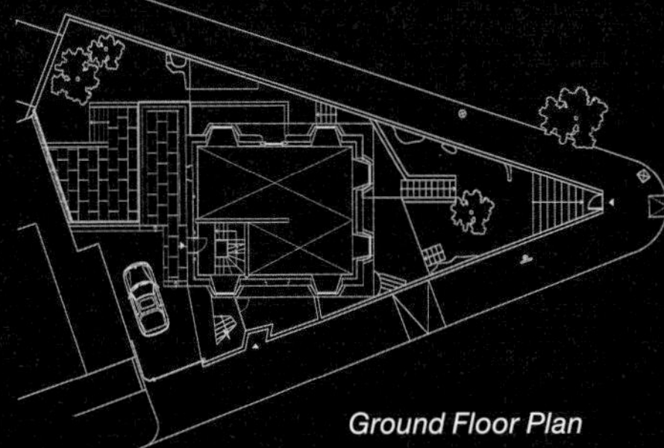

Ground Floor Plan

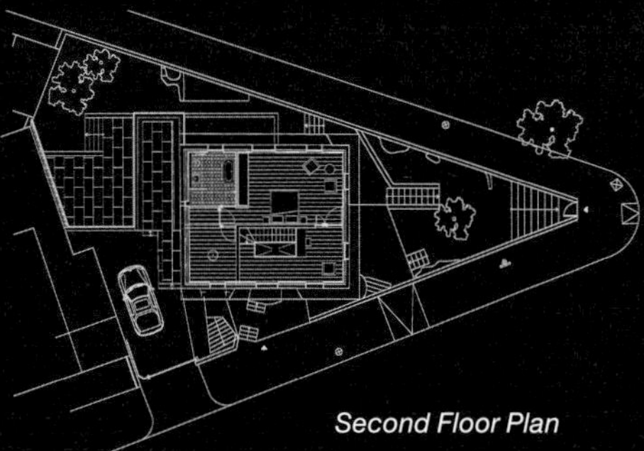

Second Floor Plan

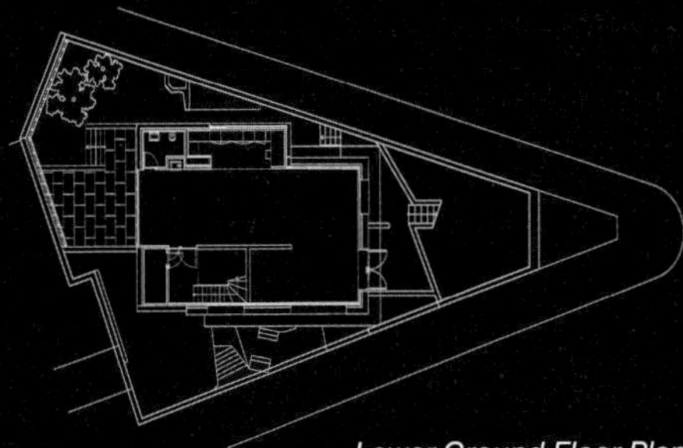

Lower Ground Floor Plan

Much of the original masonry of the house as well as the aged exterior render were conserved, while a cross-shaped concrete element was added to support the floors and divide parts of the structure.

The Mole House, located in the London Borough of Hackney, was designed as place to live and work for the artist Sue Webber. The client and the architect agreed to retain much of the character of the original detached Victorian house which was occupied for 40 years by a person known as the Hackney Mole Man. This resident created an elaborate system of tunnels beneath the house that had to be filled with 30 tons of aerated concrete to insure the stability of the house. The three-story house was expanded at the basement level. The multiple entrances of the house are an echo of the earlier tunnel excavations. The character of the house and even its time-worn appearance were retained and reinstated where necessary with reclaimed London bricks. In this respect the architectural design is both daring and yet entirely contextual, a tribute to the skills of David Adjaye. The interior walls and floors of the original house were removed to create a concrete and timber environment featuring a cantilevered staircase that leads to the generous basement artist's studio. A skylight as well as full height windows assure amply interior luminosity. According to the architects, "Mole House demonstrates a combined vision between client and architect that exalts urban, tactile and personal histories. Its design approach is defined by considered restoration, material authenticity, and elevated functionality."

Das Mole House im Londoner Stadtbezirk Hackney wurde für die Künstlerin Sue Webber als Wohn- und Arbeitsort entworfen. Bauherrin und Architekt waren sich einig, den Charakter des 40 Jahre lang von einer als „Hackney Mole Man" bekannten Person bewohnten ursprünglichen viktorianischen Einfamilienhauses weitgehend zu erhalten. Dieser Bewohner schuf ein ausgeklügeltes unterirdisches Tunnelsystem, das mit 30 Tonnen Porenbeton gefüllt werden musste, um die Stabilität des Gebäudes zu gewährleisten. Das Kellergeschoss des dreistöckigen Hauses wurde erweitert, und seine zahlreichen Eingänge erinnern an die einstigen Tunnelgrabungen. Der Charakter des Gebäudes und sogar sein veraltetes Aussehen wurden beibehalten und, wo nötig, mit wiederverwendeten Londoner Ziegeln ergänzt. In dieser Hinsicht zeigt sich der architektonische Entwurf als kühn und gleichzeitig als absolut kontextbezogen, eine Hommage an die Fähigkeiten David Adjayes. Die Innenwände und Böden des ursprünglichen Hauses wurden entfernt, um eine Umgebung aus Beton und Holz mit einer freitragenden Treppe zum Künstleratelier im Untergeschoss zu schaffen. Ein Oberlicht sowie raumhohe Fenster sorgen für reichlich Helligkeit im Inneren. Laut Adjaye „zeigt Mole House eine gemeinsame Vision von Bauherrin und Architekt, die urbane, taktile und persönliche Geschichten betont. Der Designansatz ist geprägt von durchdachter Restaurierung, Materialauthentizität und gehobener Funktionalität."

_ooking from the kitchen to the dining area, which ıas shelves requested by Sue Webster for artwork ıs opposed to closed cupboards. Opposite: the main space with a 4.8-meter-high concrete ceiling and florescent lighting.

_a Mole House, dans le quartier londonien de Hackney, a été conçue comme le lieu de vie et de travail de l'artiste Sue Webber. _a cliente et l'architecte ont convenu de conserver beaucoup du caractère de l'ancienne maison individuelle victorienne, dont l'occupant pendant quarante ans était connu sous le nom d'« homme-taupe » (Mole Man). Il y a en effet créé un réseau très élaboré de tunnels qui ont dû être comblés avec 30 tonnes de béton cellulaire pour garantir la stabilité du bâtiment. La maison de trois niveaux a été élargie au sous-sol, tandis que ses nombreuses entrées font éch0o aux anciens tunnels. Le caractère de l'ensemble, y compris son aspect usé et décrépi, a été 2conservé, et même rétabli au besoin à l'aide de briques londoniennes récupérées. L'ensemble est à cet égard à la fois audacieux et entièrement contextualisé, grâce au talent de David Adjaye.

Les murs et les sols intérieurs d'origine ont été retirés afin de créer un environnement dominé par le béton et le bois d'œuvre, avec un escalier en porte-à-faux qui mène au vaste atelier en sous-sol de l'artiste. Une lucarne et des fenêtres sur toute la hauteur de la pièce rendent l'intérieu très lumineux. Pour les architectes, « Mole Hous est le résultat d'une vision commune à la cliente et à l'architecte qui exalte le récit urbain, concre et personnel. Sa conception associe une restauration bien réfléchie, des matériaux authentiques et une grande fonctionnalité ».

ADND

Casa Feliz
Alibag, India, 2017–20
Area: 743 m²
Collaboration:
Dinesh Thakur (Senior Architect),
Benson D'Souza

he design alternates broad openings and brick walls.
)pposite: *Steel frames large, glazed surfaces that*
pen to luxuriant garden spaces.

he house is approached via a driveway that urves around dense existing trees. The impressive 6-meter wide main steel door of the house s set in a brick façade. According to the archiects, this gesture "redefines scale and acts as divider between the outside and the inside vorld." Located in the coastal town of Alibag, vhich is 120 kilometers south of central Mumbai, ne house is set on an 8100-square-meter site nd has a square central courtyard landscaped vith two green mounds and palm trees. The ouse is made up of two L-shaped blocks, one f which is solid and the other "permeable." An levated swimming pool is set on a gravel deck hat is detached from the structure. The architects xplain, "The house concentrates on encompassing nature all around, hence blurring the boundries of the inside outside experience." Built for a ost of $1,350,000, the house has floors covered with Nexion tiles, and walls are finished with polymer plaster, veneer paneling and Bombay tiles. The furniture was sourced in Bali or custom-built on site. A central element of the furnishings is the large, petrified wood table in the living area. Although broad, nearly blank brick walls characterize much of the exterior perimeter of the house its inner character is light and open, allowing residents to have the sentiment of being outside while they are in fact in a luxurious enclosed environment in this tropical setting.

ie Zufahrt zum Haus erfolgt über eine Auffahrt, ie sich durch dichten Baumbestand windet. Die eeindruckende sechs Meter breite Haustür aus tahl wurde in eine Backsteinfassade eingefügt. aut den Architekten definiert diese Geste „den Maßstab neu und fungiert als Trennwand zwischen Außen- und Innenwelt". Das Haus liegt in er Küstenstadt Alibaug, 120 Kilometer südlich es Zentrums von Mumbai, auf einem 8100 Quadratmeter großen Grundstück. Es verfügt über inen quadratischen Innenhof mit Palmen und wei begrünten Hügeln. Das Haus besteht aus wei L-förmigen Blöcken, von denen einer massiv und der andere „durchlässig" ist. Ein erhöht elegener Swimmingpool ist in ein separates Kiesdeck eingelassen. „Das Haus strebt danach, ie umliegende Natur miteinzubeziehen und so ie Grenzen zwischen innen und außen verschwimmen zu lassen", so die Architekten. Die Böden des für 1,35 Millionen Dollar erbauten Hauses sind aus Nexion-Fliesen, die Wände aus Polymerputz, Furnierverkleidungen und Bombay Fliesen. Die Möbel stammen aus Bali oder sind lokale Maßanfertigungen. Ein zentrales Einrichtungselement ist der große versteinerte Holztisch im Wohnbereich. Obwohl breite, fast leere Ziegelwände einen Großteil des Außenbereichs prägen, wirkt das Innere des Hauses hell und offen und verleiht so den Bewohnern das Gefühl, im Freien zu sein, obwohl sie sich in Wirklichkeit in einer luxuriösen, geschlossenen Umgebung inmitten dieses tropischen Umfelds befinden.

On the previous double page: *the elevated, stone-edged pool.* On this page: *the local climate permits full connections between interior spaces and the garden.* Right: *the main living area with a large, petrified wood table.*

La voie d'accès à la maison décrit une courbe autour de denses bouquets d'arbres. L'imposante porte en acier de six mètres de large est encastrée dans une façade en briques. Pour les architectes, il s'agit de « redéfinir l'échelle et de créer une division entre le monde extérieur et le monde intérieur ». Située dans la ville côtière d'Alibaug, à 120 kilomètres au sud de Mumbai, la maison occupe un terrain de 8100 mètres carrés et dispose d'une cour intérieure carrée aménagée autour de deux tertres de verdure et de palmiers. Elle est formée de deux blocs en L, dont l'un est compact et l'autre « perméable ». La piscine surélevée est posée sur une plate-forme de graviers qui se détache de l'ensemble. Les architectes expliquent que « la maison vise avant tout à enclore la nature alentour, et gomme pour cela les frontières intérieur/extérieur ». Construite pour 1,35 million de dollars, ses sols sont en carreaux Nexus et les finitions des murs en plâtre polymère, avec des panneaux de bois plaqués et des carreaux de Bombay. Le mobilier vient de Bali ou a été réalisé sur mesure sur place. L'un des éléments centraux en est la grande table en bois pétrifié du séjour. Malgré les vastes murs de briques presque aveugles qui définissent la majeure partie de son périmètre extérieur, l'intérieur de la maison présente un caractère clair et ouvert qui donne à ses habitants l'impression de se trouver à l'extérieur dans ce décor de luxe enclos dans son cadre tropical.

AIRES MATEUS

House in Campo de Ourique
Lisbon, Portugal, 2016–19
Area: 583 m²
Collaboration: Miguel Passos de Almeida (Co-author)

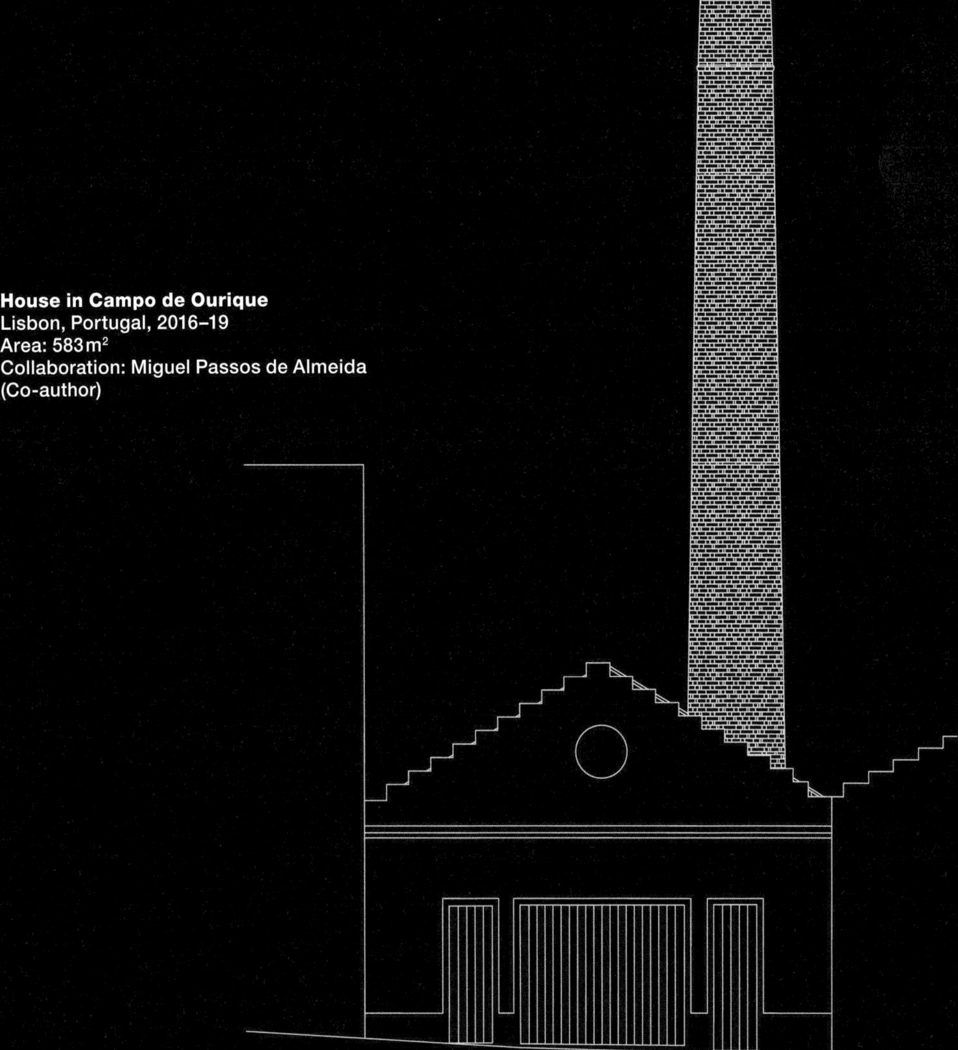

Above and opposite: *the large living space is a skillful evocation of the original building's industrial orientation while instilling the kind of surprising modernity for which the architects are well known.*

The Campo de Ourique is on one of the seven hills of the historic center of Lisbon and this house was built on a 286-square-meter site. Although the area is largely residential, this project made use of an existing factory, retaining a large living and kitchen area "in the archetypical shape of the warehouse." The bedrooms and bathrooms are situated at ground level. A high brick smokestack was retained in the design, but the architects have in a sense subverted it by opening the space beneath. Aires Mateus here again demonstrates their unique capacity to enter an existing, in this case industrial space, and to transform it into a modern building with surprising openings and generous (public) spaces. The complex way in which they handle volumes and light is surely modern, but this design succeeds in liberating former industrial space and making it light, airy and contemporary. A surprising and successful concept of a home for our time.

Der Campo de Ourique ist einer der sieben Hügel des historischen Zentrums von Lissabon, und dieses Haus wurde dort auf einer Fläche von 286 Quadratmetern erbaut. Obwohl das Gebiet größtenteils aus Wohnhäusern besteht, diente dem Projekt eine bestehende Fabrik als Konstruktionsbasis, wobei ein großer Wohn- und Küchenbereich „in der archetypischen Form eines Lagerhauses" bestehen blieb. Die Schlafzimmer und Bäder befinden sich im Erdgeschoss. Ein hoher Ziegelschornstein blieb zwar erhalten, wurde von den Architekten aber gewissermaßen unterlaufen, indem sie den darunterliegenden Raum öffneten. Aires Mateus stellen hier erneut ihre einzigartige Fähigkeit unter Beweis, einen bebauten, in diesem Fall industriellen Ort zu

Plans and a section show the smokestack on the right.

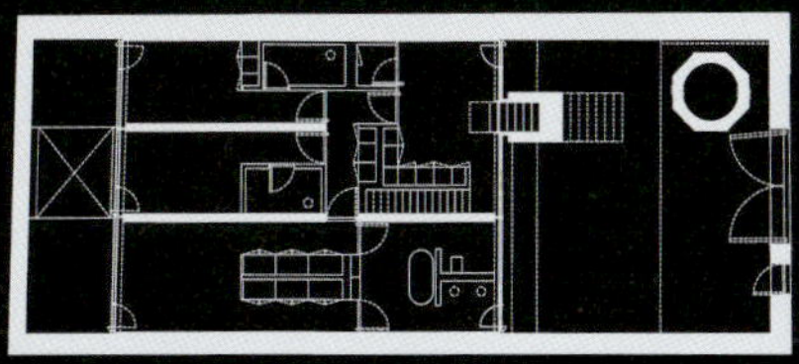

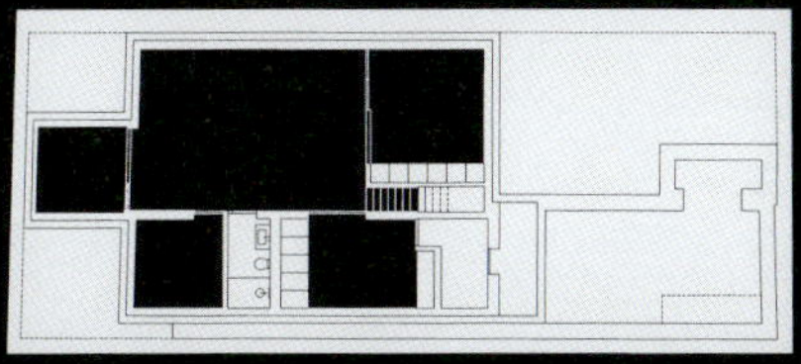

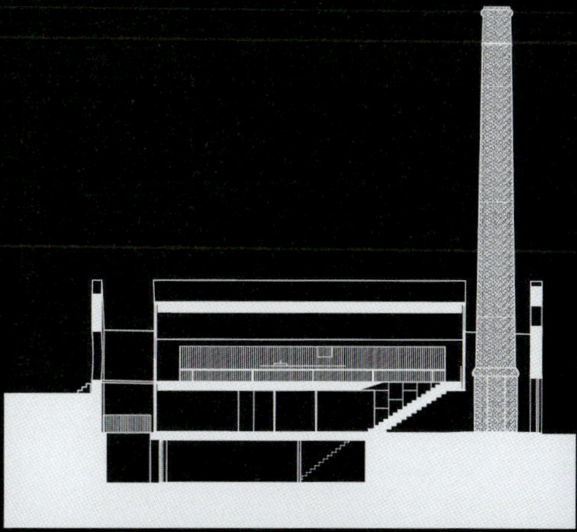

Concrete steps lead down from the main living space to the lower level where the bedrooms are located. Light and dark provide contrast, as does the choice of materials: wood, tiles, concrete and glass.

erobern und in ein modernes Gebäude mit überraschenden Öffnungen und großzügigen (öffentlichen) Räumen zu verwandeln. Die komplexe Art und Weise des Umgangs mit Raum und Licht ist sicherlich modern, doch diesem Entwurf gelingt es, einen ehemaligen Industrieort zu befreien und ihn leicht, luftig und zeitgemäß zu gestalten. Ein überraschendes und gelungenes Konzept für ein Zuhause in unserer Zeit.

Le Campo de Ourique est l'une des sept collines du centre historique de Lisbonne, la maison y a été construite sur un terrain de 286 mètres carrés. Bien que le quartier soit surtout résidentiel, le projet exploite la présence d'une usine et a conservé « la forme archétypale de l'entrepôt » avec un vaste espace séjour et cuisine. Les chambres et les salles de bains sont situées au rez-de-chaussée. Le concept inclut une grande cheminée en briques d'origine, mais les architectes l'ont pour ainsi dire renversée en ouvrant l'espace situé en dessous. Aires Mateus apporte ici une fois de plus la preuve de son talent unique à pénétrer un espace existant, dans ce cas industriel, et à le transformer en un bâtiment moderne aux ouvertures surprenantes et aux espaces (communs) généreux. Leur manière complexe de manipuler les volumes et la lumière est incontestablement moderne, mais la grande réussite de ce concept est de libérer l'ancien espace industriel pour le rendre léger, aérien et contemporain. Une vision surprenante et remarquable de maison pour notre temps.

BARCLAY & CROUSSE

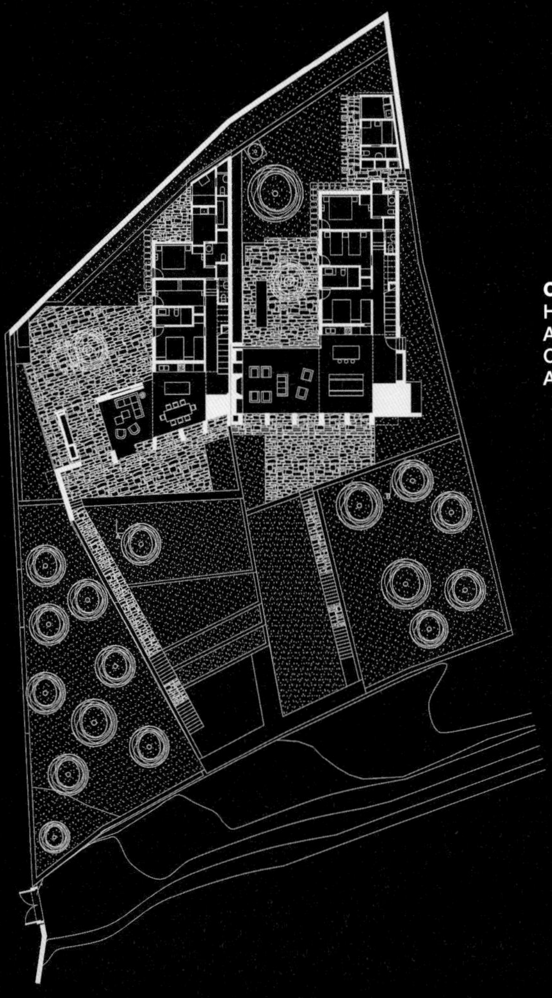

Casa Huayoccari
Huayoccari, Cusco, Peru, 2016–18
Area: 218 m²
Collaboration: Tommaso Cigarini, Andrea Otero

As the architects explain, the architecture is more closely related to the mountainous site than it is to local traditions. Opposite: *the unexpected, almost jumbled appearance of the house is underlined by a series of rough stone retaining walls and steps.*

The house was built on a 975-square-meter site. Local Andesita red stone was used as cladding including for the roof. The reinforced-concrete structure makes use of reddish puzzolanic cement. Ceramic floors are contrasted with whitewashed walls and carpentry in Aguana masha wood *(Machaerium inundatum)*. Casa Huayoccari was built at an altitude of 2950 meters above sea level in the valley of Urubamba, which is surrounded by peaks that were considered sacred by the Incas. Huayoccari is located near the Pitusiray, a 4991-meter-high mountain. According to the architects: "The project does not refer to the traditional architecture of the valley, but, instead, to the mountains that surround it." The gable roof "is decomposed into two planes that adapt to the pitch of the surrounding mountains, thus generating spatial compressions that frame the low valley and the dilatations that lead toward the Pitusiray." The inclination of the stone roof intentionally absorbs early morning sun, while the stone roof protects residents from the strong afternoon sun. The concrete and stone design is intended to use the thermal mass of the structure to preserve daytime warmth during the cool mountain nights. The mountain theme is also emphasized in the layout of the house, an L-shaped floor plan that offers a patio that faces the Pitusiray. The living and dining spaces and three bedrooms look toward the patio on the lower floor. The master bedroom is on the upper floor and includes a terrace.

)as Haus wurde auf einem 975 Quadratmeter
roßen Grundstück errichtet. Für die Verkleidung nd das Dach kam roter Andesit aus der Region um Einsatz, während für die Stahlbetonkons-
ruktion rötlicher Puzzolanzement verwendet
yurde. Die Keramikböden kontrastieren mit
en weiß getünchten Wänden und den Zimmer-
iannsarbeiten aus Aguana-Masha-Holz
Machaerium inundatum). Die Casa Huayoccari
egt auf 2950 Metern ü. NN im Urubamba-Tal,
mgeben von Gipfeln, die von den Inkas als heilig
ngesehen wurden. Huayoccari liegt in der Nähe
es Pitusiray, eines 4991 Meter hohen Berges.
Das Projekt verweist nicht auf die traditionelle
rchitektur des Tals, sondern auf die Berge,
ie es umgeben", erklären die Architekten. Das
iiebeldach „ist in zwei Ebenen zerlegt. So passt
s sich der Neigung der umliegenden Berge
n und erzeugt räumliche Verdichtungen, die
das niedrige Tal und die Ausdehnungen zum Pitusiray hin einrahmen." Dank der Neigung des Steindachs wird die Morgensonne absorbiert, während es die Bewohner vor der starken Nachmittagssonne schützt. Mit der Konstruktion aus Beton und Stein soll die thermische Masse genutzt werden, um die Tageswärme in den kühlen Bergnächten zu bewahren. Das Bergthema wird auch durch den Grundriss betont, einen L-förmigen Raumplan, der eine Terrasse mit Blic auf den Pitusiray umfasst. Die Wohn- und Essbereiche sowie die drei Schlafzimmer sind auf den Innenhof im unteren Stockwerk hin ausgerichtet. Das Hauptschlafzimmer befindet sich im Obergeschoss und verfügt über eine Terrasse.

'he ceramic-tiled floor and wood-formed concrete :eiling create a feeling of warmth and connection o the site, which is seen through large openings.)pposite below: *section/elevation drawings.*

.a maison a été construite sur un terrain de)75 mètres carrés. Le parement de ses façades, out comme du toit, est en pierre rouge d'andé- ;ite locale. La structure en béton armé comprend Ju ciment pouzzolanique de teinte rougeâtre. .es sols en céramique contrastent avec les nurs blanchis à la chaux et la charpente en bois le moutouchi des montagnes (*Machaerium nundatum*). La Casa Huayoccari a été construite ı 2950 mètres au-dessus du niveau de la mer lans la vallée d'Urubamba, entourée de mon- agnes sacrées pour les Incas. Huayoccari se rouve à proximité du Pitusiray dont le sommet :ulmine à 4991 mètres. Selon les architectes, « le projet ne fait pas référence à l'architecture raditionnelle de la vallée, mais aux montagnes qui l'entourent ». Le toit à pignon « est décom- osé en deux plans qui adoptent la pente des nontagnes environnantes et génèrent ainsi des compressions spatiales pour encadrer la basse vallée et des dilatations spatiales qui mènent au Pitusiray ». L'inclinaison du toit en pierre est délibérément conçue pour laisser passer le soleil du petit matin, tandis qu'il pro- tège les habitants du fort soleil de l'après-midi. La construction en béton et pierre exploite la masse thermique de la structure afin de conserver la chaleur du jour pendant les nuits fraîches en montagne. Le thème de la montagne est aussi mis en avant par la disposition des élé- ments de la maison, dont le plan au sol en forme de L qui ouvre un patio face au Pitusiray sur lequel donnent les espaces de vie et de repas, ainsi que trois chambres, à l'étage inférieur. La chambre principale se trouve à l'étage et com- prend une terrasse.

BAROZZI VEIGA

Private Apartment
Barcelona, Spain, 2016–17
Area: 80 m²
Collaboration: Cecilia Rueda
and Fabrizio Barozzi

Barozzi explains that his goal, working with Cecilia Rueda, was to bring luminosity into the apartment and to create a "fluid, continuous, open-plan layout to maximize" the relatively small space available.

The architects Fabrizio Barozzi and Alberto Veiga together with their respective partners Cecilia Rueda and María Díaz undertook similar projects at about the same time in 2016–17 to renovate existing apartments as their own residences in Barcelona. The process is of interest perhaps because of both the similarities and the dissimilarities of the spaces conceived by the partners.

Etwa zeitgleich, 2016/17, setzten Fabrizio Barozzi und Alberto Veiga gemeinsam mit Cecilia Rueda und María Díaz in Barcelona Projekte zur Renovierung bestehender Wohnungen in Wohnhäusern zur Eigennutzung um. Es sind die Ähnlichkeiten wie auch die Unterschiede in beiden Entwürfen, die diesen Prozess so interessant machen.

En 2016–17, ils ont tous les deux entrepris des projets similaires à peu près au même moment avec leurs partenaires respectives afin de rénover des appartements pour en faire leur domicile à Barcelone. L'intérêt de ce travail réside peut-être autant dans les ressemblances que dans les dissemblances des espaces conçus par les différents partenaires.

CECILIA RUEDA AND FABRIZIO BAROZZI
Private Apartment:
This small apartment in the Eixample area of Barcelona was finished with a concrete floor, mirror walls, a stainless-steel kitchen, and according to the architects' description, "flexible space." A palette of light gray materials "creates a sense of spaciousness, while a few mirror surfaces enhance the perspectives and reflect the outside vegetation." Mobile partitions are used to provide privacy or change the spaces as required. The architects say, "With precise and

lean interventions, the design seeks to solve the ifferent inclinations of a corner typology to reach simple neutral space, where light is the protaonist of the project."

rivate Apartment:
iese kleine Wohnung in Barcelonas Eixampleiertel wurde mit Betonboden, Spiegelwänden, iner Edelstahlküche und, so die Beschreibung er Architekten, „flexiblem Raum" ausgestatet. Eine Palette hellgrauer Materialien „schafft in Gefühl von Geräumigkeit, während einige piegelflächen die Perspektiven erweitern und ie Außenvegetation widerspiegeln". Mobile rennwände schaffen Privatsphäre oder veränern die Räume nach Bedarf. Die Architekten rläutern dazu: „Mit präzisen und sauberen ingriffen versucht das Design, die unterschiedchen Tendenzen einer Ecktypologie aufzuheben um einen einfachen neutralen Raum zu kreieren, in dem das Licht der Protagonist ist."

Private Apartment:
Ce petit appartement du quartier de l'Eixample, à Barcelone, présente un sol en béton, des murs en miroirs, une cuisine en inox et un « espace flexible », selon les termes des architectes. La gamme de matériaux gris clair utilisés « crée une impression d'espace, tandis que certaines des surfaces en miroir rehaussent les perspectives et reflètent la végétation extérieure ». Des cloison mobiles permettent d'offrir plus d'intimité ou de modifier les espaces selon les besoins. Les archi tectes déclarent : « En intervenant de manière claire et précise, le concept cherche à venir à bou des pentes différentes dans une typologie d'angl pour obtenir un espace simple et neutre, dont la lumière est l'acteur principal. »

BAROZZI V

GV Office Apartment
Barcelona, Spain, 2016
Area: 110m^2
Collaboration:
Alberto Veiga and María Díaz

Alberto Veiga's apartment is darker than that of his colleague Barozzi. He has sought, together with María Díaz to unify the originally "fragmented" aspect of his slightly larger space using painted wood, a continuous micro-cement floor, dark sheer curtains and mirrors.

ALBERTO VEIGA AND MARÍA DÍAZ

GV Office Apartment:
Explaining that the original apartment concerned reflected a typical "fragmented plan," the architects state, "The renovation pivots around the idea of getting the most from each fragment of space available to create a well-defined and bright series of rooms." A continuous "micro-cement" floor and painted wood give a feeling of continuity to the whole. Reflecting surfaces mirror the main spaces, while sheer, dark curtains divide them, contrasting with the brighter feeling of the Barozzi-Rueda apartment.

GV Office Apartment:
Mit dem Hinweis auf den „fragmentierten Grundriss" der ursprünglichen Wohnung erklären die Architekten: „Die Neugestaltung dreht sich um die Idee, das Beste aus jedem verfügbaren Raumfragment herauszuholen, um klar definierte und helle Räume zu schaffen." Ein durchgehender Boden aus „Mikrozement" und gestrichenes Holz verleihen dem Ganzen ein Gefühl von Kontinuität. Glänzende Oberflächen spiegeln die Haupträume, während durchsichtige dunkle Vorhänge sie voneinander trennen und einen Kontrast zur Helligkeit der Wohnung von Barozzi-Rueda bilden.

GV Office Apartment:
Les architectes expliquent que l'appartement d'origine reflétait un « plan morcelé » typique et que « la rénovation est centrée autour de l'idée de tirer le meilleur parti de chacun des fragments d'espace disponibles afin de créer une suite de pièces claires et bien délimitées ». Un revêtement de sol continu en « microciment » et des boiseries peintes donnent à l'ensemble une impression de continuité. Les surfaces réfléchissantes reflètent les espaces principaux, tandis que des rideaux transparents et sombres les divisent, à la différence de l'impression de plus grande clarté que donne l'appartement Barozzi-Rueda.

LUCIANO LERNER BASSO

Fortunata House
Caxias do Sul, Brazil, 2019–20
Area: 240 m²

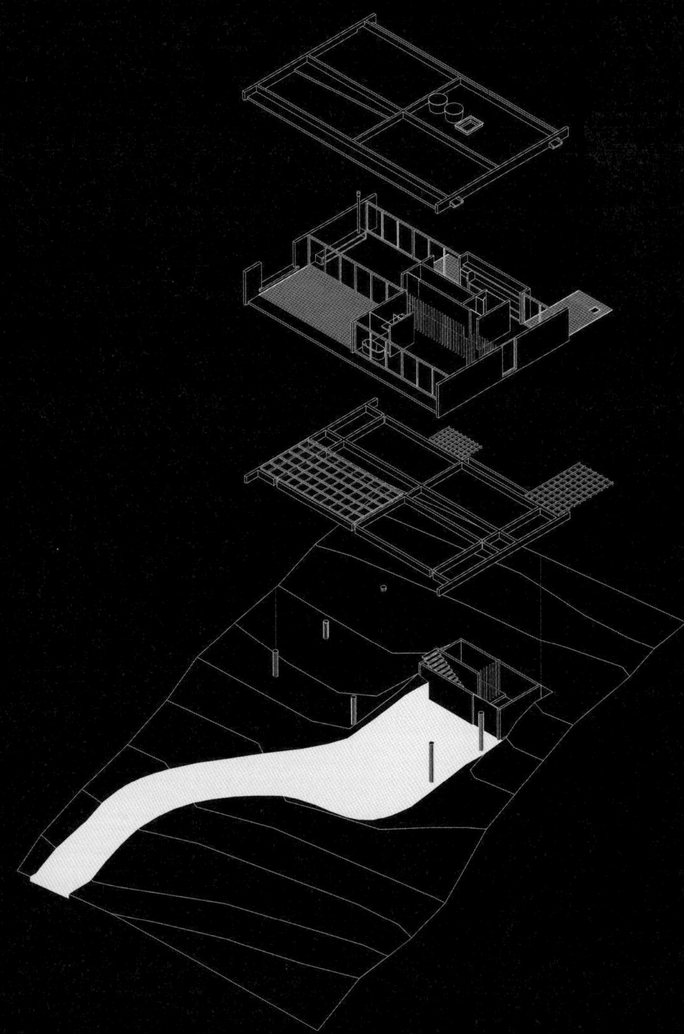

Concrete pilotis lift the house off the sloped site to conserve existing trees. Despite the modern, planar design, the many openings of the house allow it to blend into the forest setting.

Caxias do Sul is a city established by Italian immigrants in 1890 in the southern state of Rio Grande do Sul. The Fortunata House was built on a steep slope in the Atlantic Forest in an area that is characterized by relatively harsh winters. It was built around a Brazilian pine (*Araucaria angustifolia*), which is a critically endangered species, so the house was built on pilotis to avoid disturbing the terrain and the space beneath it is used as a carport. Four rectangles form the upper-level plan, and three terraces built with wood from the concrete formwork connect the house to a back patio. The main building material is exposed, reinforced concrete, which is frequently used in the region because of its low maintenance and good resistance to climate conditions there. As the architect states: "Fortunata is a structure that shows itself raw and rough both on the outside and inside." Careful attention was paid not only to the preservation of the site, but also to energy usage, with efficient cross ventilation, reuse of rainwater, natural lighting, and an ecological heating system. Built for a cost of $80 000 on a 1000-square-meter site, the house was awarded a Saint Gobain Brazil Architecture Award in 2021.

A large tree emerges from a tiled concrete terrace. The exposed concrete forms set out the limits of the architecture, but nature is omnipresent around, but also within the boundaries of the house.

Caxias do Sul ist eine 1890 von italienischen Einwanderern gegründete Stadt im südlichen Bundesstaat Rio Grande do Sul. Fortunata House liegt an einem steilen Hang im Atlantischen Regenwald, einem Gebiet mit relativ strengen Wintern. Es wurde um eine Brasilkiefer (*Araucaria angustifolia*) herum gebaut, deren Art vom Aussterben bedroht ist. Um das Terrain nicht zu beeinträchtigen, steht das Haus auf Pfeilern (*Pilotis*), und der Platz darunter wird als Carport genutzt. Vier Rechtecke bilden den Grundriss des Obergeschosses, und drei Terrassen aus dem Holz der Betonschalung verbinden das Haus mit einem rückwärtigen Patio. Das in der Region oft verwendete Hauptbaumaterial Sichtstahlbeton ist wartungsarm und sehr klimabeständig. „Fortunata ist ein Bauwerk, das sich sowohl von außen als auch von innen roh und ungeschliffen zeigt", so der Architekt. Geachtet wurde nicht nur auf den Schutz des Standorts, sondern auch auf die Energienutzung mit effizienter Querlüftung, Wiederverwendung von Regenwasser, natürlicher Beleuchtung und einem ökologischen Heizsystem. Das Haus wurde für 80 000 Dollar auf einer Fläche von 1000 Quadratmetern errichtet und erhielt 2021 einen Architekturpreis von Saint Gobain Brasilien.

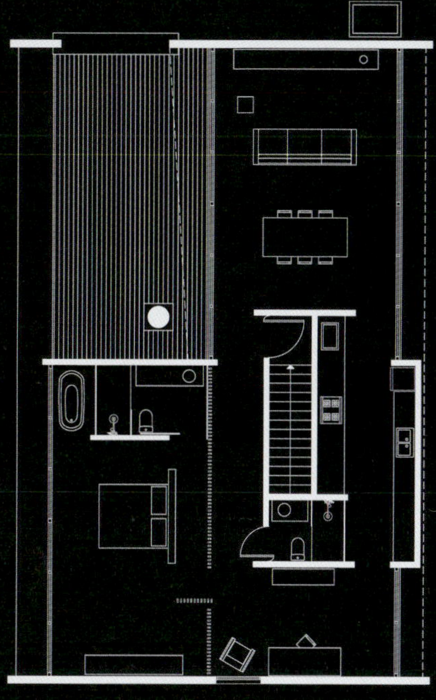

Wood-formed in situ concrete creates a mineral interior that benefits from carefully placed openings that admit natural light as seen in these images.

Top: *the rectilinear upper floor plan.*

Caxias do Sul a été créée par des immigrants italiens en 1890 à Rio Grande do Sul, dans le sud du Brésil. La maison Fortunata a été construite sur un versant escarpé de la forêt atlantique, dans une région aux hivers plutôt rudes. Elle est bâtie autour d'un pin du Paraná (*Araucaria angustifolia*), une espèce en danger d'extinction, de sorte que la maison a été montée sur des *pilotis* pour éviter d'endommager le terrain – l'espace en dessous sert d'abri à voiture. Le plan de l'étage supérieur est composé de quatre rectangles, tandis que trois terrasses construites avec le bois du coffrage utilisé pour le béton relient la maison à un patio. Le principal matériau est du béton armé apparent, fréquent dans la région où il est apprécié pour le peu d'entretien qu'il exige et pour sa résistance aux conditions climatiques. Selon les architectes : « Fortunata est une structure qui paraît brute et rude à l'intérieur comme à l'extérieur. » La préservation du site a fait l'objet d'une grande attention, de même que la consommation énergétique au moyen d'un système de ventilation croisée, de la réutilisation de l'eau de pluie, d'un éclairage naturel et d'un chauffage écologique. Construite pour 80 000 dollars sur un terrain de 1000 mètres carrés, la maison a gagné un prix d'architecture de Saint-Gobain Brésil en 2021.

BAUMRAUM

Green Dwelling
near Hanover, Germany, 2018–19
Area: 250 m²
Collaboration: Petra Pelz, Peter Berg
(Garden Design)

Above: *the new house, with the originally planned treehouse in the background.* Opposite top: *the cross-laminated timber structure allows direct access to the garden.*

Wenning's clients for this project decided to add to their existing house in which they lived with their parents, purchasing an extra 2000 square meters of land adjacent to their property. Their original request was for a tree house, but they decided to also build a new house. Space for guests, a sauna, and a closed parking area were part of the scheme. Both the clients and the architect wished to emphasize the ecological quality of the structures, and they focused on wood as the main building material. A Z-shaped plan allows for a large living area and open kitchen in the front and a bedroom, bathroom, and guest room to the rear with direct garden access. The entire structure was built with cross-laminated timber boards, using spruce and an interior layer of larch. Interior flooring is in oak planks. Heat is generated by gas-condensing boilers. The planned tree house was integrated into an oak tree at the western side of the property. Three flights of stairs lead to a terrace four meters above the ground and a square cabin a further two meters up in the tree. The solid oak tree house actually rests on laminated oak supports, while the terrace is supported using ropes anchored to the tree. Wenning used reflective stainless steel for the façades. The tree house is provided with heat and electricity for year-round use. Large windows allow for panoramic views of the garden. The tree house has an interior area of eight square meters and the terrace measures 14 square meters.

Für dieses Projekt beschlossen Wennings Kunden, ihr Haus, in dem sie mit ihren Eltern lebten, zu erweitern, indem sie ein zusätzliches 2000 Quadratmeter großes Nachbargrundstück erwarben. Ihr ursprünglicher Wunsch war ein Baumhaus, doch dann entschieden sie sich zudem für ein neues Haus mit Platz für Gäste, einer Sauna und einer geschlossenen Autostellfläche. Sowohl Bauherren als auch Architekt wollten die ökologische Qualität des Neubaus betonen und setzten auf Holz als Hauptmaterial. Ein Z-förmiger Grundriss ermöglicht einen großen Wohnbereich und eine offene Küche im vorderen Bereich sowie ein Schlafzimmer, ein Bad und ein Gästezimmer im hinteren Bereich mit direktem Gartenzugang. Die gesamte Struktur wurde mit Brettsperrholzplatten aus Fichte und einer Innenschicht aus Lärche errichtet, die Innenböden bestehen aus Eichendielen. Die Wärmeerzeugung erfolgt durch Gasbrennwertkessel. Das Baumhaus ist in eine Eiche an der Westseite des Grundstücks integriert. Drei Treppenläufe führen zu einer Terrasse in vier Metern Höhe und zu einer quadratischen, zwei Meter darüberliegenden Hütte. Während das Baumhaus aus massiver Eiche auf laminierten Eichenstützen ruht, wird die Terrasse von am Baum verankerten Seilen gehalten. Für die Fassaden verwendete Wenning reflektierenden Edelstahl. Das Baumhaus ist mit Heizung und Strom ausgestattet und kann das ganze Jahr über genutzt werden. Große Fenster bieten einen Panoramablick über den Garten. Das Baumhaus hat eine Innenfläche von acht Quadratmetern, die Terrasse misst 14 Quadratmeter.

'he generous wood-clad interiors of the house ›ffer fully-glazed sliding walls that permit a direct 'onnection to the garden.

.es clients de Wenning pour ce projet voulaient 'ajouter à la maison dans laquelle ils vivaient ıvec leurs parents et ont acheté pour cela :000 mètres carrés supplémentaires du terrain ıdjacent à leur propriété. Leur première demande :onsistait en une maison dans les arbres, mais ls ont ensuite décidé de construire aussi une ıouvelle maison. L'ensemble comprenait l'es-›ace nécessaire pour accueillir des hôtes, un ;auna et un parking fermé. Les clients et l'archi-ecte désiraient tous les deux mettre en avant a qualité écologique du projet et ont privilégié e bois comme matériau de construction prin-:ipal. Le plan en forme de Z dessine un vaste ›space de séjour et une cuisine ouverte à l'avant le la maison, une chambre, une salle de bains ›t une chambre d'hôtes à l'arrière avec accès lirect au jardin. La structure a été entièrement – de l'épicéa avec une couche intérieure de mélèze. Les sols intérieurs sont en chêne. Le chauffage est assuré par des chaudières à gaz à condensation. La maison dans les arbres a été intégrée à un chêne du côté ouest de la propriété. Trois volées de marches mènent à une terrasse à quatre mètres au-dessus du sol, puis à une cabane carrée deux mètres plus haut. La petite maison en chêne massif repose sur des supports en chêne lamellé, tandis que la terrass est fixée par des cordes fixées à l'arbre. Wenning a choisi de l'acier inoxydable réfléchissant pour les façades. La maison dans l'arbre est chauffée et électrifiée afin de pouvoir être utilisée toute l'année. De grandes fenêtres lui donnent une vue panoramique du jardin. Sa surface intérieure est de 8 mètres carrés, celle de la terrasse de 14 mètres carrés.

LINA BELLOVIČOVÁ

House LO
Chriby, Czech Republic, 2019–20
Area: 160 m²

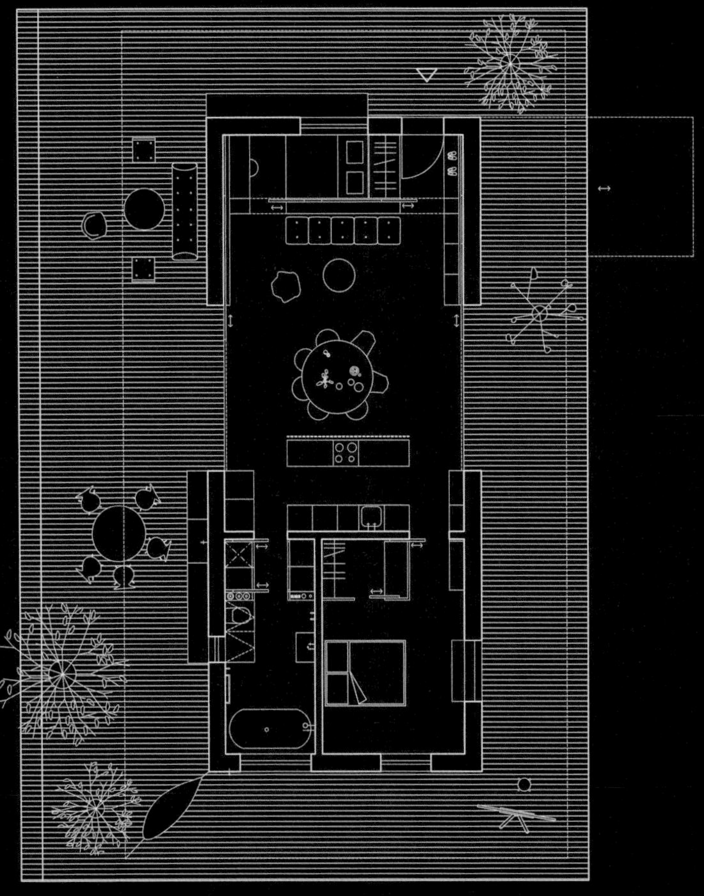

The house has walls made of hempcrete and an overhanging green roof, making it as ecologically responsible as possible.

Built for a cost of 200 000 euros, this house has a concrete basement and is made of timber and hempcrete with plywood furniture inside. The owner of this house dreamed of having a home that related to its natural setting and wanted to use hempcrete, which had never been used as a building material in the Czech Republic. Hemp is related to marijuana but does not contain high levels of THC. Hempcrete, which weighs about 12% as much as an equivalent volume of concrete, was first used for non-load-bearing walls in France in the 1990s. It has the advantage of drawing carbon dioxide from the air as it dries, and it is recyclable and resistant to pests, fire, and mold. The rectangular house opens out to its natural setting with large sliding glass walls. There are two bedrooms and a bathroom as well as a cellar that contains the owner's photography lab, technical installations, and storage space.

A large terrace runs around the house beneath the overhanging green roof. The architect explains: "The layout of the house is designed to use its space to the fullest. The house will gradually become part of the nature. First it will be a home to a family with two children, later become a family summer retreat, and even later a comfortable home for an elderly couple."

arge windows and a terrace mediate the ıteraction between the interiors and the grassy atural setting.

)as für 200 000 Euro errichtete Haus steht auf ›inem Betonsockel, ist aus Holz und Hanfbeton :onstruiert und hat Möbel aus Sperrholz. Der :igentümer träumte von einem mit seiner natür-chen Umgebung verbundenen Haus und wollte ɨanfbeton verwenden, der in der Tschechischen Republik noch nie als Baumaterial genutzt wor-len war. Hanf ist mit Marihuana verwandt, weist ıber keinen hohen THC-Gehalt auf. Hanfbeton, lessen Gewicht ca. 12 Prozent jenes einer ›ntsprechenden Betonmenge beträgt, wurde ›rstmals in den 1990ern in Frankreich für nicht ragende Wände verwendet. Er nimmt beim 'rocknen Kohlendioxid aus der Luft auf, ist recy-:elbar und resistent gegen Schädlinge, Feuer ınd Schimmel. Das rechteckige Haus öffnet sich nit großen Glasschiebewänden zur Natur hin. Es 'erfügt über zwei Schlafzimmer, ein Badezim-ner und einen Keller, in dem sich das Fotolabor des Eigentümers sowie technische Anlagen und Lagerräume befinden. Eine großzügige Terrasse unter dem überhängenden Gründach verläuft um das Haus. „Der Grundriss des Hauses ist so konzipiert, dass der Raum optimal genutzt wird“, erläutert die Architektin. „Das Haus wird nach und nach Teil der Natur werden. Zu Beginn wird es das Zuhause einer Familie mit zwei Kindern sein, dann ein Sommerhaus für die Familie und später ein komfortables Zuhause für ein älteres Ehepaar.“

The interior design emphasizes an obvious simplicity tempered by the presence of glazed walls that appear to bring the exterior closer to the tan and gray surfaces of walls, floors and ceiling.

Construite pour 200 000 euros, la maison possède un sous-sol en béton, mais est par ailleurs construite en bois et briques de chanvre, avec du mobilier en contreplaqué. Le propriétaire rêvait d'une maison en rapport avec le cadre naturel et souhaitait utiliser les briques de chanvre pour la première fois en République tchèque. Le chanvre est apparenté à la marijuana, mais sa teneur en THC est faible. Les briques de chanvre pèsent près de 12 % d'un volume de béton équivalent et ont été utilisées pour la première fois en France dans les années 1990 pour des murs non-porteurs. Elles présentent l'avantage de retenir le dioxyde de carbone de l'air en séchant, elles sont recyclables et résistent aux insectes, au feu et aux moisissures. La maison rectangulaire ouvre sur la nature par de grandes parois vitrées coulissantes. Elle comporte deux chambres et une salle de bains, ainsi qu'une cave avec le laboratoire photo du propriétaire, les locaux techniques et un espace de rangement. Une grande terrasse entoure la maison sous le toit végétalisé en surplomb. L'architecte explique que « la forme de la maison est conçue pour exploiter au maximum l'espace. Elle est appelée à s'intégrer progressivement à la nature. Elle sera d'abord une maison pour une famille de deux enfants, puis une villégiature familiale et plus tard un logis confortable pour un couple âgé ».

repello
model S
S

THIAGO BERNARDES

Triângulo House
São Paulo, Brazil, 2013–16
Area: 1430 m²

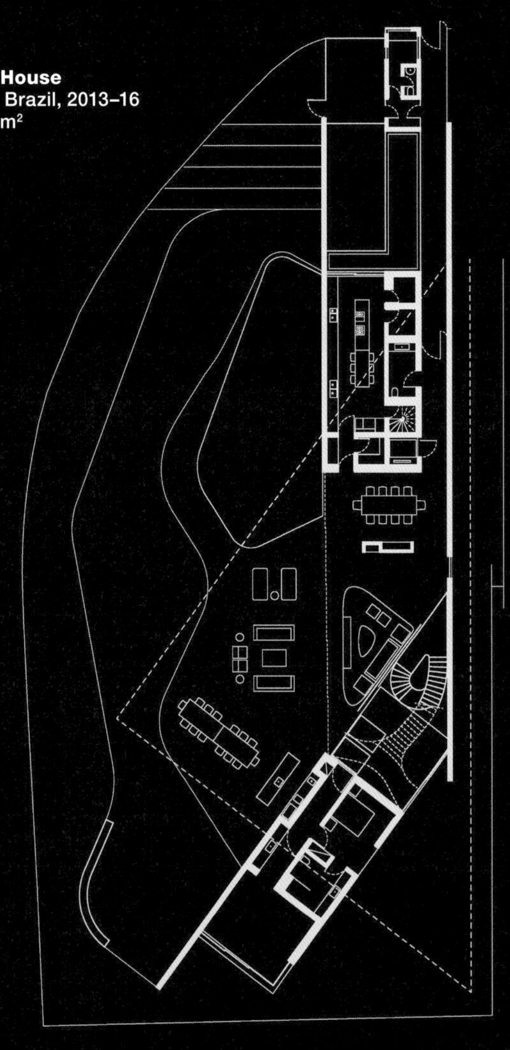

'he triangular volume of this house rests on :oncrete walls. The form was selected because ›f the shape of the 1825-square-meter site and to ›rofit from the orientation of the sun. The scheme ılso frees more space for the garden. A metallic attice around the external perimeter of the upper riangle allows for generous cantilevers. An "or- ganic" stairway beneath a large skylight connects he underground areas, the ground floor where he living and dining spaces are located, and the op level where there is another living room, bed- ooms, an office, and a secondary service core. ∖ large irregular-form swimming pool sits outside, ›pposite the living and dining areas. Large panels ›f screen-printed brise-soleil glass, which dimin- ish the effects of the sun, surround the upper volume. In the style of very large Brazilian houses ısed extensively for entertainment, this resi- lence takes advantage of a relatively restricted urban site to create a protected environment for the obviously well-off owners.

Das dreieckige Volumen des Hauses ruht auf Betonwänden. Gewählt wurde diese Struktur aufgrund der Form des 1825 Quadratmeter großen Grundstücks und um die Ausrichtung der Sonne voll auszunutzen. Zudem schafft dieses Design mehr Platz für den Garten. Ein Metallgitter um den äußeren Verlauf des oberen Dreiecks ermöglicht eine großzügige Auskragung. Eine „organische" Treppe unter einem großen Oberlicht verbindet die unterirdischen Bereiche, das Erdgeschoss, in dem sich Wohn- und Essbereich befinden, und das Obergeschoss, das ein weiteres Wohnzimmer, Schlafzimmer, ein Büro und Hauswirtschaftsräume beherbergt. Gegenüber dem Wohn- und Essbereich liegt ein großzügiger, unregelmäßig geformter Swimmingpool.

Große Paneele aus siebbedrucktem Brise-Soleil-Glas, die die Sonneneinstrahlung abschwächen, umgeben den oberen Gebäudeteil. Im Stil der sehr weitläufigen brasilianischen Häuser, meist für Freizeitaktivitäten, nutzt dieses Wohnhaus einen verhältnismäßig beschränkten urbanen Standort voll aus, um eine geschützte Umgebung für die offensichtlich wohlhabenden Eigentümer zu schaffen.

Le volume triangulaire de la maison repose sur des murs en béton. La forme a été choisie pour s'adapter à celle du site de 1825 mètres carrés et pour profiter de l'orientation du soleil. Elle permet aussi de libérer de l'espace pour un jardin. Un treillis métallique entoure le périmètre extérieur du triangle supérieur et permet de généreux surplombs. Un escalier « organique » sous une immense lucarne relie le sous-sol, le rez-de-chaussée, qui accueille les espaces séjour et repas, et l'étage avec un autre salon, les chambres, un bureau et un noyau technique secondaire. Une vaste piscine de forme irrégulière a été creusée à l'extérieur face aux espaces de séjour et de repas. Le volume supérieur est entouré de grands panneaux brise-soleil en verre sérigraphié qui atténuent les effets du rayonnement solaire. Dans la lignée des immenses maisons brésiliennes qui servent essentiellement aux loisirs, cette résidence tire profit d'un terrain urbain relativement réduit afin de créer un environnement protégé pour ses propriétaires visiblement aisés.

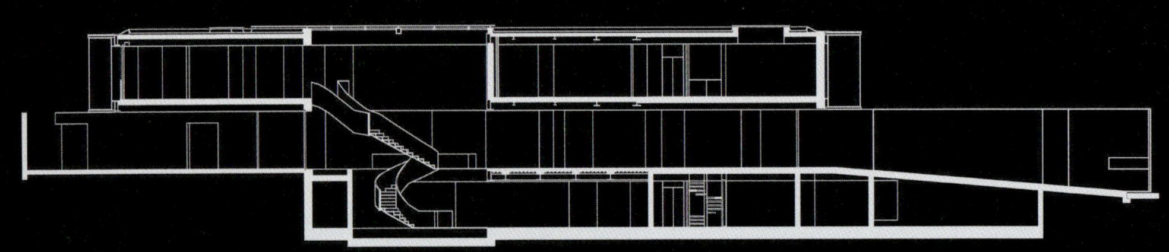

The “organic” stairway links the three levels of the house from basement to the top floor living areas. Below and left: *section drawings show how the overlapping levels of the house are related.*

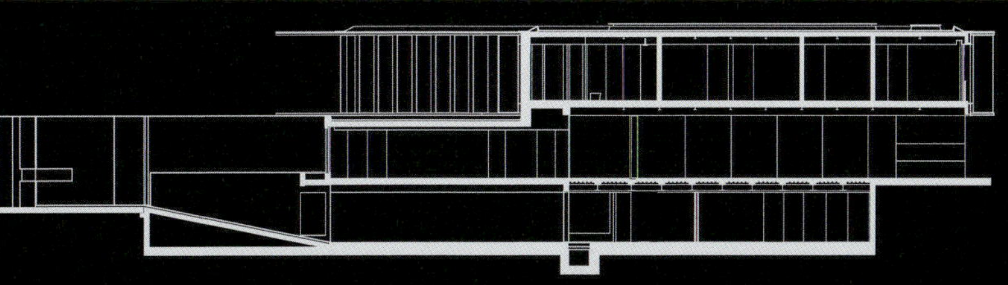

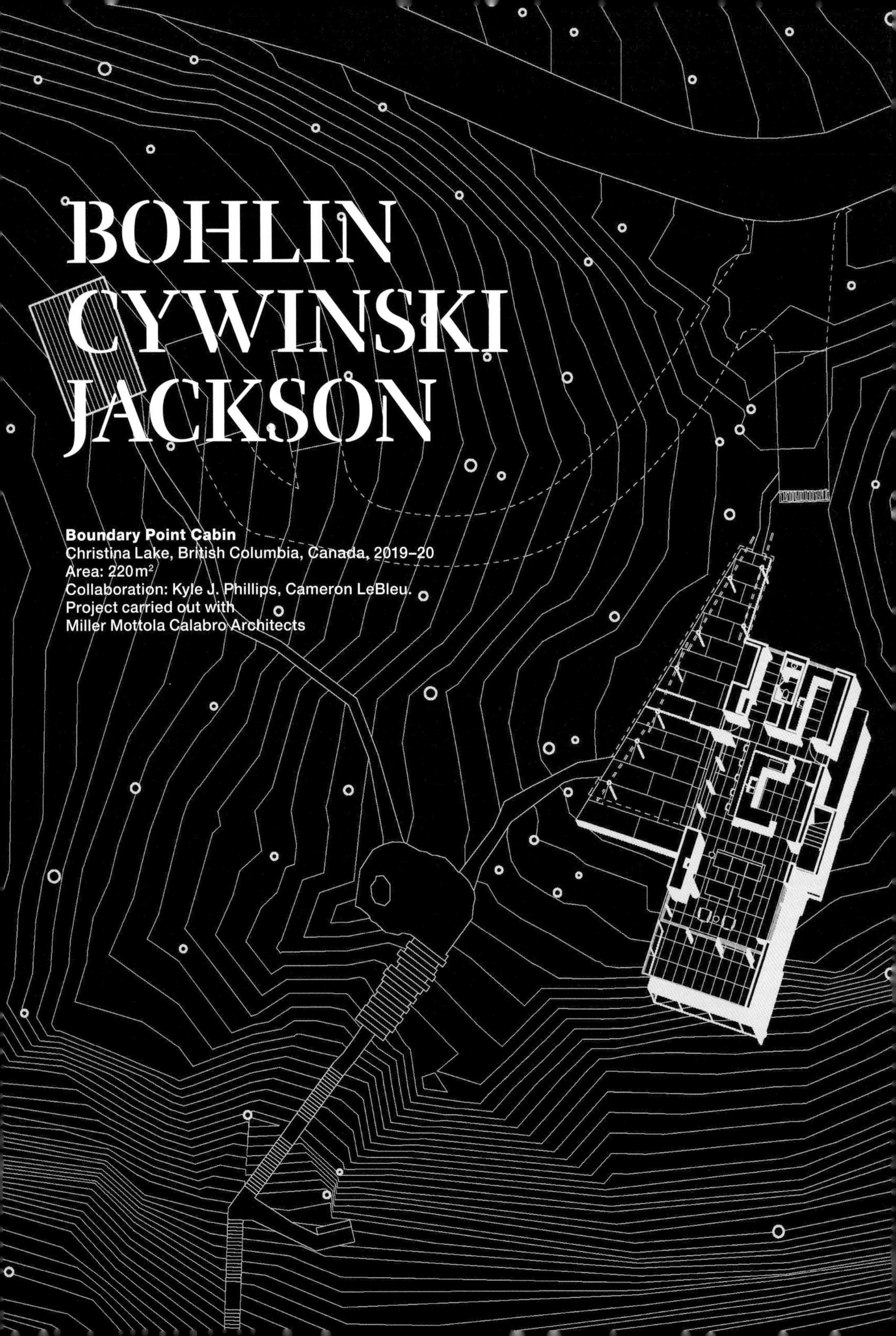

BOHLIN CYWINSKI JACKSON

Boundary Point Cabin
Christina Lake, British Columbia, Canada, 2019–20
Area: 220 m²
Collaboration: Kyle J. Phillips, Cameron LeBleu.
Project carried out with
Miller Mottola Calabro Architects

The house is deeply inserted into its wooded setting above Christina Lake. Opposite top: *a rear view shows the dark wooden volume of the cabin and the lake to the right.*

Christina Lake is in southern British Columbia, near the US border. Set above the lake, the Boundary Point Cabin is used as a summer family home. The architects explain: "Embracing the sensation of floating in the forest, we designed a cabin that cantilevers over the rock outcropping and mirrors the steep topography in its wedge-like form. The home celebrates the exhilaration of its surroundings and the communal nature of family gatherings at the lake." The exterior of the cabin was made with cast-in-place concrete, structural steel, Douglas fir laminated beams, a standing seam metal roof, Western red cedar siding, fiber-cement panels, and Loewen windows and doors. The interior materials include pre-finished birch plywood, Marbletrend porcelain tile, white oak flooring, and quartzite countertops.

Der Christina Lake liegt im Süden von British Columbia nahe der Grenze zu den USA. Die Boundary Point Cabin liegt oberhalb des Sees und dient der Eigentümerfamilie als Sommerhaus. „Wir griffen das Gefühl, im Wald zu schweben auf, um eine Hütte zu entwerfen, die über den Felsvorsprung hinausragt und mit ihrer Kleilform die Landschaft widerspiegelt", erklären die Architekten. „Das Haus zelebriert die Freude an der Umgebung und den gemeinschaftlichen Charakter von Familientreffen am See." Das Äußere der Hütte wurde aus Ortbeton, Baustahl, laminierten Douglasienbalken, einem Stehfalzmetalldach, einer Verkleidung aus Holz der westlichen Rotzeder, Faserzementplatten sowie Loewen-Fenstern und -Türen gefertigt. Für die Innenausstattung wurden u. a. vorgefertigtes Birkensperrholz, Marbletrend-Porzellanfliesen, Böden aus Weißeiche sowie Arbeitsplatten aus Quarzit verwendet.

A section drawing emphasizes the roof that is angled toward the water on the steeply sloped site.

ıteriors are largely clad in birch plywood with /hite oak floors, giving a warm feeling that is ›mphasized by the generous views of the natural etting offered by large, glazed surfaces.

.e lac Christina se trouve dans le sud de la Colombie-Britannique, près de la frontière ımericaine. La petite maison surplombe le lac et sert de villégiature familiale l'été. Les archiectes expliquent qu'ils ont « repris la sensation le flotter dans la forêt et ont conçu une cabane qui s'avance en porte-à-faux sur l'affleurement pour refléter le paysage avec sa forme en angle. .a maison célèbre l'ivresse générée par l'environnement et la nature communautaire des réunions amiliales au bord du lac ». L'extérieur est en béton coulé sur place, acier de construction, poutres amellées de sapin de Douglas, un toit métallique ı joint debout, un bardage en cèdre rouge, des panneaux de fibrociment, des portes et fenêtres .oewen. À l'intérieur, on trouve des matériaux tels que du contreplaqué de bouleau préfini, des carreaux en porcelaine Marble Trend, un sol en chêne blanc et des plans de travail en quartzite.

ALEX BRAHM AND ANTONIO POLIDURA

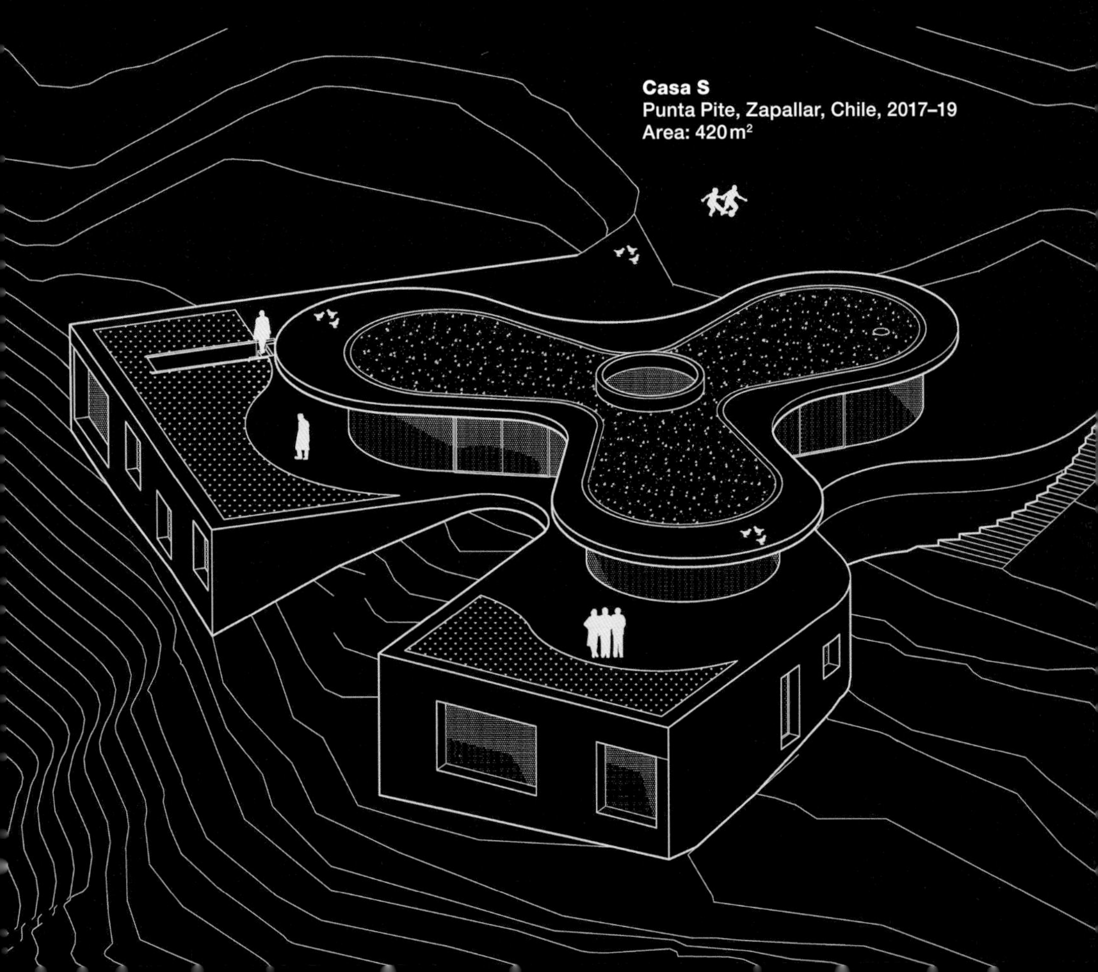

ʌs seen from above, the curving form of the house, ɔomewhat akin to a three-leafed clover, sits on its ocky site with a generous landscaped area and an ɲngular pool.

Opposite: *A rough stone path and the terrace of the house allow it to better blend into the site, while the fully glazed, curving walls seem to bring the spectacular Pacific Ocean setting inside.*

ʼhis house for friends of the architects was eveloped by two associated Santiago offices— -Arquitectos, where Alex Brahm is a Partner, ınd Gubbins+Polidura, where Antonio Polidura vorks. Punta Pite is located between Papudo ınd Zapallar on the northern coast of Chile. The 6500-square-meter site is about 100 meters long ınd slopes down toward the ocean. These facts equired the creation of a podium on which the ıouse could be built. The clients liked the idea of a simple design with soft curves from which he views could be easily enjoyed. The angular podium allows for three bedrooms and spaces for children on one side and the master bedroom on he other. The volumes of the amoeboid, glazed ıouse are arrayed above, around the central core that has a spiral staircase leading to the ower-floor private spaces. The kitchen area is to he southeast, a living space with a suspended fireplace is set to the southwest, and the dining area is on the northern side. The architects designed the furniture for the residence in part because of the complexity of its forms. The roof of the house is supported by 21 steel columns, each 2.3 meters high. The house was built in concrete, steel, and glass on a 6500-square-meter site for a construction budget of $750 000.

The spiral staircase that seems very much in place given the curved forms of the house connects the main level living area with the lower level private zone of the residence.

Dieses Haus wurde für Freunde der Architekten von zwei miteinander verbundenen Architekturbüros in Santiago entwickelt: von +Arquitectos mit Alex Brahm als Teilhaber und von Gubbins+ Polidura mit Antonio Polidura. Punta Pite liegt zwischen Papudo und Zapallar an der Nordküste Chiles. Das 6500 Quadratmeter große Grundstück ist etwa 100 Meter lang und fällt zum Meer hin ab. Dies machte die Errichtung eines Podiums erforderlich, auf dem das Haus gebaut werden konnte. Den Bauherren gefiel die Idee eines schlichten Designs mit sanften Kurven, das freie Sicht auf die Umgebung bietet. Das eckige Podium bietet Raum für drei Schlafzimmer sowie Bereiche für die Kinder auf der einen und das Hauptschlafzimmer auf der anderen Seite. Die verschiedenen Abschnitte des amöboiden, verglasten Hauses gruppieren sich auf der oberen Ebene um den zentralen Kern, von dem aus eine Wendeltreppe zu den unteren privaten Räumen führt. Die Küche ist nach Südosten ausgerichtet, im Südwesten liegt ein Wohnzimmer mit offenem Kamin, und auf der Nordseite befindet sich der Essbereich. Die Einrichtungsgegenstände für das Haus entwarfen die Architekten auch aufgrund der Komplexität seiner Formen. 21 Stahlstützen von jeweils 2,3 Meter Höhe tragen das Hausdach. Das Budget für dieses Haus aus Beton, Stahl und Glas auf dem 6500 Quadratmeter großen Grundstück betrug 750 000 Dollar.

A bedroom with large sliding glass doors has a corner view of the ocean below.

Cette maison destinée à des amis des architectes a été créée par deux agences associées de Santiago, +Arquitectos, dont Alex Brahm est un partenaire et Gubbins+Polidura où travaille Antonio Polidura. Punta Pite se trouve entre Papudo et Zapallar, sur la côte nord du Chili. Le terrain de 6500 mètres carrés est long d'une centaine de mètres et descend vers l'océan. Cette configuration a exigé de créer une plate-forme sur laquelle construire la maison. Les clients aimaient l'idée d'un concept simple aux courbes douces pour admirer facilement la vue. La plate-forme anguleuse a permis d'aménager trois chambres et des espaces pour les enfants d'un côté, et la chambre principale de l'autre. Les volumes de la maison vitrée à la forme amiboïde sont déployés autour et au-dessus du noyau central qui présente un escalier en colimaçon vers les espaces privés de l'étage inférieur. La cuisine est au sud-est, un espace salon avec une cheminée suspendue au sud-ouest et le coin repas au nord. Les architectes ont aussi conçu le mobilier de la résidence, en raison notamment de ses formes complexes. Le toit de la maison est porté par 21 colonnes d'acier hautes chacune de 2,3 mètres. La maison en béton, acier et verre a été construite sur un terrain de 6500 mètres carrés pour un budget de 750 000 dollars.

EDUARDO CADAVAL

The Theater
Barcelona, Spain, 2019–20
Area: 330 m²

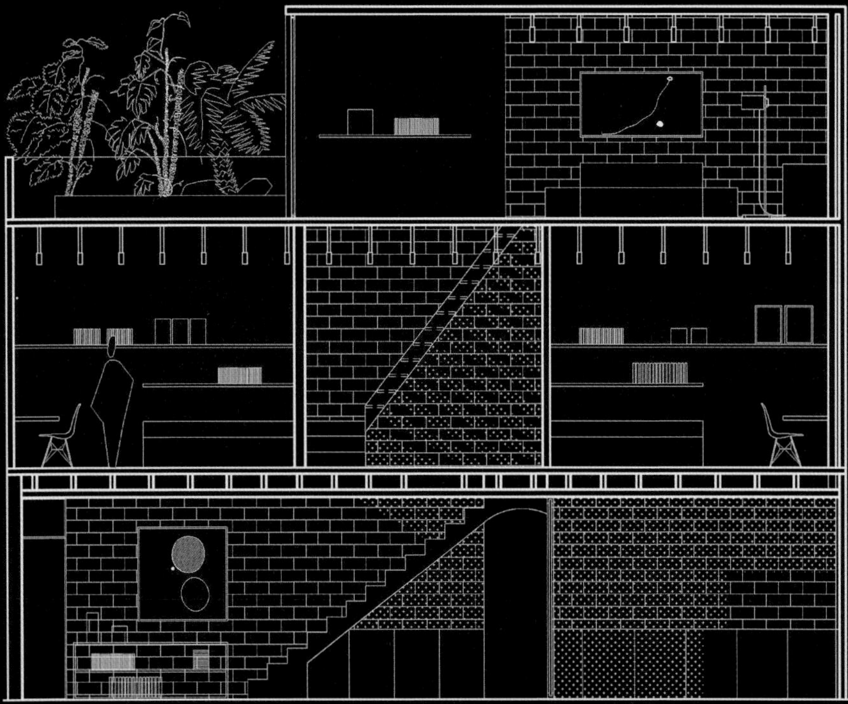

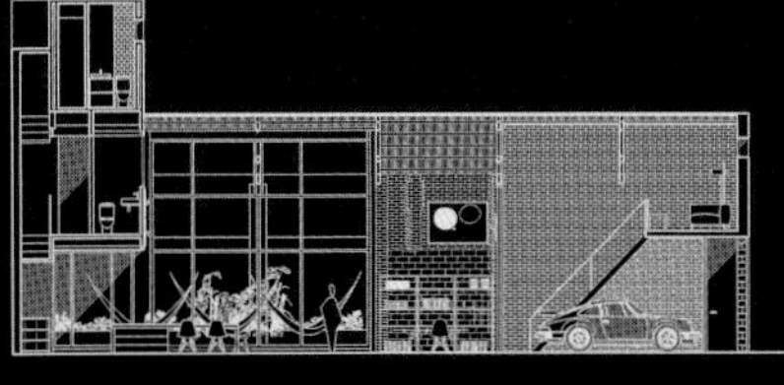

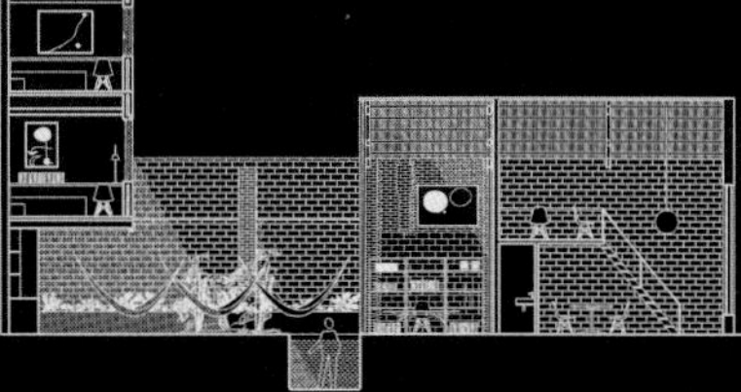

\ façade view does not disguise the fact hat this structure was originally intended o be a theatre.

Built as a theater in the late nineteenth century, converted into a barn and then into a toilet paper warehouse, The Theater is in the center of Barcelona in the Poblenou area near the Avinguda Diagonal. A hall near the entrance opens onto two double-height studios and the main part of the house. A classical car is exhibited like a sculpture near the central space of the residence. The high, bright central space is used as a living and dining area and includes a kitchen and a study. Part of the roof of the original warehouse was removed to create a patio, which is now an extension of the main space. At the back of the former warehouse, there are two rooms on the first floor and a third with a terrace on the uppermost level. The concept of the architects was to convert the former theater/warehouse into a home without changing the original structure, on the "understanding that over time the theater will surely have another use and another life." The Theater was built, or rather rebuilt, for a cost of $500 000 using brick, steel, concrete, and wood

Im 19. Jahrhundert als Theater erbaut, später in eine Scheune und schließlich in ein Lager für Toilettenpapier umgewandelt, befindet sich The Theater im Zentrum Barcelonas, im Stadtteil Poblenou nahe der Avinguda Diagonal. Eine Eingangshalle öffnet sich zu zwei Ateliers mit doppelter Höhe sowie zum Hauptteil des Hauses. Ein Oldtimer ist wie eine Skulptur in der Nähe des zentralen Wohnraums ausgestellt. Der hohe helle zentrale Ort dient als Wohn- und Essbereich und umfasst neben einer Küche auch ein Arbeitszimmer. Ein Teil des ursprünglichen Lagerhausdaches wurde entfernt, um einen Innenhof zu schaffen, der nun eine Erweiterung des Hauptraums darstellt. Im hinteren Teil des ehe

naligen Lagerhauses befinden sich zwei Räume m ersten und ein drittes Zimmer mit Terrasse m obersten Stockwerk. Das Konzept der Archi- ekten bestand darin, das ehemalige Theater/ .agerhaus in ein Wohnhaus umzuwandeln, ohne lie ursprüngliche Struktur zu verändern, in der Zuversicht, dass das Theater im Laufe der Zeit icherlich noch eine andere Nutzung und ein nderes Leben haben wird". Das Theater wurde ür 500 000 Dollar mit Ziegeln, Stahl, Beton und łolz ge-, oder besser gesagt: umgebaut.

Construit pour servir de théâtre à la fin du XIXe siècle, puis reconverti en grange et ensuite n entrepôt de papier toilette, le Théâtre est itué au centre de Barcelone, dans le quartier le Poblenou, près de l'Avinguda Diagonal. Un all près de l'entrée ouvre sur deux studios louble hauteur et la partie principale de la maison. Une vieille voiture est exposée comme une sculpture à côté de l'espace central. Haut e clair, ce dernier sert de salon et de salle à manger et comprend une cuisine et un bureau. Le toi de l'entrepôt d'origine a été en partie retiré pour créer un patio qui prolonge l'espace principal. À l'arrière de l'ancien entrepôt, on trouve deux pièces au premier étage et une troisième avec terrasse au dernier étage. Le concept imaginé par les architectes a consisté à transformer en domicile l'ancien théâtre/entrepôt sans en modifier la structure originale, « considérant qu'avec le temps, le Théâtre connaîtra certainement un autre usage et une autre vie ». Il a été construit, ou plutôt reconstruit, pour 500 000 dollars en briques, acier, béton et bois.

The double-height living space takes advantage of the original typology of the structure while creating comfortable, generous living space in the heart of Barcelona.

MINO CAGGIULA

Atelier Alice Trepp
Origlio, Switzerland, 2016–19
Area: 454 m²
Collaboration: Alberto Bernasconi
(Project Architect)

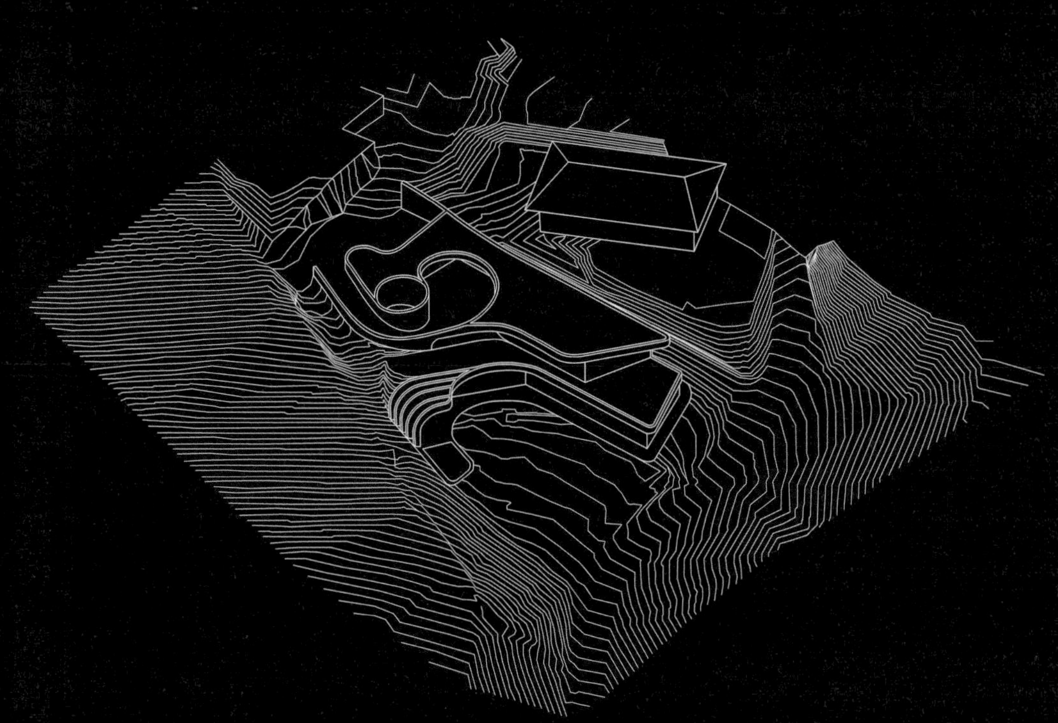

The unusual curving forms of the house and its green roof make it almost seem to disappear into its green, hilly site.

A side view of the residence gives a different impression of the ribbed partial colonnade and extensive green terraced garden spaces.

Origlio is a town of about 1500 inhabitants located in the district of Lugano in the Canton of Ticino. The house and studio were built for Alice Trepp, who is an Ecuadorian painter and sculptor. Wedged into the sloped site, the structure is in part underground with a green roof that emphasizes its connection to the site. The very forms of the house appear to be a physical manifestation of the topographical lines that one usually sees on a site map. A plaster room, spa, studio, kitchen, living room, bedroom, and "bio-pool" are located on the first floor. Broad openings and large glazed surfaces fill the house with light and views of the mountainous countryside. The design also incorporates a "cenote," which signifies a natural pit or solutional cave. The architect explains: "The cenote in Atelier Trepp is a space of contemplation and communion with nature. Reflected, refracted light playing on water is conducive to a multisensorial awareness of the passing of time." The Atelier Alice Trepp was built for a cost of 6.5 million euros.

Origlio ist eine Kleinstadt mit etwa 1500 Einwohnern im Bezirk Lugano des Kantons Tessin. Das Haus und das Atelier wurden für Alice Trepp gebaut, eine ecuadorianische Malerin und Bildhauerin. Das in das abschüssige Gelände eingebettete Gebäude ist zum Teil unterirdisch und hat ein begrüntes Dach, das die Verbindung mit dem Gelände betont. Seine Grundformen wirken wie eine physische Manifestation typischer Höhenlinien topografischer Pläne. Im ersten Stock befinden sich ein Gipsraum, ein Spa, ein Studio, eine Küche, ein Wohnzimmer, ein Schlafzimmer und ein „Bio-Pool". Dank großzügiger Wandöffnungen und großer Glasflächen ist

he "cenote" or sinkhole at the rear of the house, een left, connects the sky to a reflecting pool and is ntended to provide a place for calm contemplation. bove: a carefully designed intersection of curves, ifferent materials and views.

as Haus lichtdurchflutet und bietet Ausblicke uf die Berglandschaft. Das Design umfasst auch ine „Cenote", eine natürliche Grube bzw. ein arsthöhle. „Die Cenote im Atelier Trepp ist ein aum der Kontemplation und des Einklangs mit er Natur", erklärt der Architekt. „Das reflektierte, ebrochene Licht, das auf dem Wasser spielt, ördert ein multisensorisches Bewusstsein für as Verstreichen der Zeit." Das Atelier Alice Trepp vurde für 6,5 Millionen Euro gebaut.

)riglio est une ville d'environ 1500 habitants ans le district de Lugano, dans le canton du essin. La maison et le studio ont été construits our Alice Trepp, une peintre et sculptrice équaorienne. Encastrée dans le terrain en pente, a construction est en partie souterraine avec n toit végétalisé qui met en avant son rapport la nature. Les formes mêmes de la maison semblent la traduction concrète des courbes de niveau qu'on voit sur les cartes. Le premier étage accueille une salle de plâtre, un spa, un studio, une cuisine, un salon, une chambre et un « bassin bio ». De grandes ouvertures et de vastes surfaces vitrées emplissent la maison de lumière et des vues sur le paysage de montagnes. Le concept inclut également un « cénote », soit un puits naturel ou un gouffre karstique. L'architecte explique que « le cénote de l'atelier Trepp est un espace dédié à la contemplation et à la communion avec la nature. Le jeu des reflets et des réfractions de la lumière sur l'eau est propice à une perception multisensorielle du temps ». L'atelier Alice Trepp a été construit pour un coût de 6,5 millions d'euros.

A spiral staircase circles a column in the living room, a space seen at the top center of the floor plan below.

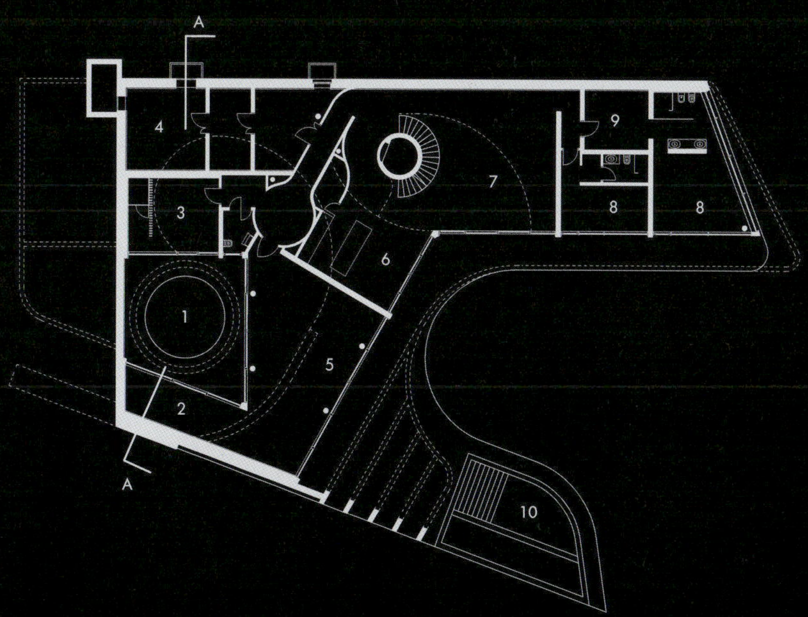

1. Cenote
2. Plaster room
3. Spa
4. Utility room
5. Artist's studio
6. Kitchen
7. Living room
8. Bedroom
9. Closet
10. Biopool

VICTOR CAÑAS

House for a Ceramist (The Guanacastes)
Orotina, Costa Rica, 2018–19
Area: 521 m²
Collaboration: Andres Cañas, Sara Araya

Although the structure is complex, it sits lightly in its green site. Below: *a section and the east elevation of the house.*

'he glazed volume seen above has a sloping roof ınd is slightly lifted off the ground, preserving existing ree roots and connecting it to the wooded exterior.

'he site of this house, which slopes down toward he Gulf of Nicoya, an inlet of the Pacific Ocean, ncludes numerous mature Guancaste trees *Enterolobium cyclocarpum)*, a fact that determined the precise location of the residence and ts design. The house had to be lifted 80 centimeters off the ground to protect the roots of the rees. Inside, there are four bedrooms, public ıreas, a TV/studio, ceramic workshop, and service volumes, and it is long and narrow to ıllow sea views from every room. An enclosed jarden links the kitchen, ceramic workshop, ınd the studio. The living and dining areas ›pen to the terrace and pool, and the kitchen extends outdoors, an arrangement that is possible because of the local climate. The pool is inished in black stone so that it reflects the mage of the trees. The roof of the house, with ts generous eaves, is covered with zinc alloy. Cross ventilation was planned to reduce energy consumption, which is provided entirely by photovoltaic panels.

Dass auf dem Grundstück dieses Hauses, das zum Golf von Nicoya, einem Meeresarm des Pazifischen Ozeans, hin abfällt, zahlreiche ausgewachsene Guancaste-Bäume (*Enterolobium cyclocarpum*) stehen, bestimmte den genauen Standort des Hauses und dessen Gestaltung. Zum Schutz der Baumwurzeln musste das Haus 80 Zentimeter vom Boden angehoben werden. Es beherbergt vier Schlafzimmer, gemeinschaftlich genutzte Bereiche, ein TV-Studio, eine Keramikwerkstatt und Hauswirtschaftsräume. Das Gebäude ist lang und schmal, sodass jeder Raum Meerblick bietet. Ein eingezäunter Garten verbindet die Küche mit der Keramikwerkstatt und dem Atelier. Die Wohn- und Essbereiche

Generous partially covered spaces, such as the kitchen and neighboring black infinity pool seen on this page, allow residents to be both inside and out at the same moment. Trees such as the one seen near the pool (below) were preserved and integrated into the design.

The kitchen space seen on the left page is viewed here from a different angle, emphasizing the transparency and depth of the house.

öffnen sich zur Terrasse und zum Pool, und die Küche erstreckt sich dank des lokalen Klimas ins Freie. Der Pool ist mit schwarzem Stein verkleidet und spiegelt die Bäume wider. Das Hausdach mit seiner großzügigen Traufe ist mit einer Zinklegierung gedeckt. Um den Energieverbrauch zu senken, wurde eine Querlüftung vorgesehen, die vollständig durch Fotovoltaikpaneele gedeckt wird.

Le terrain sur lequel est construite la maison descend vers le golfe de Nicoya, une crique de l'océan Pacifique, et comporte de nombreux guanacastes (*Enterolobium cyclocarpum*) âgés, ce qui a déterminé l'emplacement précis de la construction et sa conception. La maison a dû être surélevée à 80 centimètres au-dessus du sol pour protéger les racines des arbres. Elle comprend quatre chambres, des espaces publics, une salle de télé/studio, un atelier de céramique et des espaces techniques. Elle est longue et étroite afin d'offrir une vue sur la mer depuis chaque pièce. Un jardin clos relie entre eux la cuisine, l'atelier de céramique et le studio. Les espaces destinés au séjour et aux repas ouvrent sur la terrasse et la piscine, tandis que la cuisine se prolonge à l'extérieur, disposition que permet le climat local. Le revêtement en pierre noire de la piscine reflète l'image des arbres. Le toit de la maison aux avant-toits généreux est recouvert d'un alliage de zinc. Le projet comporte une ventilation croisée pour réduire la consommation d'énergie, entièrement fournie par des panneaux photovoltaïques.

CARMODY GROARKE

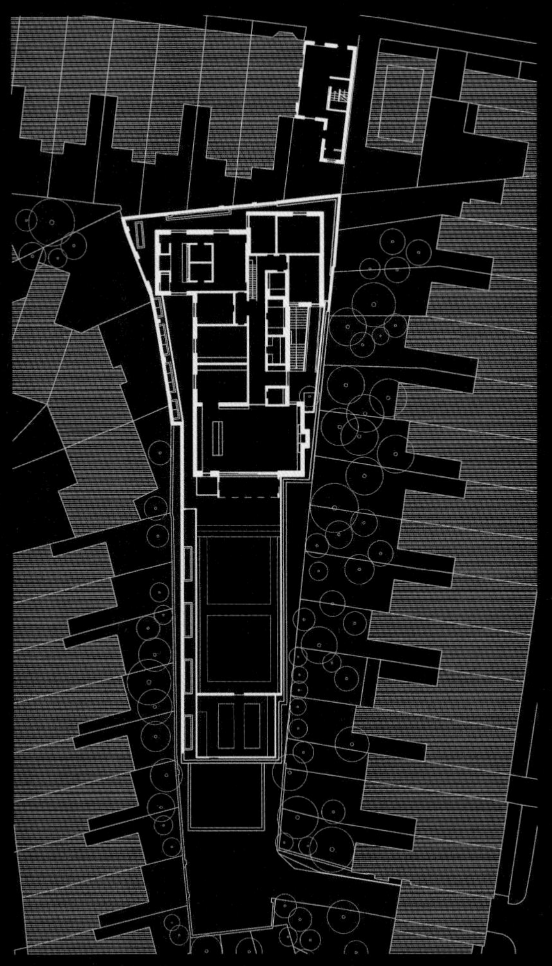

House and Studio
Lambeth, London, UK, 2015–18
Area: 1300 m²

Above: *the minimally furnished living room and concrete fireplace.* Right: *the master bedroom is sharply defined and filled with natural light.*

Opposite: *the cast-in-place concrete of the house is contrasted with the rougher surfaces of the Victorian brick structure.*

This project combines a home and an office in a repurposed Victorian-era brick warehouse, which is surrounded by 19th-century housing. Rather than demolishing the existing structure, the architects chose to use it as a kind of "skin" for their newly designed concrete interior volumes. The studio area is on the ground floor. As the architects explain: "Above, the architecture of the 'pavilion' is broken down into a cluster of small buildings, brick externally and exposed concrete inside—each designed according to the sensitivities of the neighboring Victorian houses. The residence nestles within a landscaped roof garden to give a visual amenity to the neighbors and character to the new house." Carmody Groarke succeeds in creating very contemporary interiors and space within this formerly crumbling Victorian brick building, not a small achievement, especially since their work does not conflict with the environment in externally visible ways. The project was built for a cost of £3.5 million.

Dieses Projekt kombiniert ein Wohnhaus mit einem Büro in einem umgenutzten viktorianischen Backsteinlager, dessen Gebäudehülle noch aus dem 19. Jahrhundert stammt. Anstatt die bestehende Struktur abzureißen, entschieden sich die Architekten dafür, sie als eine Art „Haut" für ihre neu gestalteten Innenräume aus Beton zu nutzen. Das Atelier befindet sich im Erdgeschoss. „Im oberen Bereich gliedert sich die Architektur des Pavillons' in eine Gruppe kleiner Gebäude, die außen aus Ziegeln und innen aus Sichtbeton bestehen", so die Architekten. „Dabei wurde jedes in seinem Design den benachbarten viktorianischen Häusern angepasst. Das Wohnhaus schmiegt sich unter einen begrünten Dachgarten, der für die Nachbarn eine

optische Bereicherung darstellt und dem neuen Haus Charakter verleiht.“ Carmody Groarke ist es gelungen, in diesem ehemals dem Verfall preisgegebenen Gebäude höchst zeitgemäße Räume und Platzverhältnisse zu schaffen – keine geringe Leistung, vor allem da ihre Arbeit optisch in keinem Konflikt mit der Umgebung steht. Die Kosten betrugen 3,5 Millionen Pfund.

Le projet associe une maison et un bureau dans un entrepôt victorien en briques reconverti, entouré des logements datant du XIXe siècle. Plutôt que de démolir la structure existante, les architectes ont choisi de l'utiliser comme une « seconde peau » pour les nouveaux volumes intérieurs en béton. Le studio occupe le rez-de-chaussée. Les architectes expliquent qu'« au-dessus, l'architecture du "pavillon" est brisée en une grappe de petits bâtiments en briques et béton apparent à l'intérieur, chacun conçu en fonction des sensibilités des maisons victoriennes voisines. La résidence est nichée dans un jardin paysager sur le toit qui crée une vue agréable pour les voisins et lui donne du caractère ». Carmody Groarke a réussi à créer des intérieurs et un espace très contemporain dans ce bâtiment victorien en briques qui tombait en ruines, une belle réussite, notamment parce que la construction n'entre pas en conflit avec à son environnement de manière visible. Le projet a coûté 3,5 millions de livres.

ARTHUR CASAS

JY House
Fazenda Boa Vista, Porto Feliz, São Paulo, Brazil, 2014–18
Area: 4992 m²
Collaboration: Beto Cabariti

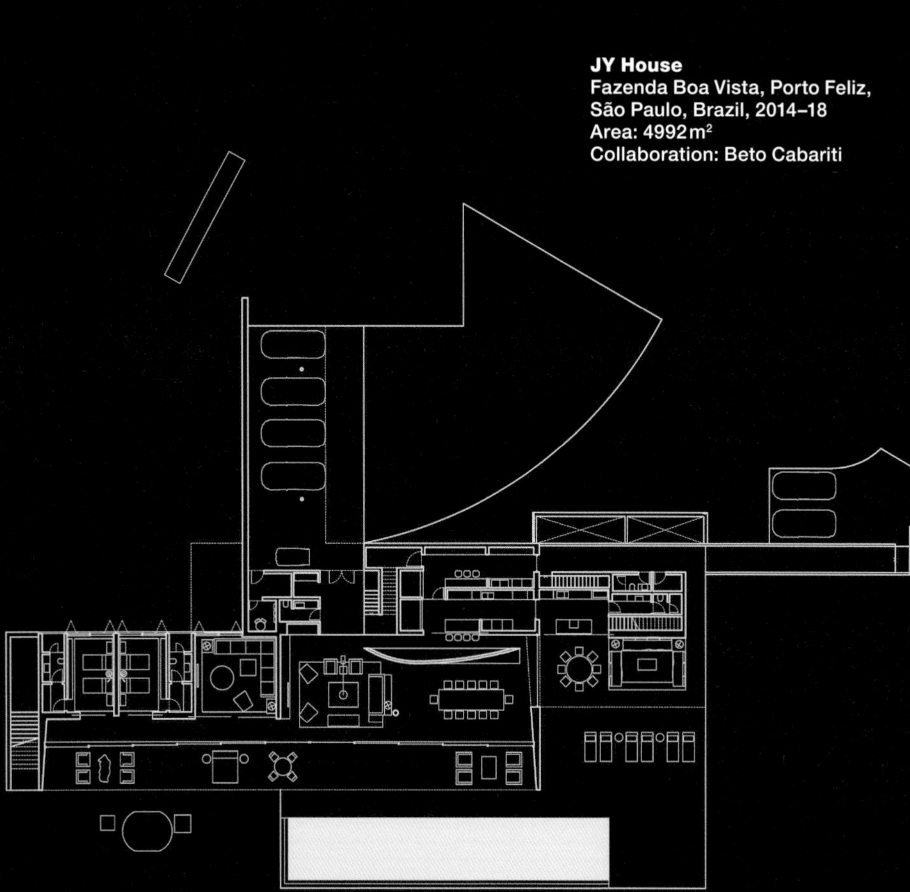

'he JY House was built on a 1127-square-meter site in Fazenda Boa Vista, which is a residential and hospitality complex located on a 750-hectare property in Porto Feliz, 120 kilometers southeast of the city of São Paulo. The JY House is located opposite the golf course of the domain. The public areas of the house are on the ground floor, with the three bedroom suites and other private areas set in the upper volume, which is clad in gray (leaded) aluminum. This upper section is set back from the lower element and looks out on the green roof of the public volume. There are, however, two guest suites on the ground level. A long curved freijó wood screen divides the dining and living areas from the kitchen. In fact, this is the only curve in the design, which is otherwise strictly rectilinear. The living area opens entirely on the side of the rectangular pool. The house has solar water heating, a green roof, and passive cross-air circulation. As is always the case in the work of Arthur Casas, the JY House was conceived and decorated with the architect's refined and almost minimal aesthetic sense, allowing residents to fully profit from the green site in an environment of luxury.

With living spaces on the ground floor, the house has an upper block for the bedroom suites that is covered in gray aluminum.

iround level and aerial views of the house emphasize 's sculptural composition of rectangular blocks.)pposite below: *seen from above, the long, equally ectangular pool participates in the overall design.*

)as JY House wurde auf einem 1127 Quadrat- neter großen Grundstück in der Fazenda Boa 'ista errichtet, einem Wohn- und Hotelkomplex uf 750 Hektar in Porto Feliz, 120 Kilometer üdöstlich von São Paulo. Das JY House liegt egenüber dem Golfplatz der Anlage. Die iemeinschaftsbereiche befinden sich im Erd- eschoss, während die drei Schlafsuiten und ndere private Räume im oberen Teil unter- ebracht sind, der mit grauem (verbleitem) luminium verkleidet wurde. Dieser obere Ab- chnitt ist etwas zurückgesetzt und blickt uf das begrünte Dach der gemeinschaftlich enutzten Räume. Im Erdgeschoss befinden ich zudem zwei Gästeappartements. Ein langer eschwungener Paravent aus Freijó-Holz trennt len Ess- und Wohnbereich von der Küche. 'atsächlich ist dies die einzige Kurve in dem nsonsten streng geradlinigen Entwurf. Der Wohnbereich öffnet sich auf einer Seite vollständig zum rechteckigen Pool. Das Haus verfügt über eine solare Warmwasserbereitung, ein Gründach sowie eine passive Luftzirkulation. Wie immer bei Arthur Casas wurde das JY House mit dem raffinierten und nahezu minimalästhetischen Gespür des Architekten konzipiert und dekoriert, sodass die Bewohner, von Luxus umgeben, voll von der grünen Umgebung profitieren können.

As is often the case in such large Brazilian houses, a large part of the interior can be opened almost entirely to the outside—here living spaces connect smoothly to the exterior deck and to the swimming pool.

La maison JY est construite sur un terrain de 1127 mètres carrés à Fazenda Boa Vista, un complexe résidentiel et hôtelier situé dans une propriété de 750 hectares à Porto Feliz, à 120 kilomètres au sud-est de São Paulo. Elle fait face au golf du domaine. Les espaces communs sont situés au rez-de-chaussée, les trois suites et autres espaces privés à l'étage, qui présente un parement d'aluminium gris (au plomb). Cette partie supérieure est en retrait par rapport à l'élément du bas et donne sur le toit végétalisé du bâtiment commun. Le rez-de-chaussée compte cependant aussi deux suites pour les hôtes. Un long panneau incurvé de bois *freijó* sépare le coin repas et le salon de la cuisine. C'est la seule courbe de l'ensemble sinon strictement rectiligne. Le salon s'ouvre entièrement du côté de la piscine rectangulaire. La maison possède un système de chauffage solaire de l'eau, une toiture végétalisée et un système passif de ventilation transversale. Comme toujours dans les réalisations d'Arthur Casas, elle a été conçue et décorée dans le style esthétique raffiné et presque minimaliste de l'architecte afin que ses habitants puissent profiter pleinement du décor naturel dans un cadre luxueux.

BERGENDY COOKE

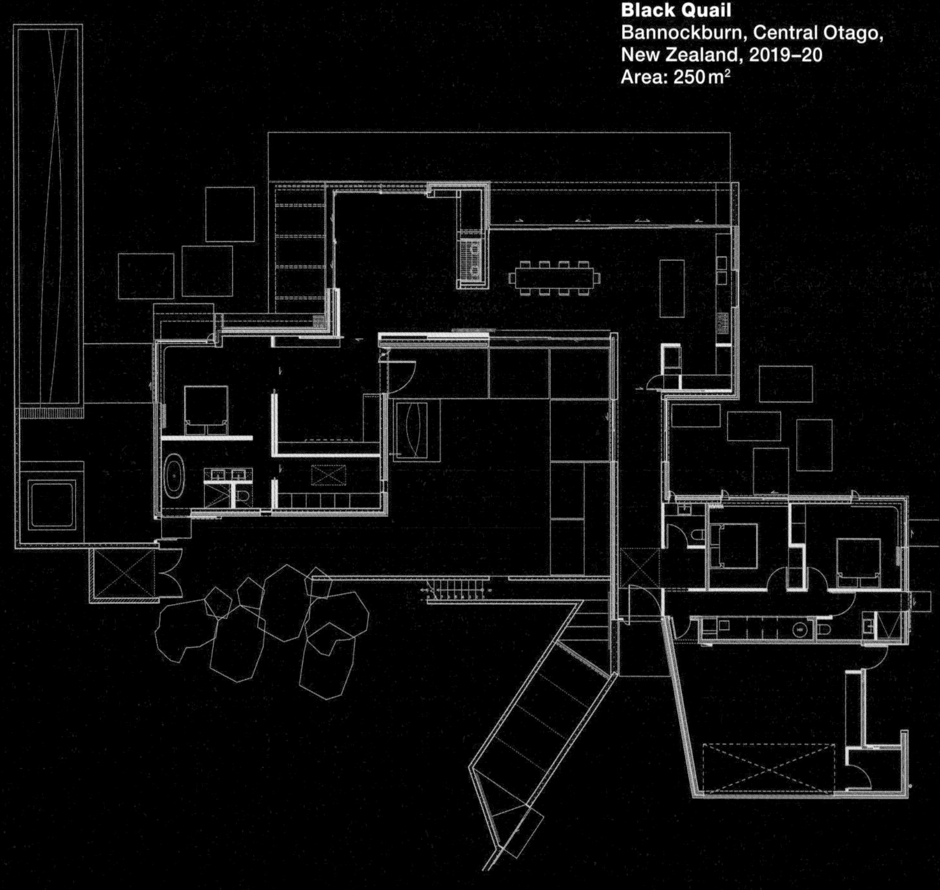

Black Quail
Bannockburn, Central Otago, New Zealand, 2019–20
Area: 250 m^2

Emerging from a landscape formed from local rocks, the house is clad with weathered steel near its entrance.

The Black Quail was built in "historic mining tailings in a craggy, dry and at times inhospitable landscape." It is in the former gold-mining town of Bannockburn on South Island. The house is wedged into a hillside beneath a vineyard to protect it and to allow views of the nearby Kawarau River and mountains beyond. Its stone shingle roof (from the site) increases the impression that the residence is quite literally part of the landscape. The floor plan is orthogonal, and the living area and courtyard open entirely to the garden and beyond to the rocky, mountainous landscape. Smaller courtyards were created to the east and west to "offer varying extended living scenarios and enhance the transparency throughout the building." Built for a cost of 900 000 euros with precast-concrete panels and weathered steel cladding near the entrance and garage, the house has concrete floors and interior timber panelling and wood joinery. The concrete used in the house was washed and tinted by hand with a color derived from local soil. The house, built for a Sri Lankan client who admires the courtyard homes of Geoffrey Bawa, won the 2021 "Home of the Year" award from *HOME* magazine (NZ).

ull-height sliding glass doors and a large window ring the landscape inside the house.

)as Black Quail wurde in der ehemaligen Gold- räberstadt Bannockburn (Neuseeland) auf historischen Abraumhalden in einer zerklüfteten, rockenen und zuweilen unwirtlichen Landschaft" rrichtet. Das Haus liegt geschützt eingebet- et in einen Hang unterhalb eines Weinbergs nd bietet Ausblicke auf den nahe gelegenen (awarau River und die dahinterliegenden Berge. ein Dach aus Steinschindeln (vom Grundstück elbst), lässt das Haus als Teil der Landschaft virken. Der Grundriss ist rechtwinklig, und owohl Wohnbereich als auch Innenhof öffnen ich vollständig zum Garten sowie zur felsigen 3erglandschaft. Kleinere Innenhöfe im Osten und Vesten „bieten verschiedene erweiterte Wohns- enarien und erhöhen im gesamten Gebäude lie Transparenz". Das 900 000 Euro teure Haus esteht aus Betonfertigteilen und verwitterten Stahlverkleidungen im Eingangs- und Garagen- bereich, hat Betonböden und ist im Inneren mit Holzverkleidungen ausgestattet. Der innen ver- wendete Beton wurde gewaschen und von Hand mit einer aus örtlicher Erde gewonnenen Farbe eingefärbt. Das Haus, für einen sri-lankischen Kunden und Bewunderer von Geoffrey Bawas Hofhäusern errichtet, wurde 2021 von der Zeit- schrift *HOME* (Neuseeland) zum „Haus des Jahres" gekürt.

;omfortable furniture and a fireplace temper the mooth, unified surfaces of the living space.

3lack Quail est construite en « résidus miniers istoriques dans un paysage accidenté, sec t parfois inhospitalier » – l'ancienne ville de a mine d'or de Bannockburn, sur l'île du sud le Nouvelle-Zélande. La maison est encastrée ans le flanc d'une colline sous un vignoble pour ıne meilleure protection et pour la vue sur la ivière Kawarau toute proche et les montagnes lus lointaines. Son toit en pierres (du site) et bar- leaux renforce l'impression qu'elle fait partie du aysage. Le plan au sol est orthogonal, le salon t la cour s'ouvrent entièrement sur le jardin et le aysage rocheux et montagneux qui le prolonge. Des cours plus petites ont été ajoutées à l'est t à l'ouest pour « permettre des existences et xpériences d'habitat variées et accroître la ransparence dans tout le bâtiment ». Construite our 900 000 euros en panneaux de béton pré- abriqués et revêtement d'acier patiné au niveau de l'entrée et du garage, la maison a des sols en béton et un intérieur en panneaux de bois et menuiserie. Le béton a été lavé et teint à la main dans un coloris dérivé du sol local. Réalisée pou un client sri-lankais admirateur des maisons à cours de Geoffrey Bawa, elle a gagné le prix de la « Maison de l'année » 2021 du magazine *HOME* (NZ).

DE KORT VAN SCHAIK

House on the Raboes
Eemnes, The Netherlands, 2018–20
Area: 220 m²
Collaboration: Karbouw Bouwonderneming (Contractor), Sabine Marcelis (Bathroom)

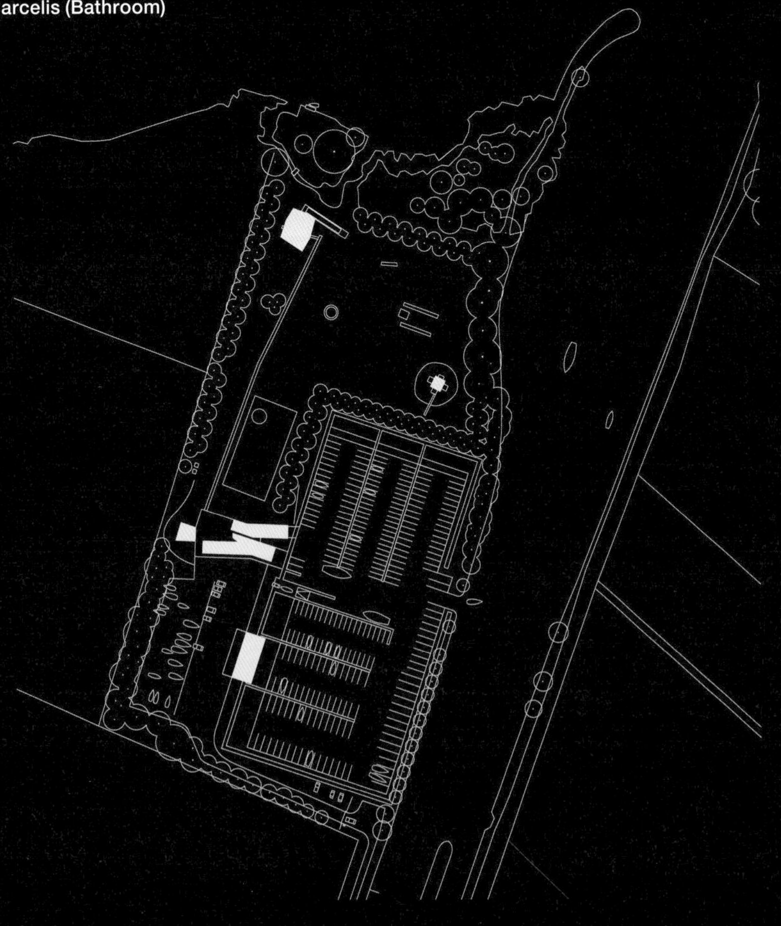

'he site includes the House on the Raboes, a guest ouse and a number of buildings that support the narina. Opposite: *the concrete structure gives an mpression of protective strength tempered by the arge glazed openings seen both in the aerial image nd opposite.*

Eemnes is in the province of Utrecht and is ocated 36 kilometers southeast of Amsterdam. 'his country retreat was built in a polder land-scape where the Eem River flows into Eem Lake at the marina of Jachthaven 't Raboes, which has been regenerated to create an area for water-sports and some residences. The clients wanted both an open house and shelter from the winter elements. According to the architects: "The seemingly monolithic house stands like a boulder n the flat expanse of grassland." The design is nade up of three "loosely grouped volumes" and three covered terraces forming a T-shaped space. In situ concrete walls and floors transi-ion from exterior to interior. Untreated timber was used for the ceilings and roof. Large square windows can open entirely, sliding into the walls. nterior walls are covered with large ceramic bricks with a thin, rough-plaster coating. Other materials such as natural stone in the kitchen and sculpted yellow epoxy washbasin, shower, and bath contrast with the rest of the house. Photovoltaic cells on the roof of the nearby marina building produce electricity for both the marina and the house. A heat pump connected to the lake is used to warm the house and swimming pool. Wood-burning stoves used for heating in winter are fueled with locally grown timber, and the thermal mass of the concrete structure participates in a responsible energy strategy.

Eemnes liegt in der Provinz Utrecht, 36 Kilometer südöstlich von Amsterdam. Errichtet wurde dieses Landhaus in einer Polderlandschaft, wo die Eem am Jachthafen 't Raboes in das Eemmeer mündet, das zu einem Wassersportgebiet mit einigen Wohnhäusern umgestaltet wurde. Die Bauherren wünschten sich sowohl ein offenes Haus als auch Schutz vor dem Winter. „Einem Felsbrocken gleich steht das scheinbar monolithische Haus auf der flachen Wiese“, schildern die Architekten. Der Entwurf setzt sich aus drei „locker gruppierten Teilen“ sowie drei überdachten Terrassen zusammen, die zusammen ein T bilden. Wände und Böden aus Ortbeton gestalten den Übergang von außen nach innen. Für die Decken und das Dach wurde unbehandeltes großen, mit dünnem Rauputz überzogenen Keramikziegeln verkleidet. Andere Materialien wie der Naturstein in der Küche und das gelbe Epoxidharz, aus dem das Waschbecken, die Dusche und die Badewanne gefertigt wurden, kontrastieren mit dem Rest des Hauses. Fotovoltaikzellen auf dem Dach des nahe gelegenen Jachthafens erzeugen Strom für sowohl den Jachthafen als auch das Haus. Eine an den See angeschlossene Wärmepumpe beheizt Haus und Pool. Die Holzöfen, die im Winter zum Heizen verwendet werden, werden mit lokalem Holz befeuert, und die thermische Masse der Betonstruktur trägt zu einer verantwortungsvollen Energiestrategie bei.

Above: *the sculpted yellow epoxy washbasin, shower, and bath.* Below and opposite: *the gray palette of the interiors is complemented by relatively sparse furnishings and contrasts with the large openings that give views of the exterior landscape.*

Eemnes est une ville de la province d'Utrecht à 36 kilomètres au sud-est d'Amsterdam. Cette retraite à la campagne a été bâtie sur un polder à l'endroit où le fleuve Eem se jette dans le lac Eemmeer à la marina de Jachthaven 't Raboes – qui a été remise en état pour accueillir un centre de sports nautiques et quelques résidences. Les clients souhaitaient une maison qui soit à la fois ouverte et qui les abrite des intempéries en hiver. Le résultat, selon les architectes, est « une maison d'apparence monolithique qui ressemble à un rocher au milieu d'une prairie ». Le concept consiste en trois « volumes groupés librement » et trois terrasses couvertes qui forment un espace en T. Les murs et les sols en béton *in situ* assurent la transition entre l'extérieur et l'intérieur. Les plafonds et le toit sont en bois non traité. De grandes fenêtres carrées peuvent être entièrement ouvertes en coulissant à l'intérieur des murs, recouverts à l'intérieur de grandes briques céramiques et d'un revêtement fin en plâtre à hourdis. Quelques autres matériaux comme la pierre naturelle dans la cuisine et la résine époxy jaune dans laquelle sont sculptés le lavabo, la douche et la baignoire contrastent avec le reste de la maison. Les cellules photovoltaïques sur le toit de la marina voisine fournissent l'électricité aux deux, tandis qu'une pompe à chaleur connectée au lac chauffe la maison et la piscine, que les poêles à bois utilisés en hiver sont alimentés avec du bois cultivé localement et que la masse thermique de la structure en béton contribue à une stratégie énergétique responsable.

DECA ARCHITECTURE

Hourglass Corral
Milos, Cyclades, Greece, 2017–20
Area: 280 m²

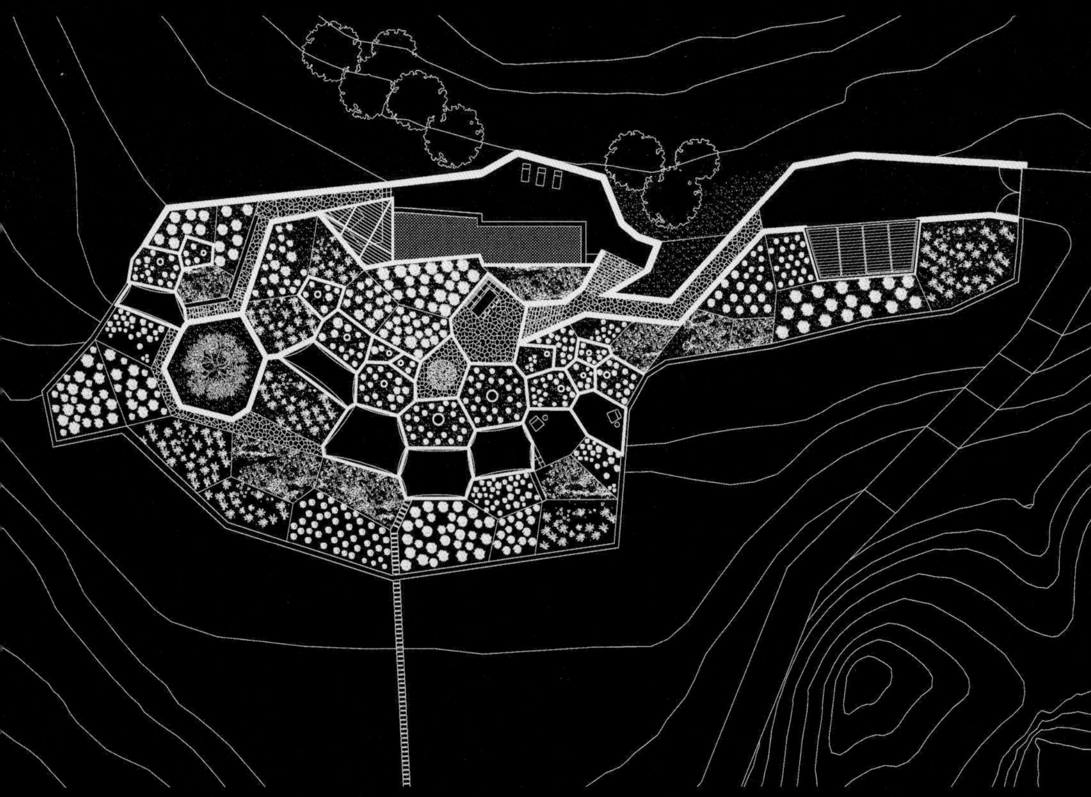

Voronoi cells or diagrams also called tessellations were first defined by the Ukrainian mathematician Georgy Voronoy (1868–1908) and have applications in architecture as seen here but also in such areas as computer graphics and video games.

The Hourglass Corral is the fifth part of Voronoi's Corrals, a project that the architects started working on 2011 and that encompasses an area of about 90 000 square meters. The architects of DECA Architecture explain that this larger project is "an ongoing investigation of what it means to integrate the domestic scale using sustainable strategies into its rural landscape." The architects started with an examination of the use of Voronoi cells, consisting of all designated points of a plane closer to a "seed" (i.e., a designated point) than to any other. They explain: "Each cell corresponds to a clearly defined use, be it an exterior courtyard, a shading canopy, a common space, a bedroom, or an auxiliary space." Each cell in the house is marked by an operable, circular skylight. Green roofs, exterior shading, and thick walls are used to reduce energy needs. The property is surrounded by a stone fence that separates it from "the wild and the agricultural areas."

Hourglass Corral ist der fünfte Teil von Voronoi's Corrals, einem Projekt, an dem die Architekten seit 2011 arbeiten und das inzwischen eine Fläche von etwa 90 000 Quadratmetern umfasst. Die Architekten von DECA Architecture erklären, dass es sich bei diesem umfangreichen Projekt um „eine fortlaufende Untersuchung dessen handelt, was es bedeutet, ein Einfamilienhaus mittels nachhaltiger Strategien in seine ländliche Landschaft zu integrieren". Die Architekten untersuchten zunächst Voronoi-Zellen, die alle festgelegten Punkten einer Ebene beinhalten, die näher an einem „Keim" (d. h. einem festgelegten Punkt) liegen als an jedem anderen. „Jede Zelle entspricht einer klar definierten Nutzung", erklären sie, „sei es ein

ɩußenhof, ein schattenspendendes Vordach, ɜin Gemeinschaftsraum, ein Schlafzimmer ɔder ein Nebenraum.“ Jede Zelle des Hauses st durch ein bedienbares, rundes Oberlicht ȷekennzeichnet. Gründächer, Außenbeschattungen und dicke Mauern dienen dazu, den Ξnergiebedarf zu senken. Das Grundstück ist ɾon einem Steinzaun umgeben, der es von den Wild- und Agrarflächen“ trennt.

.e corral du Sablier est l'ajout le plus récent aux ɔorrals de Voronoï, un projet sur lequel les architectes ont commencé à travailler il y a dix ans ɜt qui englobe aujourd'hui une surface d'environ) hectares. Les architectes décrivent ce vaste ɔrojet comme « une exploration en continu ɬe l'effet sur le paysage rural d'intégrer l'échelle ɬomestique dans des stratégies durables ». Ils ɔnt commencé par s'intéresser au diagramme de Voronoï dont les cellules sont chacune composées des points d'un plan plus proches d'un « germe » (un point désigné) que d'aucun autre. Ils expliquent que « chaque cellule correspond à un usage clairement défini, tel qu'une cour intérieure, un auvent d'ombrage, un espace commun, une chambre ou un espace secondaire ». Les cellules possèdent chacune une lucarne circulaire qui peut être ouverte. Les toits végétalisés, les ombrages extérieurs et les murs épais permettent de réduire les besoins énergétiques. La propriété est entourée d'une barrière en pierre qui la sépare des « zones sauvages et agricoles ».

The unusual design of the house is evident in the ground floor plan below, but both inside and outside, it develops generous agreeable spaces and appears to integrate perfectly into its Cycladic landscape.

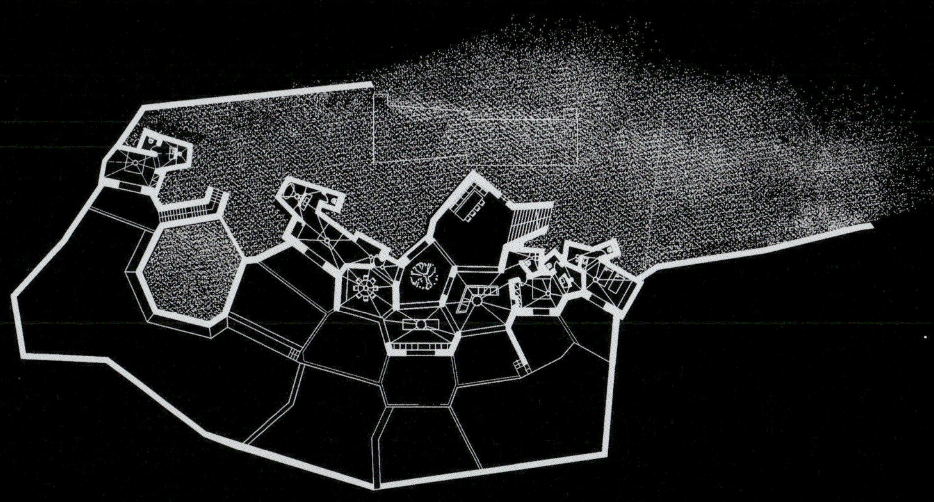

ELEMENTAL

Ochoquebradas House
Los Vilos, Chile, 2017–18
Area: 289 m²
Collaboration: Suyin Chia

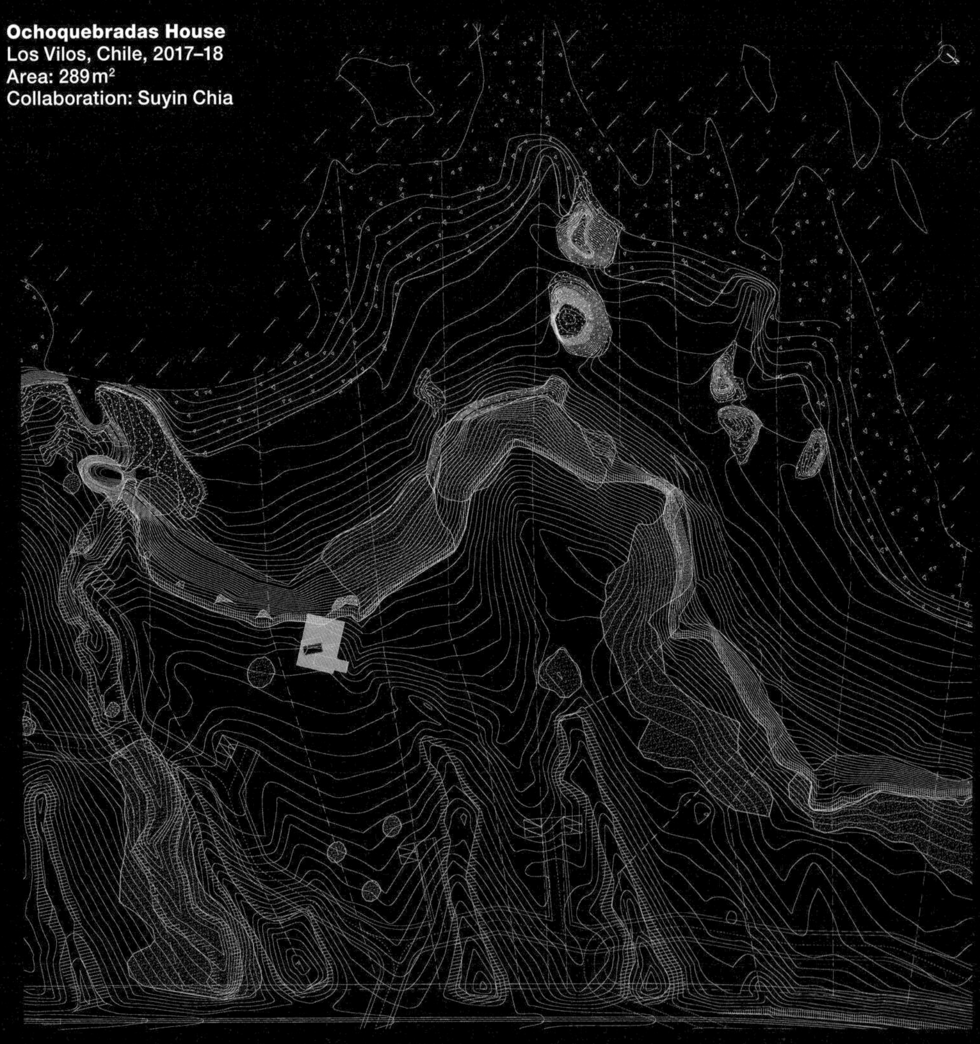

The house stands like an enigmatic or "archaic" monolith in its spectacular oceanside site. The wood seen on the upper façade (opposite above) was used for the concrete formwork.

Built with a reinforced-concrete structure on a 5450-square-meter site located 250 kilometers north of Santiago, the Ochoquebradas (eight ravines) house is part of a broader scheme that has brought together eight Japanese architects and eight Chileans. The program proposed to each of the architects was the same—a four bedroom house with a living and dining area, kitchen, bathrooms, and a wine cellar with an overall budget ($500 000) that each architect was asked to build with otherwise complete freedom. ELEMENTAL imagined their structure as a weekend house, with a "certain primitiveness" inspired by the rough site. As the architects explain, they used the fact that there was as yet no specific client for the house to reduce the forms to a powerful (elemental) expression. They state: "We chose to move backward toward the archaic, not as a nostalgic escape but as a natural filter against the clichés. In an era where the hunger for novelty is threatening architecture to become immediately obsolete, we looked for timelessness." There are three volumes: a horizontal one containing the basics for one couple, that slightly cantilevers over the cliff; a vertical one containing the other spaces requested by the organizer of the project, as well as a rooftop terrace; and between these two blocks "a slightly leaning and hollowed one containing a fire—not a chimney (which is already something civilized), but a fire (which is one of the most revolutionary yet oldest achievements of man)." Five sides of the pieces are made of poured concrete; the sixth one is made out of the wood used as formwork. They conclude: "We expect these pieces to age as a stone, acquiring some of the brutality of the place but still being gentle for people to enjoy nature and life in general."

)as Haus Ochoquebradas (Acht Schluchten) vurde in Stahlbetonbauweise auf einem 450 Quadratmeter großen Grundstück 250 Kiloneter nördlich von Santiago errichtet und ist 'eil eines umfassenderen Projekts, an dem sich ıcht japanische und acht chilenische Architekten)eteiligten. Alle erhielten dieselben Vorgaben: ein Haus mit vier Schlafzimmern, Wohn- und Essbeeich, Küche, Badezimmern und Weinkeller für ein Gesamtbudget von 500 000 Dollar, über das jeder Architekt frei verfügen sollte. Inspiriert vom rauen Standort, schwebte ELEMENTAL für ihr Gebäude ein Wochenendhaus von „gewisser Primitivität“ vor. Wie die Architekten erklären, nutzten sie lie Tatsache, dass es noch keinen konkreten Käufer für das Haus gab, um die Formen auf einen starken (elementaren) Ausdruck zu reduzieren. Wir wollten uns auf das Archaische zurückbeinnen, nicht als nostalgische Flucht, sondern als natürlichen Filter gegen Klischees. In einer Zeit, ir der der Hunger nach Neuem die Architektur sofor zu veralten droht, suchten wir nach Zeitlosigkeit.“ Das Haus besteht aus drei Blöcken: einem horizontalen für die Grundbedürfnisse eines Paares, das leicht über die Klippe hinausragt; einem vertikalen für die weiteren vom Projektorganisato vorgegebenen Räumen sowie einer Dachterrasse und dazwischen „ein leicht geneigter und ausgehöhlter Block mit einer Feuerstelle – keinem Kami (der bereits etwas Zivilisiertes darstellt), sondern ein Feuer (eine der revolutionärsten und ältesten Errungenschaften des Menschen)“. Fünf Seiten sind aus gegossenem Beton, die sechste wurde aus dem Schalungsholz gefertigt. „Wir erwarten, dass diese Stücke wie Stein altern und etwas vor der Brutalität des Ortes annehmen, aber dennoch sanft bleiben, damit die Menschen die Natur und das Leben generell genießen können“.

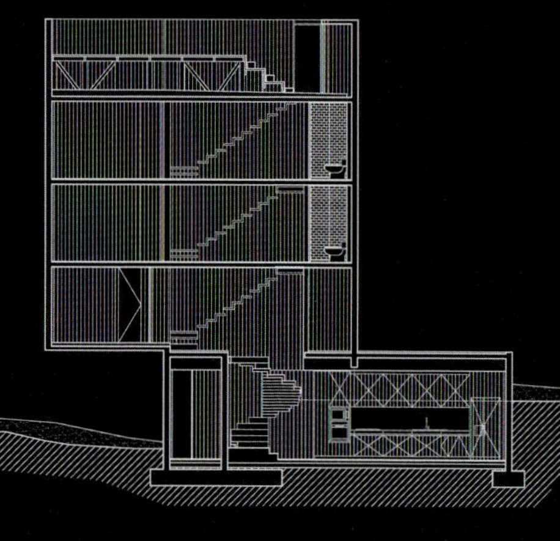

The rough in situ concrete surfaces emphasize the "elemental" nature of the house, corresponding to the rocky shoreline where it is situated, almost as though it had always been there. Right: *section drawing.*

Construite à partir d'une structure en béton armé sur un terrain de 5450 mètres carrés à 250 kilomètres au nord de Santiago, la maison Ochoquebradas (« huit ravins ») fait partie d'un ensemble plus important auquel ont collaboré huit architectes japonais et huit chiliens. Le programme a proposé la même chose à chacun : une maison de quatre chambres avec lieux de vie et de repas, cuisine, salles de bains et cave à vin pour un budget global (500 000 Dollar) avec lequel chacun était libre de construire. ELEMENTAL a imaginé une maison pour les week-ends, dont la « nature quelque peu primitive » s'inspire de la rudesse du terrain. Les architectes ont profité de l'absence de client spécifique pour réduire les formes à une expression (élémentaire) puissante. Ils déclarent « avoir choisi de reculer vers l'archaïsme, non pour une évasion nostalgique, mais pour servir de filtre naturel contre les clichés. À une époque où la faim de nouveauté menace l'architecture de devenir immédiatement obsolète, nous avons cherché l'intemporalité ». La maison compte trois volumes : un bloc horizontal qui contient le nécessaire pour un couple et s'avance légèrement en surplomb au-dessus de la falaise ; un bloc vertical avec les autres espaces exigés par l'organisateur du projet et un toit en terrasse, et entre les deux, un bloc « légèrement incliné et évidé où se trouve un feu – pas une cheminée (qui serait déjà un élément civilisé), mais un feu (qui est l'un des acquis les plus révolutionnaires, et l'un des plus anciens, de l'être humain) ». Cinq côtés sont en béton coulé, le sixième est fait du bois utilisé pour le coffrage. « Nous comptons que ces éléments vieilliront comme la pierre et acquerront ce faisant un peu de la nature brute de l'endroit, tout en demeurant agréables pour permettre à leurs occupants d'apprécier la nature et la vie en général. »

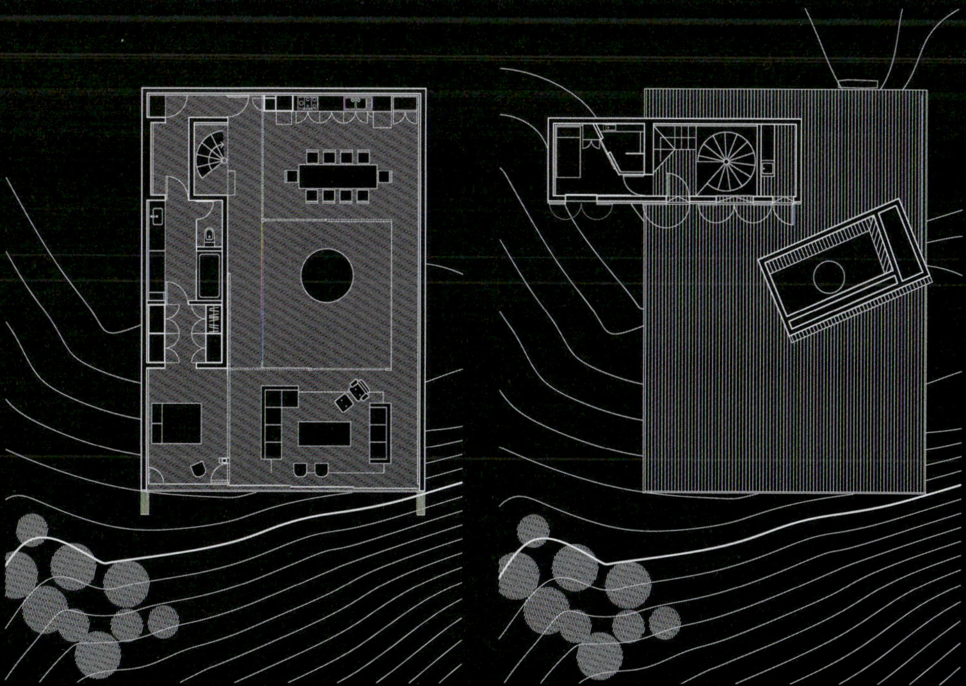

ENSAMBLE STUDIO

Ca'n Terra
Menorca, Spain, 2018–20
Area: 1000 m²

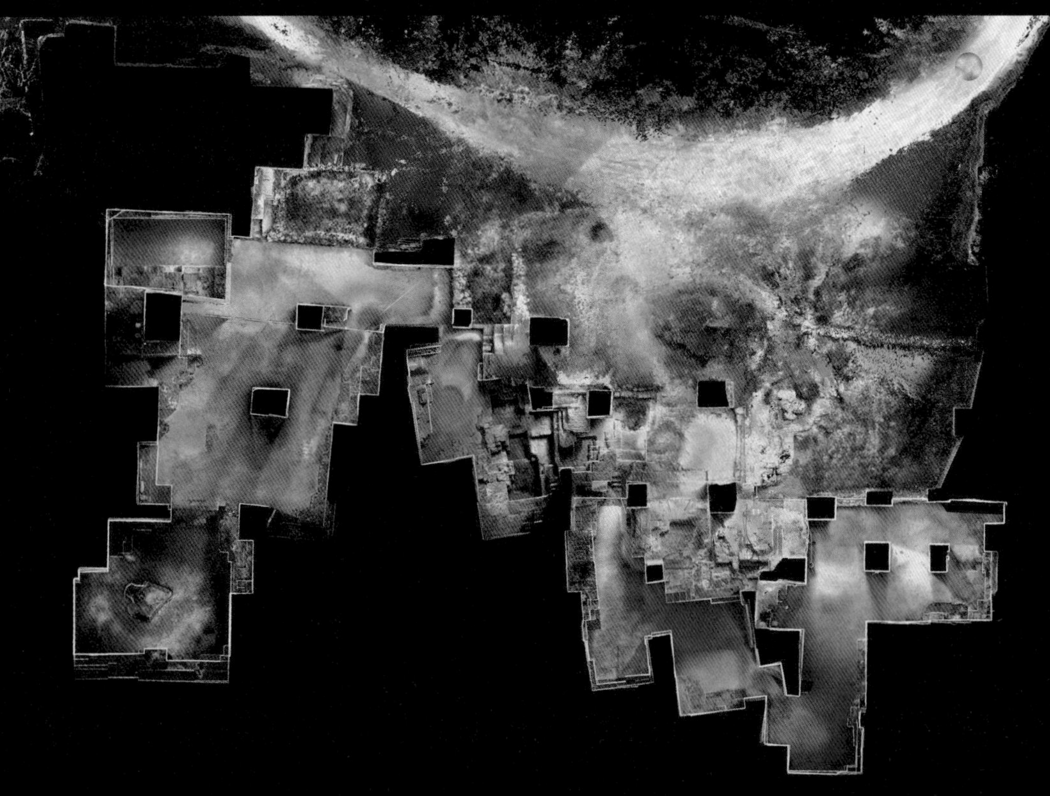

he abandoned quarry and ammunition dump seems o be naturally inscribed in its rough setting. It is hardly liscernable as a house in the image above.

he Ca'n Terra was built in what remains of a juarry, which was used as an ammunition dump uring the Spanish Civil War. Abandoned for nany years, the hand-carved spaces were rediscovered by Antón García-Abril and his team. hree skylights were carved from the rock o bring in natural illumination, and the stone urfaces were thoroughly cleaned. Translucent curtains are used to create a degree of intimacy where required. Mixing cement with powdered tone of the type found in the area, spaces for nechanical systems were introduced. Solar panels, a septic tank, and a water cistern give he new residence a high degree of autonomy. he architect says: "Ca'n Terra is the house of he earth: first just that, earth, after quarried vith industrial logic, voided and abandoned, o be rediscovered 100 years later and come o be architecture.... This is a project that boldly seeks a balance between nature and artifice, between histories and times, between people and the environment."

Das Ca'n Terra wurde in den Überresten eines Steinbruchs errichtet, der während des Spanischen Bürgerkriegs als Munitionslager genutzt worden war. Die seit vielen Jahren vernachlässigten handgegrabenen Räume wurden von Antón García-Abril und seinem Team wiederentdeckt. Sie schlugen drei Oberlichter in den Fels, um natürliches Licht einzulassen, und unterzogen die Steinoberflächen einer gründlichen Reinigung. Lichtdurchlässige Vorhänge schaffen dort, wo es nötig ist, eine gewisse Intimität. Mit Material, das durch Mischen von Zement mit pulverisiertem, lokal vorkommendem Stein gewonnen wurde, schufen sie Platz für mechanische Systeme. Solarpaneele, eine

With artificial light emerging and a modern space visible within, the unusual nature of the design becomes more apparent.

Klärgrube und eine Wasserzisterne verleihen dem neuen Wohnhaus ein hohes Maß an Autonomie. „Ca'n Terra ist das Haus der Erde", so die Architekten. „Zuerst ist da einfach nur Erde, die – nachdem sie mit industrieller Logik abgebaut, entleert und verlassen wurde – 100 Jahre später wiederentdeckt und zu Architektur wird ... Dies ist ein Projekt, das kühn nach einem Gleichgewicht zwischen Natur und Künstlichkeit, zwischen Geschichten und Zeit, zwischen Mensch und Umwelt sucht."

Ca'n Terra a été construit dans ce qui reste d'une carrière utilisée comme dépôt de munitions pendant la guerre d'Espagne. À l'abandon pendant des années, les salles taillées à la main ont été redécouvertes par Antón García-Abril et son équipe. Trois lucarnes ont été percées dans la roche pour un éclairage naturel et la surface de la pierre a été nettoyée en profondeur. Des rideaux translucides créent une certaine intimité aux endroits où c'est nécessaire. Du ciment a été mélangé à de la poudre de pierre du type de celle trouvée sur place afin de créer des espaces destinés à des systèmes mécaniques. Des panneaux solaires, une fosse septique et une citerne d'eau confèrent une certaine autonomie à l'habitation. Selon les mots de l'architecte : « Ca'n Terra est la maison de la terre : c'est d'abord seulement cela, de la terre, qui a ensuite été exploitée selon une logique industrielle, évidée, puis abandonnée et redécouverte centans plus tard pour devenir architecture… C'est un projet audacieux qui cherche un équilibre entre nature et artifice, entre les histoires et le temps, entre les hommes et l'environnement. »

The carved surfaces of the original quarry are combined with willful additions to make the house using concrete and local powdered stone. The spaces are quite literally cavernous.

Like a subterranean world, the house is developed within existing cave-like volumes. The section drawing below shows both the pool (opposite) and the rubble-filled space with a tree seen right on this page.

ESCOBEDO SOLIZ

Nakasone House
Mexico City, Mexico, 2019
Area: 105 m²

Interior and exterior walls are fashioned from stone in a similar way—as seen in the images above, including the stairway leading to the upper floor from ground level.

This small house located on the periphery of the Mexican capital was built for a cost of just 29 565 euros using bricks, concrete, and wood. Originally, two identical houses were planned on the site, but the sister of the owner decided not to build her pavilion, leaving a relatively large garden space open. Anticipating substantial informal construction in the neighborhood within five to seven years, the architects decided to protect the plot with a stone wall and concentrate openings in an inner patio. Volcanic stone found on site was used for the wall, foundations, platform, and stairs of the residence, which is reinforced with a concrete frame for seismic reasons. The presence of this stone and public spaces below. In good weather, the patio opens easily towards the living and dining area. The architects explain: "Each space of the house is provided with a different type and intensity of light according to the activities taking place within. The honesty on the use of materials, construction systems, and structure are a homage to Rudolf Schwarz's beautiful and powerful churches of the Post War period." Schwarz, the architect of the Wallraf Richartz Museum in Cologne (1957), also designed the St. Antonius Church in Essen-Frohnhausen (1959), which makes use of a concrete frame and brick walls.

Brick, stone, and wood create a solid, yet warm atmosphere in the kitchen and dining area, which has ample natural light and windows.

Dieses kleine Haus am Rand der mexikanischen Hauptstadt wurde für nur 29 565 Euro aus Ziegeln, Beton und Holz errichtet. Ursprünglich waren für das Grundstück zwei identische Häuser geplant, aber die Schwester des Eigentümers entschied sich gegen den Bau ihres Pavillons, sodass eine relativ große Gartenfläche frei blieb. Da die Architekten von einer umfangreichen Bebauung innerhalb von fünf bis sieben Jahren in der Nachbarschaft ausgingen, beschlossen sie, das Grundstück mit einer Steinmauer zu schützen und die Gebäudeöffnungen auf einen Innenhof auszurichten. Für die Mauer, Fundament, Plattform und Treppe des aus seismischen Gründen mit einem Betonrahmen verstärkten Gebäudes, wurde vor Ort gefundener Vulkanstein verwendet. Dieser Stein und die Ziegelsteine verleihen dem Haus eine thermische Masse, die zu seiner Kühlung beiträgt. Auf einem Holzdeck, das auch als Decke für die Gemeinschaftsräume darunter dient, sind zwei Schlafzimmer untergebracht. Bei schönem Wetter lässt sich der Innenhof leicht zum Wohn- und Essbereich hin öffnen. „Jeder Raum des Hauses wird mit einer anderen Lichtart und -intensität versorgt, je nachdem, welche Aktivitäten darin stattfinden", so die Architekten. „Die Offenheit, mit der beim Einsatz von Materialien, Bausystemen und der Struktur verfahren wurde, ist eine Hommage an die wunderschönen und beeindruckenden Kirchen der Nachkriegszeit von Rudolf Schwarz." Schwarz, Architekt des Wallraf-Richartz-Museums in Köln (1957), entwarf auch die Pfarrkirche St. Antonius in Essen-Frohnhausen (1959), die aus einem Betonskelett und Backsteinwänden besteht.

Brick walls mark the modest living room space (above), while the stairway wall (opposite) made of rough stone contrasts with the relatively light wooden shelving and guard rail. A blue wall in the background breaks the otherwise gray and brown color scheme.

La construction en briques, béton et bois de cette maison en périphérie de la capitale mexicaine a coûté seulement 29 565 euros. Deux maisons identiques étaient prévues à l'origine sur le même site, mais la sœur du propriétaire a finalement décidé de ne pas construire son pavillon, ce qui a libéré un espace pour le jardin. Anticipant les constructions anarchiques dans le voisinage au cours des cinq à sept ans à venir, les architectes ont choisi de protéger la parcelle avec un mur de pierre et de concentrer les ouvertures dans un patio intérieur. Le mur est construit en pierre volcanique trouvée sur place, ainsi que les fondations, la dalle et les escaliers de l'habitation qui sont renforcées par une charpente en béton pour des raisons sismiques. Cette pierre et les briques confèrent à la maison une masse thermique qui l'aide à conserver sa fraîcheur. Deux chambres à l'étage ont été aménagées sur un plancher en bois qui tient lieu de plafond aux espaces communs en dessous. Par beau temps, le patio peut être ouvert sur le salon et l'espace destiné aux repas. Les architectes expliquent que « chacun des différents espaces de la maison dispose d'un type et d'une intensité d'éclairage différents en fonction des activités qui s'y déroulent. L'honnêteté en ce qui concerne les matériaux utilisés, les systèmes de construction et la structure sont un hommage aux belles et puissantes églises construites par Rudolf Schwarz pendant l'après-guerre » – l'architecte du musée Wallraf Richartz de Cologne (1957) a également conçu l'église St. Antoine d'Essen-Frohnhausen (1959) avec une charpente en béton et des murs de briques.

STACEY FARRELL

The Coast House
Omaui, New Zealand, 2018
Area: 97 m² (not including outdoor shed)

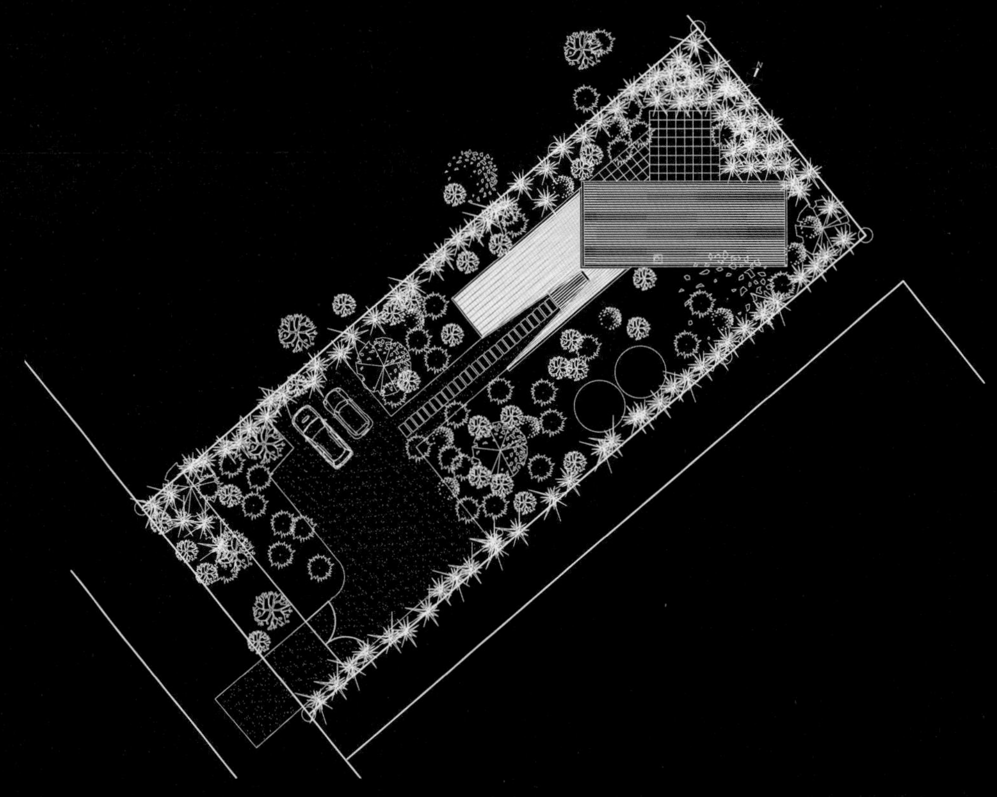

Built on a camping site near the shore of the Foveaux Strait the house is not far from the southern tip of the South Island.

Designed by the architect for her own use, The Coast House is in Omaui, a coastal village in the Southland region of New Zealand. Stacey Farrell camped on the site with her husband, the cinematographer Ben Ruffell, to get to know it better, even climbing in trees to imagine views from the future floors. She decided to place the house at the northern end of the site and wrapped it around a windswept, leaning beech tree. As she says: "This house was designed to hide discretely, hunker down into its harsh southerly environs. Landscape was a priority." There are two forms: the "grounded" one is clad in brown Lignite corrugate, and the upper one with black vertical trapezoid profile. Passive energy savings were a priority and sustainably sourced materials were privileged. New Zealand wool was used for roof insulation. Heating is provided by a wood-burning stove in the lounge and "some panel heaters" in the bedrooms.

Das von der Architektin für den Eigengebrauch entworfene The Coast House liegt in Omaui, einem Küstendorf in der neuseeländischen Region Southland. Um das Gelände besser kennenzulernen, zeltete Stacey Farrell dort mit ihrem Ehemann, dem Kameramann Ben Ruffell, und kletterte sogar auf Bäume, um sich die Aussicht von den künftigen Stockwerken vorstellen zu können. Sie beschloss, das Haus am nördlichen Ende des Geländes um eine windschiefe Buche herum zu bauen. „Dieses Haus sollte sich unauffällig verstecken, sich in die rau südliche Umgebung kauern", sagt die Architektin. „Der Landschaft wurde Priorität eingeräumt." Zwei Formen herrschen vor: Die ebenerdige ist mit lignitfarbenem Wellblech verkleidet, die

A small triangular terrace contrasts with the dark façade of the house. Both seem relatively fragile or ephemeral in the undulating brush setting.

obere mit einem schwarzen vertikalen Trapezprofil. Wichtig waren zudem passive Energieeinsparungen und Materialien aus nachhaltiger Produktion. Neuseeländische Wolle dient zur Dachdämmung. Geheizt wird mit einem Holzofen im Wohnzimmer und „einigen Flächenheizungen" in den Schlafzimmern.

Conçue par l'architecte pour son usage personnel, The Coast House est située à Omaui, un village côtier de la région du Southland. Stacey Farrell a campé sur place avec son compagnon, le cinéaste Ben Ruffell, pour mieux connaître l'endroit, et a même grimpé aux arbres pour imaginer les vues des futurs étages. Elle a décidé de placer la maison à l'extrémité nord du terrain et de l'enrouler autour d'un hêtre penché et battu par les vents. Selon elle, « cette maison est conçue pour se cacher discrètement, tapie dans le rude décor du Sud. Le paysage était une priorité ». On distingue deux formes : la forme « à la terre » est revêtue de lignite brun ondulé, et celle du haut présente des profilés verticaux noirs et trapézoïdaux. Les économies d'énergie passives étaient également une priorité pour l'architecte qui a privilégié des matériaux issus de sources durables. L'isolation est en laine de Nouvelle-Zélande. Le chauffage est assuré par un poêle à bois dans le séjour et « quelques panneaux chauffants » dans les chambres.

FAULKNER ARCHITECTS

Miner Road House
Orinda, California, USA, 2015
Area: 346 m²
Collaboration: DZINE Concept w/ Faulkner Architects (Interiors), Thuilot Associates (Landscape), Ethan Allen Construction (Contractor)

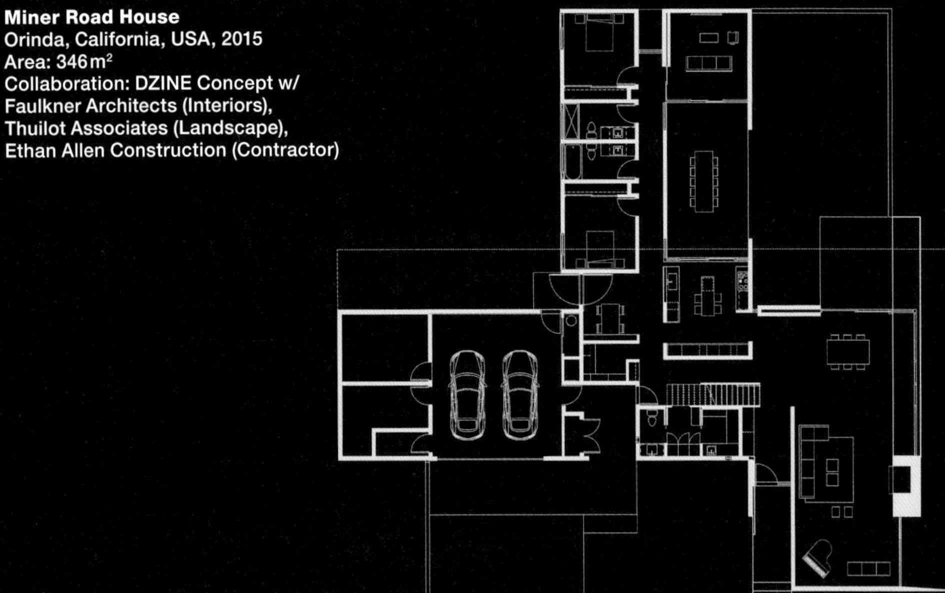

he Corten weathered steel screen that envelops he house allows it to fit into the hilly natural setting vithout aggressivity.

he clients for this house requested annual et-zero energy performance. Their idea was o remodel an existing 1954 ranch house on the ite, but, in the end, only the fireplace of that ouse wrapped in concrete was used as a struc-ural support. A mezzanine design provides for double-height family space with the master edroom and study above the kitchen. Other edrooms are located on the lower level near an utdoor dining area which is between the kitchen nd the family room. A 14-gauge (2-mm) Corten ain screen forms the exterior skin of the house, vhich was built on a shotcrete foundation. Inside, nfinished oak ceilings and walls contribute to willful roughness in the material palette. As or the environmental strategy of the house, the rchitects explain: "An 8.1kW photovoltaic system rovides on-site renewable energy and produced nore electrical energy than the house used the first year. Electronically commutated motors and variable speed heat pumps are used to further limit energy use and control heating and cooling. An energy recovery ventilator is used to provide fresh air." Orinda, in California, is located east of Berkeley and is home to suburban professionals who commute to San Francisco or Oakland.

'he entrance is marked by a high canopy and a jeometric composition of steel forms that make its esidential function less immediately evident than night be expected.

ür dieses Haus wünschten sich die Bauherren eine jährliche Netto-Null-Energieeffizienz. Vom ırsprünglichen Ranchhaus von 1954 wurde ediglich der mit Beton ummantelte Kamin ıls strukturelle Stütze weiterverwendet. Ein Aezzanin-Design sorgt für einen doppelt hohen 3ereich für die Familie mit Hauptschlafzimmer ınd Arbeitszimmer über der Küche. Die andeen Schlafzimmer befinden sich auf der unteren Ebene nahe einem Essbereich im Freien zwischen Küche und Familienraum. Die Außenhülle des lauses, das auf einem Spritzbetonfundament errichtet wurde, besteht aus einer zwei Millimeter licken vorgehängten Fassade aus Cortenstahl. m Inneren tragen unbehandelte Eichenholzlecken und -wände zu einer eigenwilligen Rauheit der Materialpalette bei. Zur Umweltstrategie des Gebäudes führen die Architekten us: „Eine 8,1-kW-Fotovoltaikanlage liefert vor Ort erneuerbare Energie und produzierte mehr elektrische Energie, als das Haus im ersten Jahr verbrauchte. Elektronisch kommutierte Motoren und Wärmepumpen mit variabler Drehzahl begrenzen den Energieverbrauch weiter und steuern Heizung und Kühlung. Ein Ventilator mit Energierückgewinnung sorgt für Frischluft." Das kalifornische Orinda liegt östlich von Berkeley und ist die suburbane Heimat von Pendlern nach San Francisco und Oakland.

'he spectacular, high interior spaces are placed in 'irect contact with the wooded setting through a 'eometric composition forming a glass wall (left). This 'eature echoes the outside appearance, much as the 'nfinished oak walls and ceiling seem to be the ideal 'ounterpart to the exterior Corten walls.

.es clients de cette maison ont exigé un ren-'ement énergétique annuel net zéro. Leur idée 'onsistait à reconfigurer un ranch de 1954, mais 'inalement, seule la cheminée enrobée de béton 'été utilisée comme soutien structurel. Un 'oncept avec mezzanine fournit un logement 'amilial double hauteur avec la chambre prin-'ipale et le bureau au-dessus de la cuisine.)'autres chambres sont situées au niveau 'nférieur à côté d'un espace repas extérieur 'ntre la cuisine et la pièce familiale. Un écran 'are-pluie de 2 mm en acier Corten forme 'enveloppe extérieure de la maison construite 'ur des fondations en béton projeté. Les pla-'onds et les murs en chêne non finis ajoutent 'la nature rustique des matériaux. Concernant 'a stratégie environnementale, les architectes 'xpliquent qu'un « système photovoltaïque de '1 kW fournit de l'énergie renouvelable produite sur place et a produit plus d'énergie électrique que la consommation de la première année. Des moteurs à commutation électronique et des pompes à chaleur à vitesse variable permettent de limiter la consommation et de contrôler le chauffage et le refroidissement, tandis qu'un ventilateur à récupération d'énergie apporte de l'air frais ». Orinda, se trouve à l'est de Berkeley, ses habitants font chaque jour la navette vers San Francisco ou Oakland pour travailler.

FORMAFATAL

Atelier Villa
Bahia Ballena, Playa Hermosa,
Costa Rica, 2016–19
Area: 326 m²

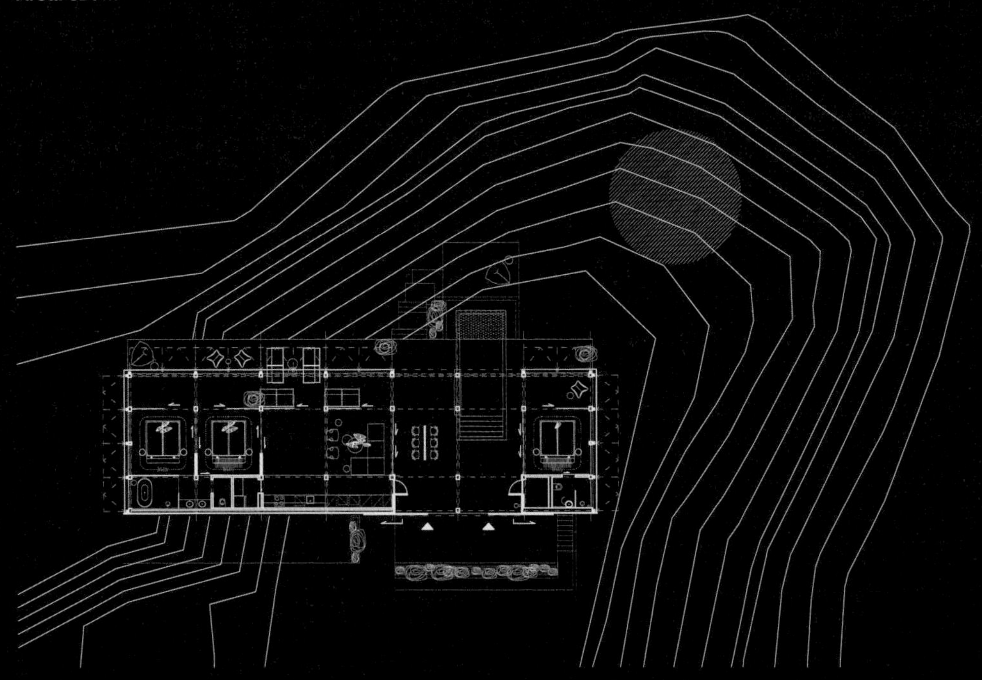

Partially lifted off the ground and cantilevered to correspond to the site, the long, low form of the house is complemented by a green roof that allows it to blend into the natural environment.

The Atelier Villa is part of a small resort located in the jungle near Uvita, Costa Rica, above the Playa Hermosa beach. Villas and pavilions were created on a two-hectare site. The resort also includes five tree house-like egg-shaped structures called CoCo Houses—designed by Archwerk.cz. The Atelier Villa was conceived as the private residence of the owner of the resort. The 26-meter-long steel-frame structure appears to partially "levitate" above the tropical vegetation on the site. The façades facing the ocean and jungle were made with perforated aluminum that is coated to resemble Corten steel. The back wall of the house is clad in charred timber using the Japanese *shou sugi ban* technique. The utility spaces and kitchen are arrayed on the back wall. The interior is fitted with sliding partition walls in another reference to Japanese architecture. The furnishing of the house, aside from lounge and dining chairs, was in large part custom-made by local craftsmen for the house. The exterior landscaping is by Atelier Flera.

Die Atelier Villa ist Teil eines kleinen Resorts im Dschungel bei Uvita, Costa Rica, oberhalb des Strandes Playa Hermosa. Seine Villen und Pavillons wurden auf einem zwei Hektar großen Gelände errichtet, ebenso fünf eiförmige Baumhäuser, die sogenannten CoCo Houses von Archwerk.cz. Die Atelier Villa wurde als private Residenz des Resorteigentümers konzipiert. Die 26 Meter lange Stahlrahmenkonstruktion scheint teilweise über der tropischen Vegetation des Geländes zu „schweben".Die Fassaden Richtung Ozean und Dschungel sind aus perforiertem, speziell beschichteten Aluminium, das aussieht wie Cortenstahl. Die Hausrückseite ist mit geflammtem Holz in der japanischen

The covered spaces open almost entirely to the warm exterior while the pool actually enters the villa.

;hou-Sugi-Ban-Technik verkleidet. Wirtschafts-äume und Küche sind an der Gebäuderückwand ıngeordnet. Der Innenraum ist mit verschieb-ɔaren Trennwänden ausgestattet – eine weitere Referenz an die japanische Architektur. Die Einrichtung wurde, abgesehen von den Lounge-ınd Esszimmerstühlen, größtenteils von lokalen Handwerkern eigens für das Haus angefertigt. ᴧtelier Flera gestaltete die Außenanlagen.

L'Atelier Villa fait partie d'un petit complexe ouristique dans la jungle près d'Uvita (Costa Rica), au-dessus de la plage Playa Hermosa. Les villas et les pavillons y ont été construits sur ın terrain de deux hectares. Le complexe com-orend aussi cinq structures ovoïdes rappelantl des maisons dans les arbres baptisées CoCo Houses — créées par Archwerk.cz. L'Atelier Villa était destiné à servir de résidence privée au propriétaire. La structure de 26 mètres de long à charpente métallique semble en partie « léviter » au-dessus de la végétation tropicale. Les façades face à l'océan et à la jungle sont en aluminium perforé ce qui rappelle l'acier Corten. Le mur arrière est recouvert de bois carbonisé à l'aide de la technique japonaise *shou sugi ban*. Les espaces de rangement et la cuisine sont disposés le long de ce mur. L'intérieur est divisé par des cloisons coulissantes en référence à l'architecture japonaise. Le mobilier, à l'exception des fauteuils et des chaises, a été en grande partie réalisé sur mesure par des artisans locaux. L'aménagement paysager extérieur est l'œuvre d'Atelier Flera.

FRANKIE PAPPAS

House of the Big Arch
Waterberg, South Africa, 2019
Area: 120 m²

As seen from above, the house is immersed in its forest environment, with no trees having been cut during construction. Opposite: outdoor terraces extend the living space well into the surrounding environment.

The House of the Big Arch is in the 223 000-square-kilometer Bushveld nature reserve in the Waterberg mountains of north Limpopo Province in South Africa. The architects call it "a home that disappears into the landscape; that sits among the rocks and trees and birds; that offers animals and plants and humans equal opportunity to find shelter; that treats the bushveld with its deserved respect." The scheme seeks to "bridge the landscape between riverine forest and sandstone cliff." No trees were cut during the construction despite the dense growth on the site. Rough brick selected to match weathered sandstone on the site, sustainably grown timber, and glass and aluminum for non-structural walls were main materials. The ground floor has courtyards, a study, a library, and a swing bench. The first floor includes a courtyard, lounge and dining area, the kitchen, an outdoor deck, and a small pool. The building is just 3.3 meters wide, but its overall plan was at least in part dictated by the presence of trees. The site was laser-scanned and converted into a 3D digital model to allow for the complex fitting into the natural environment. The house is entirely off grid, and has 16 square meters of solar panels, as well as a design intended to create breeze and shade.

Das House of the Big Arch liegt im 223 000 Quadratkilometer großen Naturschutzgebiet Bushveld in den Waterberg-Bergen der nördlichen Limpopo-Provinz von Südafrika. Die Architekten bezeichnen es als „ein Wohnhaus, das in der Landschaft verschwindet; das zwischen Felsen, Bäumen und Vögeln hockt; das Tieren, Pflanzen und Menschen gleichermaßen die Möglichkeit bietet, Schutz zu finden; das Bushveld mit dem verdienten Respekt

ɔehandelt". Während der Bauarbeiten wurden
ceine Bäume gefällt. Grobe Ziegelsteine,
ɔassend zum verwitterten Sandstein des
Geländes ausgewählt, Holz aus nachhaltigem
Anbau sowie Glas und Aluminium für die nicht-
ragenden Wände sind die Hauptbaustoffe.
m Erdgeschoss befinden sich Innenhöfe,
ein Arbeitszimmer, eine Bibliothek und eine
Schaukelbank. Der erste Stock beherbergt
einen Innenhof, einen Lounge- und Essbereich,
die Küche, eine Außenterrasse und einen kleinen Pool. Form und Größe des nur 3,3 Meter
breiten Gebäudes wurden zumindest teilweise
dem vorhandenen Baumbestand angepasst.
Der Standort wurde mit einem Laser gescannt
und in ein digitales 3-D-Modell umgewandelt,
um den Komplex in die natürliche Umgebung
einfügen zu können. Das Haus ist völlig netzunabhängig und verfügt über 16 Quadratmeter
Solarpaneele sowie eine Konstruktion, die für
Wind und Schatten sorgt.

La maison se trouve dans la réserve naturelle
de 22,3 hectares du Bushveld, dans les montagnes du Waterberg, au nord de la province
sud-africaine du Limpopo. Les architectes en
parlent comme d'« une maison qui disparaît dans
le paysage ; posée parmi les rochers, les arbres
et les oiseaux, qui offre aux animaux, aux plantes
et aux hommes les mêmes possibilités de trouver
un abri ; qui traite le Bushveld avec le respect
qu'il mérite ». Le projet cherche à « jeter un pont
sur le paysage entre la forêt fluviale et la falaise
de grès ». Aucun arbre n'a été coupé pendant
la construction. Les principaux matériaux sont
la brique crue, choisie pour s'accorder avec
le grès érodé du site, du bois issu de cultures
durables, le verre et l'aluminium pour les murs

A long wooden dining table leading toward the kitchen is surrounded by full height glazing. Right: *a ground-level ceiling plan and below, isometric drawings of the exterior seen from different angles.* Opposite: *a brick-lined wine cellar.*

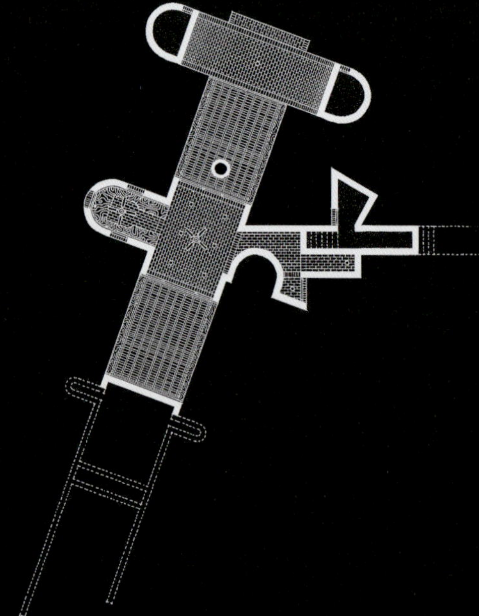

non porteurs. Le rez-de-chaussée comprend des cours, un bureau, une bibliothèque et une balancelle. Le premier étage comporte une cour, un salon et un coin repas, la cuisine, une plateforme extérieure et une petite piscine. Le bâtiment ne dépasse pas 3,3 mètres de large, mais son plan d'ensemble a été dicté en partie par la présence d'arbres. Le terrain a été balayé au laser et converti en un modèle numérique 3D pour venir à bout de la tâche difficile qui consistait à le placer dans le décor naturel. La maison est hors-réseau et possède 16 mètres carrés de panneaux solaires, ainsi qu'un système pour fournir air frais et ombre.

TREES
BRYSON
CAPITAL
IDEAS

WILL GAMBLE

The Parchment Works
Northamptonshire, UK, 2017–18
Area: 200 m²

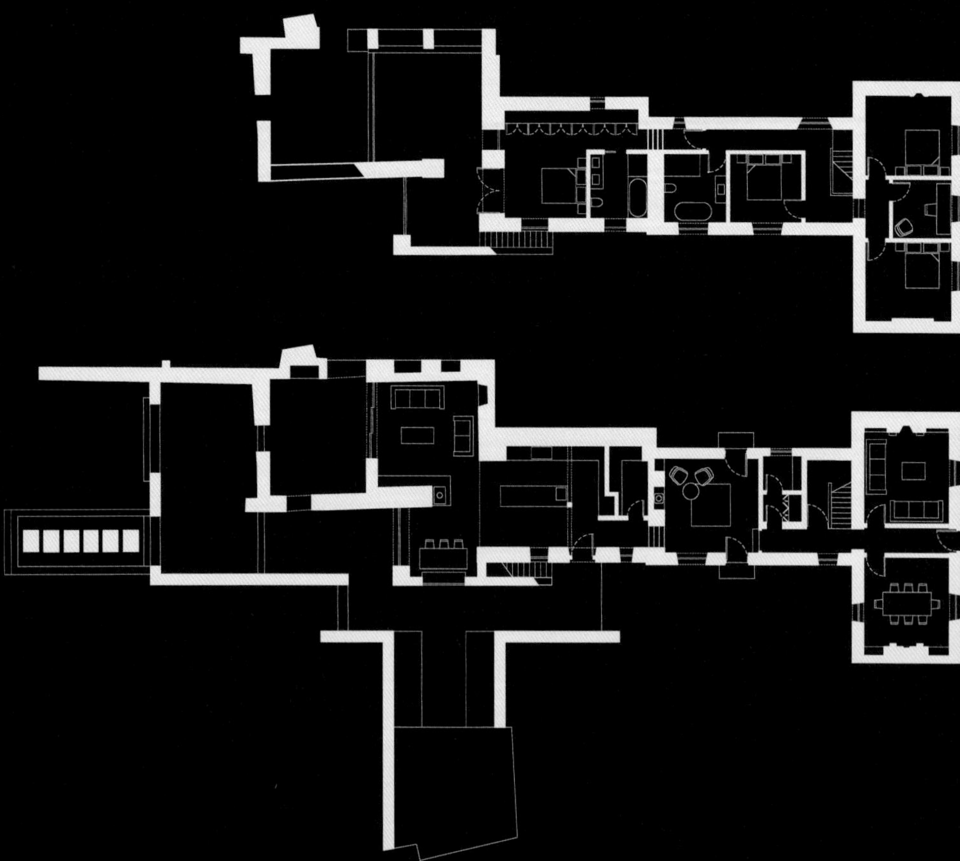

Reclaimed brick volumes have been added in a skillful and almost seamless manner to the consolidated and restored ruins of the factory.

The architect worked with a Grade 2-listed double-fronted Victorian house. The ruin of a former parchment factory (scheduled monument) is located nearby. The client sought to demolish the ruins to make space for a new extension, but the architect proposed, instead, to insert two lightweight volumes into the existing brick walls. Corten steel, reclaimed brick, and oak were used for the new elements. An existing cattle shed was reworked to expose structural beams and stone walls, with the addition of a concrete plinth. A modern kitchen serves to juxtapose the old and new in this instance as well. Built for a relatively low cost of 295 000 euros, this project shows how the reminiscence of the past can be made entirely compatible with a modern dwelling.

Als Ausgangsbasis diente dem Architekten ein viktorianisches, unter Denkmalschutz (Stufe 2) stehendes Zweifrontenhaus. In der Nähe befindet sich die Ruine einer ehemaligen, ebenfalls denkmalgeschützten Pergamentfabrik. Der Bauherr wollte die Ruine abreißen, um Platz für einen neuen Anbau zu schaffen, doch schlug der Architekt stattdessen vor, zwei leichte Baukörper in die bestehenden Backsteinmauern einzufügen. Konstruiert wurden diese mit Cortenstahl, wiederverwendeten Ziegeln und Eichenholz. Ein vorhandener Viehstall erhielt einen Betonsockel und wurde renoviert, um die tragenden Balken und Steinmauern freizulegen. Auch in der modernen Küche stehen sich Alt und Neu gegenüber. Realisiert mit einem relativ geringen Budget von 295 000 Euro, zeigt dieses Projekt, wie die Reminiszenz an die Vergangenheit mit einem modernen Wohnhaus in Einklang gebracht werden kann.

Interiors contrast rough stone walls, old oak ceilings and the smooth surfaces of a modern kitchen designed for the house. Opposite: *a dining table next to a large square window.*

L'architecte a ici travaillé à une maison victorienne à double fronton classée niveau 2. Les ruines d'une ancienne fabrique de parchemins (bâtiment d'importance nationale) se trouvent à proximité. Le client souhaitait les démolir pour faire place à une nouvelle extension, mais l'architecte lui a proposé d'insérer plutôt deux volumes légers dans les murs de briques. Les nouveaux éléments sont en acier Corten, en briques récupérées et en chêne. Une étable a été retravaillée pour en rendre apparentes les poutres porteuses et les murs de pierre et un socle en béton lui a été ajouté. Une cuisine moderne permet là aussi de juxtaposer l'ancien et le nouveau. Avec un coût relativement bas de 295 000 euros, le projet montre comment les vestiges du passé peuvent être rendus parfaitement compatibles avec un habitat moderne.

FRANK O. GEHRY

Santa Monica House
Santa Monica, California, USA, 2014–17
Area: 836 m²
Collaboration: Tensho Takemori (Partner), Sam Gehry (Project Designer), Brian O'Laughlin (Project Architect)

1. *Geothermal System*
2. *Radiant Floor Cooling and Heating*
3. *Natural Wind Ventilation*
4. *Gravity Wall Cooling System*
5. *Low-E Fabric Shading*
6. *Wind Scoop – Solar Chimney*
7. *Solar Photovoltaic System*

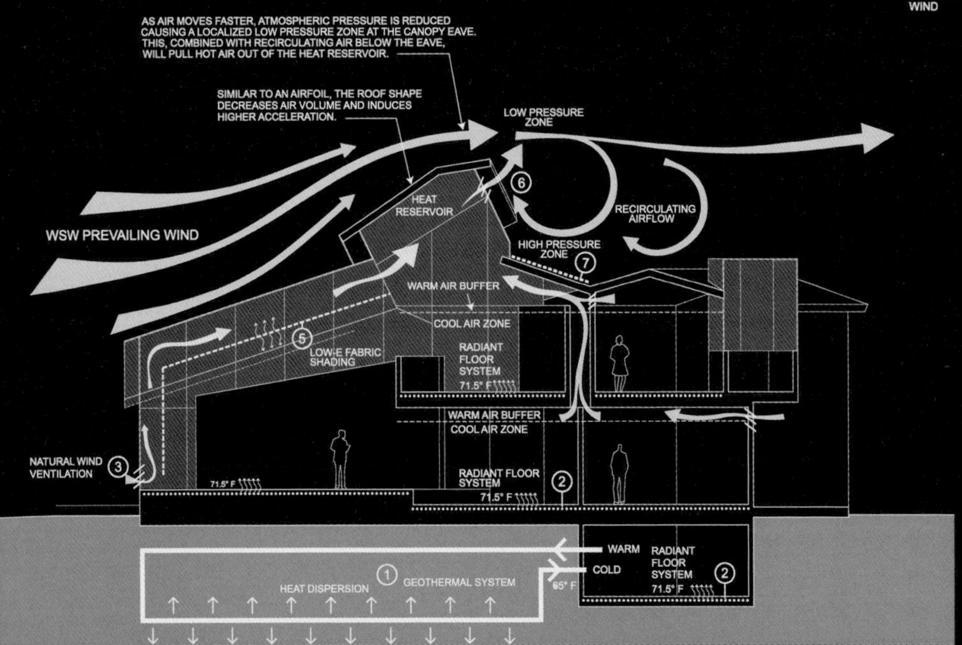

1 THERMAL DIAGRAM DURING SUMMER

Although the design can immediately be identified as being the work of Frank Gehry, it also pays homage to the Spanish style of the previous residence on the site, a style that is of course typical of the region.

This house's structure is made of solid 30.5 × 30.5-centimeter Douglas fir timber, glass walls to maximize the views, and a corrugated metal roof with a copper finish. The corrugated roof material is "designed to pay homage to the Spanish tile roof of the previous house on the site." Another reference to that house is the Churrigueresque (late Spanish Baroque) front door from the original house that was retained for the entrance. The design makes use of prevailing winds to create passive ventilation. Radiant floor heating operated with geothermal well water is another sustainability element of the house. The Santa Monica House is located to maximize views toward Santa Monica Canyon and the Pacific coastline. Readers will note numerous elements of furniture and art designed by Frank O. Gehry. So too, the design of the house has clear and present references to Gehry's slightly earlier Louis Vuitton Foundation in Paris (2008–14).

Die Struktur dieses Hauses besteht aus massivem Douglasienholz (30,5 × 30,5 cm), aus Glaswänden, um die Aussicht zu maximieren, sowie einem Wellblechdach mit Kupferbeschichtung. Das gewellte Dachmaterial ist „eine Hommage an das spanische Ziegeldach des früher auf dem Grundstück stehenden Hauses". Eine weitere Anspielung auf jenes Haus ist dessen churriguereske (im Stil des spätspanischen Barock gestaltete) Eingangstür, die für den derzeitigen Eingang erhalten wurde. Die passive Belüftung des Gebäudes macht sich die vorherrschenden Windverhältnisse zunutze. Die Fußbodenheizung, mit geothermischem Brunnenwasser betrieben, ist ein weiteres nachhaltiges Element des Hauses. Das Santa Monica

'he angled glass surfaces of the house bring to ıind the design of other Gehry projects like the Louis 'uitton Foundation in Paris, albeit on a smaller scale.

Iouse ist so ausgerichtet, dass der bestmögliche ˌusblick auf den Santa Monica Canyon und die ˀazifikküste erzielt wird. Dem Leser werden zahl-eiche von Frank O. Gehry entworfene Möbel und ˂unstwerke auffallen. Das Design des Hauses viederum weist deutliche und aktuelle Bezüge zu ɜehrys etwas früher fertiggestellter Louis Vuitton ˀoundation in Paris (2008–14) auf.

.a structure de la maison est en sapin de Douglas nassif de 30,5 × 30,5 cm, avec des parois en verre ɔour optimiser la vue et un toit de métal ondulé finition cuivrée. Le matériau ondulé du toit est conçu pour rendre hommage au toit en tuiles ɜspagnoles de la maison précédente ». La porte le devant churrigueresque (baroque espagnol ardif) qui a été conservée pour l'entrée constitue ıne autre référence à cette maison. Le concept ient compte des vents dominants pour créer une ventilation passive, il comporte d'autres éléments durables comme un chauffage au sol à rayonnement qui exploite l'eau de puits géo-thermique. La maison est orientée pour optimise les vues sur le canyon de Santa Monica et la côte Pacifique. Les lecteurs noteront les nombreux éléments de mobilier et d'art créés par Frank O. Gehry. De même, la conception de la maison présente des références claires et bien présentes à la Fondation Louis Vuitton qu'il a réalisée peu auparavant à Paris (2008–14).

The complex interior volumes are characterized by an extensive use of wood, and of course the generous glazed surfaces that include the ceilings in the living spaces seen above and opposite. Cross Check chairs by Gehry are seen below, with a version of the Little Beaver armchair on the left page.

DAVID HERTZ

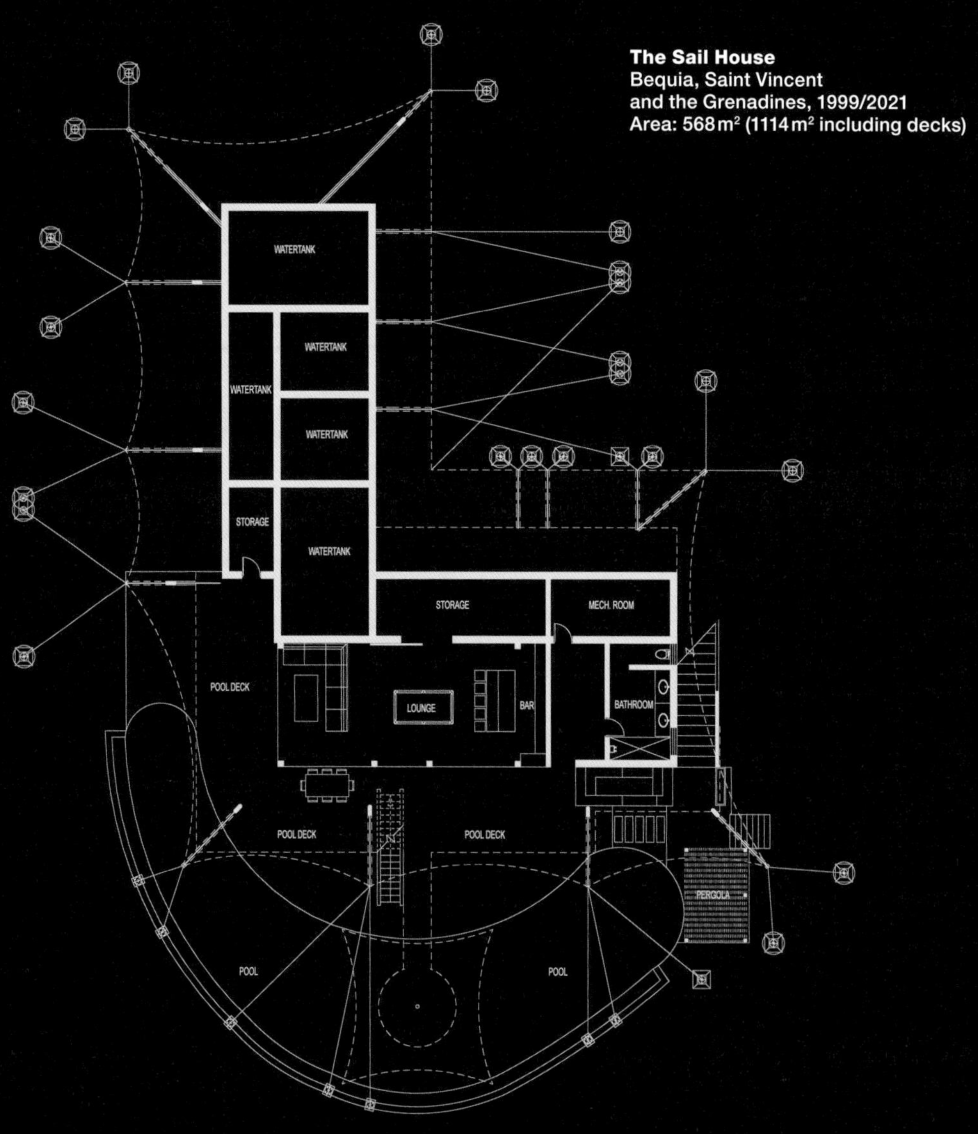

The Sail House
Bequia, Saint Vincent
and the Grenadines, 1999/2021
Area: 568 m² (1114 m² including decks)

The fabric membrane roof of the house certainly justifies the architect's description of it as a "land yacht," sitting here at the top of its densely wooded site.

The architect calls the Sail House a "land yacht" located on a ridge on the island of Bequia. A main residence, several guesthouses and a caretaker's residence are all part of the project. The forms of the fabric membrane collect rainwater and create a thermal chimney that draws heat out the top of the structures. Rainwater and dew are for appropriate reuse on the property. Over 3000 individual custom-extruded aluminum profiles were used for the prefabricated structural system of this house. Iron wood planking was reclaimed from a pier in Borneo. The tensile fabric membrane materials and custom stainless-steel rigging were all prefabricated and assembled in Java and Bali and flat-pack shipped to Bequia and reassembled. The prefabricated elements arrived in 15 shipping containers and were assembled in about two months on top of the concrete box that serves as a water cistern.

Wall panels made of woven palm and coconut shell fragments are part of the crafted materials prepared by Javanese and Balinese craftsmen. The Sail House generates its own electricity and "provides for a truly indoor/outdoor relationship conducive to the local microclimate." Construction cost was about $2700 per square meter.

A wooden bridge leads to a suspended round exterior seating area. The angled stainless-steel rigging of the house together with the fabric covering give it a decidedly unique appearance and a lightness that seems appropriate to the natural setting.

Eine „Landjacht" nennt der Architekt das auf einem Bergrücken der Insel Bequia gelegene Sail House. Das Projekt umfasst ein Hauptwohnhaus, mehrere Gästehäuser und eine Hausmeisterwohnung. Eine Gewebemembran fängt das Regenwasser auf und bildet einen thermischen Schornstein, der die Wärme aus den oberen Gebäudeteilen ableitet. Regen- und Tauwasser werden auf dem Grundstück wiederverwendet. Mehr als 3000 individuelle, stranggepresste Aluminiumprofile wurden im vorgefertigten Struktursystem verarbeitet. Die Eisenholzplanken stammen von einem Pier auf Borneo. Die Membranen aus dehnbarem Gewebe und die speziell angefertigten Edelstahlseile wurden auf Java und Bali vorgefertigt und zusammengebaut, als Flatpack nach Bequia verschifft und wieder zusammengebaut. Die Fertigelemente wurden in 15 Schiffscontainern angeliefert und in rund zwei Monaten auf der als Wasserzisterne fungierenden Betonbox montiert. Wandpaneele aus geflochtenen Palmen- und Kokosnussschalenfragmenten gehören zu den von javanischen und balinesischen Handwerkern handgefertigten Materialien. Das Sail House erzeugt seinen eigenen Strom und „sorgt für eine echte Innen-außen-Beziehung, die dem örtlichen Mikroklima zuträglich ist". Die Baukosten betrugen etwa 2700 Dollar pro Quadratmeter.

The tensile membrane roof extends broadly over both the interior spaces and the exterior terraces. Opposite bottom: *ground and upper level plans of the house.*

L'architecte définit la Sail House comme un « yacht terrestre » ancré sur une crête de l'île de Bequia. Le projet comporte une résidence principale, plusieurs maisons d'hôtes et le logement du gardien. Les formes de la membrane textile utilisée permettent de récupérer l'eau de pluie et créent une cheminée thermique qui draine la chaleur vers le haut de la structure et l'extérieur. L'eau de pluie et la rosée sont destinées à être réutilisées comme il se doit sur la propriété. La structure préfabriquée de la maison a nécessité plus de 3000 profilés en aluminium extrudé sur mesure. Le bardage en bois de fer a été récupéré sur un ponton abandonné à Bornéo. Les matériaux de la membrane textile résistante et le gréement en acier inoxydable ont tous été préfabriqués et assemblés à Java et Bali, puis acheminés en kit par bateau jusqu'à Bequia et réassemblés. Ils sont arrivés dans 15 conteneurs maritimes et ont été montés en deux mois environ au sommet du cube en béton qui sert de citerne d'eau. Les panneaux muraux en palmier tressé et fragments de noix de coco ont également été confectionnés par des artisans javanais et balinais. Sail House produit son électricité et « permet un véritable échange intérieur/extérieur propice au microclimat local ». La construction a coûté environ 2700 dollars par mètre carré.

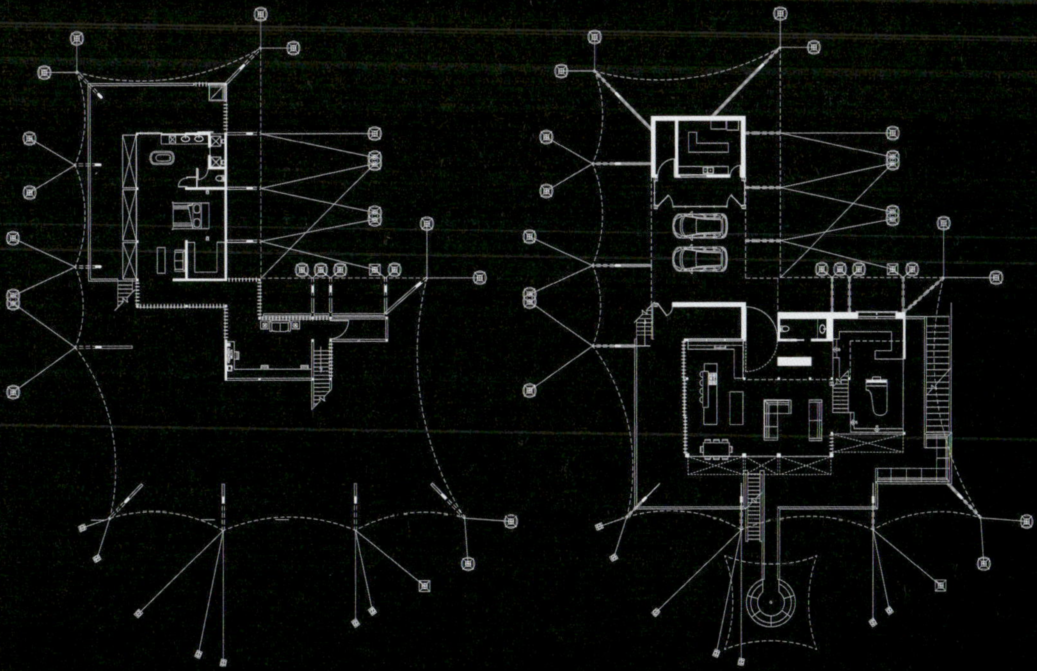

ROBERT HUTCHISON ARCHITECTURE & JSa ARQUITECTURA

Rain Harvest Home
Temascaltepec, Mexico, 2019
Area: 158 m²

Covered exterior terraces run around the house, leaving space for vegetation even within the limits of the architectural footprint.

This self-sufficient house in the mountains west of Mexico City includes a main residence, a detached art studio, and a bathhouse. The home collects rainwater which is purified and stored above and below ground in five cisterns, providing all of the water required. The design includes a 10-kW photovoltaic array, and fruits and vegetables are also grown on site. The three structures were built on Recinto volcanic stone foundations and have green roofs. Two-thirds of the main building consist of covered interior space, in keeping with local climate. The circular bathhouse includes a hot bath, sauna, steam shower, and wash and has an open-air cold plunge pool. Stained tongue-and-groove pine siding is used for the buildings.

Dieses autarke Haus in den Bergen westlich von Mexiko-Stadt umfasst ein Hauptwohnhaus, ein freistehendes Kunstatelier und ein Badehaus. Das Wohnhaus sammelt Regenwasser, das gereinigt und ober- wie auch unterirdisch in fünf Zisternen gespeichert wird, um den gesamten Wasserbedarf zu decken. Das Projekt nutzt eine 10-kW-Fotovoltaikanlage; auch Obst und Gemüse werden vor Ort angebaut. Die drei Gebäude wurden auf Fundamenten aus Recinto-Vulkangestein errichtet und verfügen über begrünte Dächer. Zwei Drittel des Haupthauses bestehen aus überdachten, dem örtlichen Klima angepassten Innenräumen. Im runden Badehaus befinden sich ein Heißluftbad, eine Sauna, eine Dampfdusche, eine Waschgelegenheit sowie ein kaltes Tauchbecken im Freien. Die Gebäude sind mit gebeizter Kiefer mit Nut und Feder verkleidet.

'he low, simple design of the house is visible in
ıe image above.

;ette maison autosuffisante des montagnes
, l'ouest de Mexico comprend une résidence
ɪrincipale, un studio artistique séparé et des
hermes. L'eau de pluie est récupérée, purifiée
ɪt stockée au-dessus et en dessous du sol
lans cinq citernes qui suffisent aux besoins.
'ensemble comprend 10 kW de panneaux
hotovoltaïques. Des fruits et des légumes sont
ultivés sur place. Les trois structures ont été
ɪrigées sur des fondations en pierre volcanique
ecinto avec des toits végétalisés. Les deux tiers
lu bâtiment principal sont formés d'un espace
ıtérieur couvert adapté au climat local. La mai-
on de bain circulaire comporte une baignoire
'eau chaude, un sauna, une douche de vapeur
ɪt un bassin de plongée extérieur froid. Le revê-
ement extérieur des bâtiments est en planches
le pin teinté à rainures et languettes.

Although the house is notable because of its self-sufficiency, it exudes a comfortable modernity that sometime ago would have seemed antithetical with ecological awareness. Below: a plan and an elevation drawing show the rectangular grid underlying the disposition of the main elements.

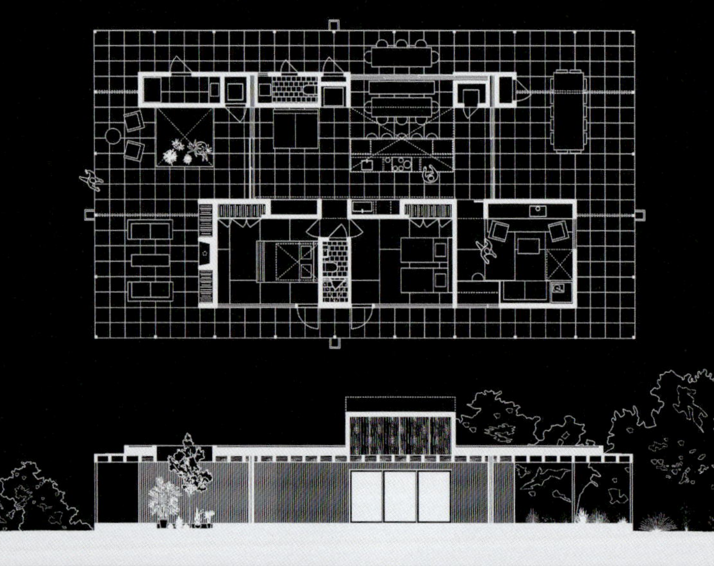

The circular bathhouse is seen on this double page with plan and section drawings below. Grayed pine siding covers the exterior.

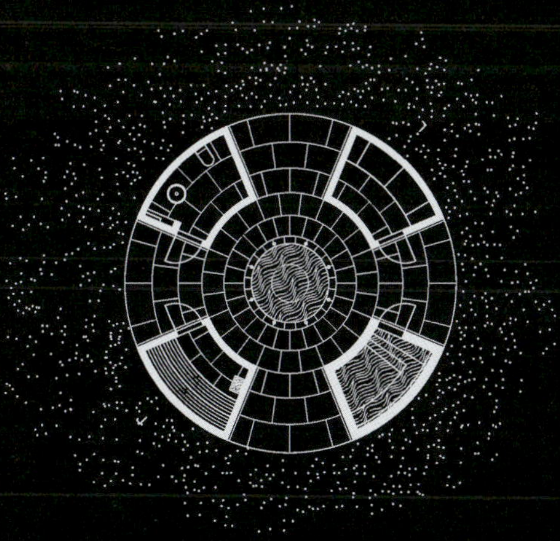

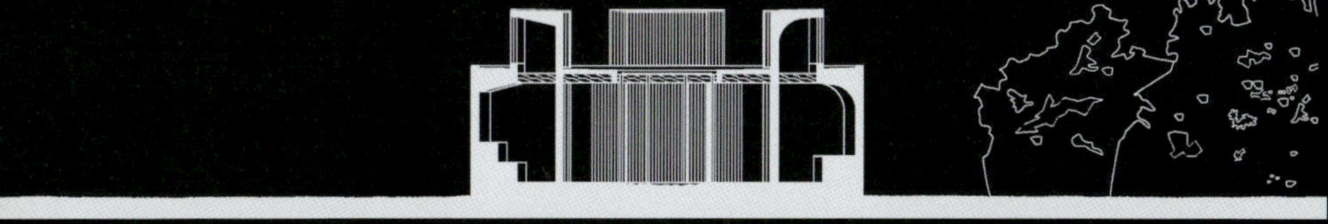

PAULO AND BERNARDO JACOBSEN

RN House
Minas Gerais, Brazil, 2016–20
Area: 1250 m²

An aerial view shows that the basic form of the house is that of an asymmetrical "T" with a further platform extending beneath the large existing tree seen in the plan (page 268) and the picture above.

The RN residence was designed for a couple and their family for weekends and vacations on a site located near a large dam. The project was developed around an existing Vinhático tree (*Plathymenia reticulata*). The asymmetrical ground floor frames a courtyard with one wing devoted to bedrooms and another with living spaces. A wooden deck was built under the tree connecting the house and garden "in a natural way." The covered living spaces open entirely to this outdoor deck under the enormous tree. The architects used materials that are usually associated with Brazilian farmhouses. Granite was employed for wall cladding and for the floors of the public areas. Freijó (*Cordia goeldiana*) wood covers the ceiling and panels of the bedrooms. The house, typical of large Brazilian weekend residences conceived by Jacobsen and other architects, is set on a generous 26 650-square-meter site.

Das RN House wurde für ein Ehepaar und seine Familie als Wochenend- und Ferienresidenz auf einem Grundstück in der Nähe eines großen Staudamms entworfen. Es wurde um einen bestehenden Vinhático-Baum (*Plathymenia reticulata*) herum konstruiert. Das asymmetrische Erdgeschoss umrahmt einen Innenhof mit einem Flügel für die Schlafzimmer und einem anderen für die Wohnräume. Unter dem Baum befindet sich ein Holzdeck, das Haus und Garten „auf natürliche Weise" miteinander verbindet. Der überdachte Wohnbereich öffnet sich vollständig zu dieser unter dem gewaltigen Baum gelegenen Außenterrasse. Die Architekten verwendeten Materialien, die für brasilianische Farmhäuser typisch sind: Granit für die Wandverkleidung und für die Böden der Gemeinschaftsbereiche, Freijó (*Cordia goeldiana*) für die Decke und die Paneele in den Schlafzimmern. Das Haus, ein typischer Vertreter

der von Jacobsen und anderen Architekten entworfenen großen brasilianischen Wochenendhäuser, steht auf einem weitläufigen Grundstück von 26 650 Quadratmetern.

La résidence RN a été conçue pour un couple et leur famille pendant les week-ends et les vacances sur un terrain à côté d'un barrage. Le projet a été développé autour d'un arbre vinhático (*Plathymenia reticulata*). Le plan asymétrique encadre une cour dont une aile accueille les chambres et une autre les espaces à vivre. Une plate-forme en bois a été construite sous l'arbre et relie « naturellement » la maison et le jardin. Les espaces couverts ouvrent entièrement sur ce ponton sous l'immense arbre. Les architectes ont choisi des matériaux souvent associés aux fermes brésiliennes : du granite pour le revêtement des murs et les sols des espaces communs, du bois de freijo (*Cordia goeldiana*) pour le plafond et les panneaux muraux des chambres. La maison typique des grandes villégiatures brésiliennes déjà construites par Jacobsen et d'autres architectes occupe un vaste terrain de 2,6 hectares.

The expansive house features gardens in close proximity to the interiors, in particular in the area extending out to the large wooden deck seen on the right page.

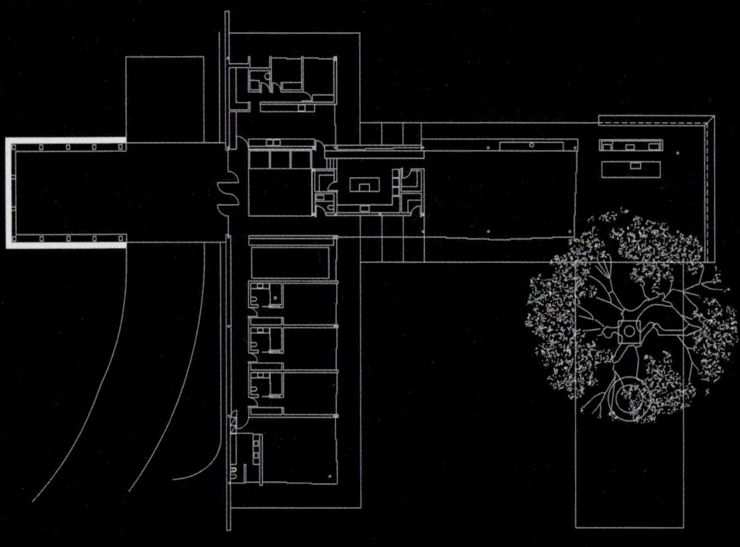

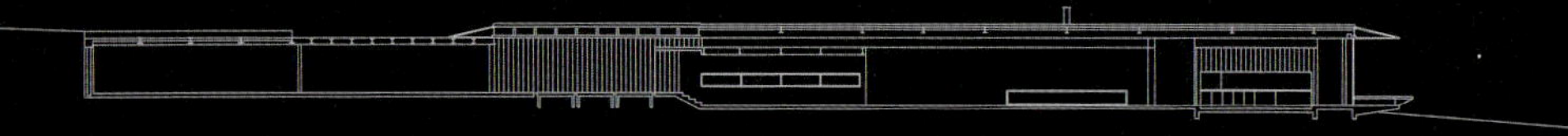

As is the custom in large Brazilian houses, covered interior spaces blend seamlessly with the outdoor environment. More than an architectural gesture, this is a natural reaction to the climate.

The generous covered spaces allow residents to feel that they are outdoors even in times of typical rain.

JK-AR

The House of Three Trees
Sangju, Gyeongsangbuk-do, South Korea, 2018
Area: 85 m²
Collaboration: Jae Kyung Kim,
Yesøl Lee, Seongbum Heo

This small house represents a willful combination of traditional structural and decorative elements with an advanced use of contemporary design and building techniques.

This house is a reinterpretation of the wooden bracket systems once ubiquitous in East Asia's timber architecture—called *Gong-po* in Korea and *Dougong* in China. The architect sees this work as a critique of contemporary interest in traditional architecture since it usually imitates only expressions and remains "too abstract." Rather, tradition implies a combination of structure and ornamentation according to Jae K. Kim, albeit advanced in this instance with the use of digital design and fabrication. This small structure, built for a cost of $126 000, explores the meaning of the house, defining it as "a room or space for a basic unit of society called family." The three trees referred to in the case of this house create an interior space, responding to a hexagonal building footprint, whose form is related to the site. The number of trees is defined as being a "minimum requirement to support the roof."

A gap between walls and the roof allows sunlight to filter in, as it does in a forest. No fastener (nails etc.) was used for the construction, which was carried out with 4006 pieces of engineered wood but traditional methods. Corrugated polycarbonate panels were used to finish the exterior walls, an element that contributes to a feeling of "ethereal lightness." The polycarbonate also improves the insulation qualities of the house and protects the interior plywood from rain.

ieses Haus ist eine Neuinterpretation der ölzernen Klammersysteme, wie sie einst in er ostasiatischen Holzarchitektur allgegenwärtig waren: *Gong-po* in Korea bzw. *Dougong* n China. Der Architekt sieht diese Arbeit als ine Kritik am zeitgenössischen Interesse an raditioneller Architektur, da dieses meist nur usdrucksformen imitiere und „zu abstrakt“ leibe. Tradition bedeutet für Jae K. Kim vielmehr ine Kombination von Struktur und Ornament, ie in diesem Fall allerdings durch den Einsatz on digitalem Design und digitaler Fertigung weierentwickelt wurde. Dieses kleine Bauwerk, das 26 000 Dollar gekostet hat, erforscht die Bedeuung des Hauses und definiert es als „Raum oder latz für eine gesellschaftliche Grundeinheit amens Familie“. Die drei namensgebenden äume bilden einen Innenraum als Reaktion auf en sechseckigen Gebäudegrundriss, dessen Form durch den Standort mitbestimmt wurde. Die Anzahl der Bäume ist als „Mindestanforderung zur Stützung des Daches“ festgelegt. Eine Lücke zwischen Wänden und Dach lässt wie in einem Wald das Sonnenlicht eindringen. Die Konstruktion weist keine Befestigungsmittel (Nägel usw.) auf, sondern wurde mit 4006 Holzwerkstoffteilen nach traditionellen Methoden montiert. Gewellte Polycarbonatplatten verkleiden die Außenwände, schützen vor Regen und verbessern die Isolierfähigkeit.

Drawings and photos show the transformation of the inspiration of the natural form of trees into a viable structural concept.

La maison réinterprète le système de crochets en bois autrefois omniprésent dans l'architecture d'Asie orientale, appelé *Gong-po* en Corée et *Dougong* en Chine. L'architecte voit ce travail comme une critique de l'intérêt actuel pour l'architecture traditionnelle qui n'imite que certaines expressions et reste « trop abstrait ». Or, la tradition suppose pour Jae K. Kim d'associer la structure et l'ornementation, même si l'exemple présenté ici est très avancé – du fait de la conception et de la fabrication numériques. La structure de petite taille, dont le coût de construction s'est élevé à 126 000 dollars, explore la signification même de la maison qu'elle définit comme « une pièce ou un espace pour une unité fondamentale de la société appelée famille ». Les trois arbres auxquels le nom fait référence créent un espace intérieur en écho à la surface hexagonale dont la forme est apparentée à celle du site. Le nombre d'arbres est « le minimum exigé pour tenir le toit ». Un intervalle entre les murs et le toit laisse filtrer la lumière comme dans une forêt. La construction n'a nécessité aucune fixation (clous, etc.), mais 4006 éléments de bois manufacturé assemblés selon des méthodes traditionnelles. Les finitions des murs extérieurs sont des panneaux de polycarbonate ondulés qui contribuent au sentiment de « légèreté éthérée ». Le polycarbonate permet une meilleure isolation et protège le contreplaqué de l'intérieur.

ALBERTO KALACH

Hacienda Tzalancab
Mérida, Yucatan, Mexico, 2012
Area: 400 m² (house), 1100 m² (including pool and other outdoor areas)

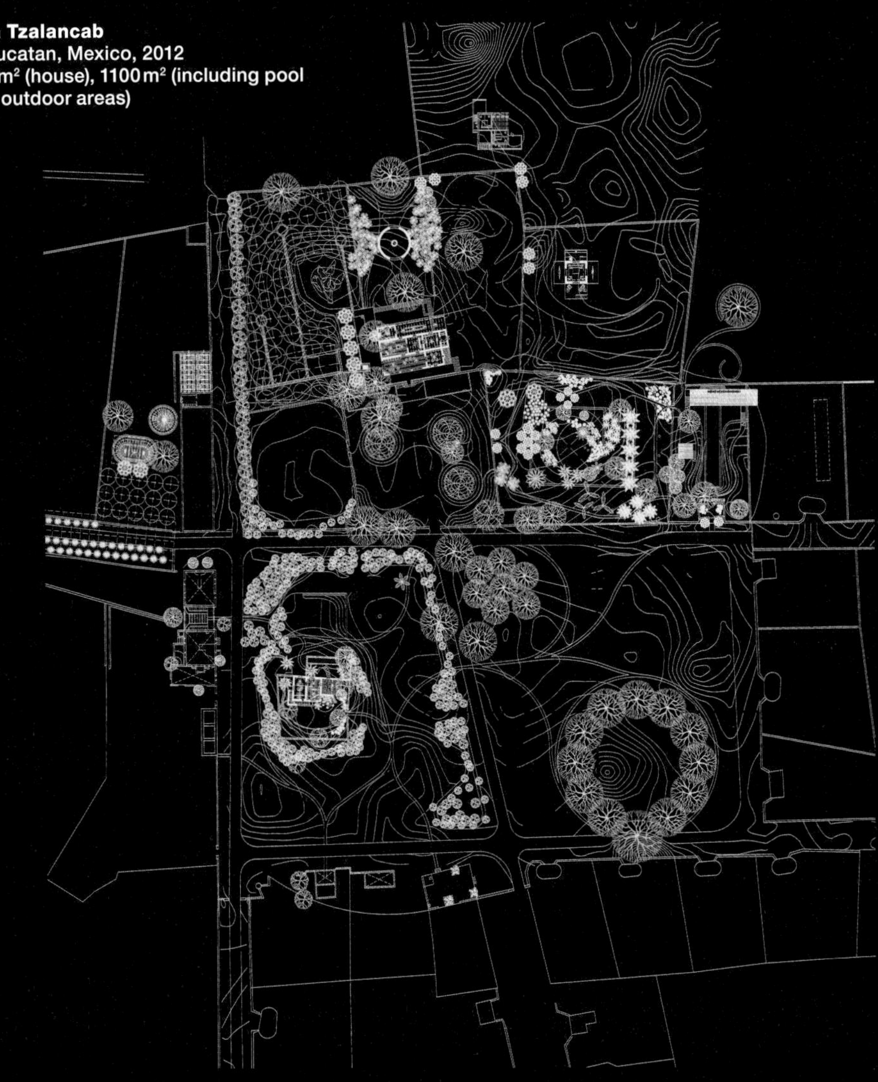

The architect insists that he did as little as possible to modernize and restore this historic house, focusing on terraces, stairways, and the garden. Opposite: *a long dining table under a canopy.*

Deeply inserted into dense vegetation on this 2.5-hectare site, the architect was involved not only in the "responsible and authentic" restoration of existing buildings, but also in "sustainable" work on the landscape. A green roof including a wooden deck was created on top of the main house. Solar panels power fountains and watercourses on the property. External staircases were added to this house and to a guesthouse. Alberto Kalach has taken a willfully light approach in this case. He says: "For the Tzalancab hacienda project I tried to leave things as close to what they were as possible. We added a pergola to take advantage of the roof and just a staircase; other than that, my intention is that visitors cannot identify the architectural intervention. I understand the intervention as fixing the structure, not so much as invasively intervening in this place." He refers to the landscape work that he did in a similar way: "We intervened near the pool with a few plants to create a composition with the landscape. I think that a composition of plants is like a musical orchestra, with different sounds in tune." In a sense he sees this project as a kind of ruin on which he has sought to intervene only lightly. "Time and dirt bring a unique dimension to architecture. Imagine a painting by Leonardo da Vinci. You want it to be preserved over the years in the best possible way. However, architecture over time gets ruined and that is unique and very special. To see what you did ruined or ruining in line with life, as we humans grow older, that's nature."

ıngesichts der Lage der bestehenden Gebäude, ˌie tief in die dichte Vegetation des 2,5 Hektar ıroßen Geländes eingebettet sind, ging es dem ırchitekten nicht nur um deren „verantwortungs-olle und authentische" Restaurierung, sondern ıuch um die „nachhaltige" Arbeit. Das Haupthaus ɹrhielt ein Gründach samt Holzdeck. Solarpaneele ersorgen die Brunnen und Wasserläufe des Grundstücks. Außentreppen wurden am Haupt-ıaus und an einem Gästehaus angebracht. Kalach ıat hierfür einen bewusst leichten Ansatz gewählt. Bei dem Tzalancab-Hacienda-Projekt habe ich ersucht, die Dinge möglichst so zu belassen, wie ie waren", so der Architekt. „Um das Dach zu ıutzen, fügten wir eine Pergola hinzu und sonst ıur noch eine Treppe. Davon abgesehen, sollen ˌie Besucher die architektonische Intervention ıicht erkennen können. Ich verstehe den Eingriff ıle Fixierung der Struktur nicht so sehr als inva-sives Eingreifen in diesen Ort." Ähnlich verhält es sich für ihn mit den durchgeführten Landschafts-arbeiten: „In der Nähe des Schwimmbeckens griffen wir mit einigen Pflanzen in die Natur ein, um ein Arrangement mit der Landschaft zu kreie-ren. Ich denke, ein Pflanzenarrangement ist wie ein Musikorchester, in dem verschiedene Klänge aufeinander abgestimmt sind." In gewisser Weise betrachtet er dieses Projekt als eine Art Ruine, in die er nur leicht eingreifen wollte. „Zeit und Schmutz verleihen der Architektur eine einzigar-tige Dimension. Stellen Sie sich ein Gemälde von da Vinci vor. Man möchte, dass es im Laufe der Jahre so gut wie möglich erhalten bleibt. Aber Architektur zersetzt sich mit der Zeit, und dies ist etwas Einzigartiges und ganz Besonderes. Zu sehen, wie das, was man schuf, im Laufe unseres Lebens zerfällt, während wir Menschen älter wer-den – das ist Natur."

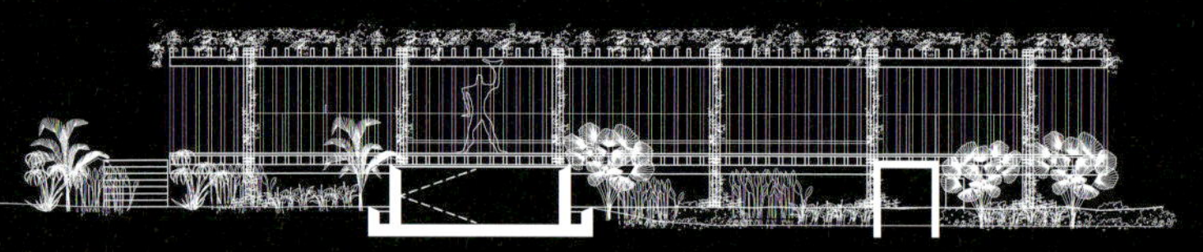

Opposite top: *a photo of the pool itself and a drawing of the poolside structure.* Opposite below: *The elevated pool and covered lounging structure at its head.*

The kitchen and a bathroom are at once modernized and yet not in contradiction with the existing building.

La maison est profondément enfoncée dans la végétation dense du terrain de 2,5 hectares, l'architecte ayant cherché, outre la restauration « responsable et authentique » des constructions existantes, à réaliser un travail « durable » sur le paysage. Un toit végétalisé en bois à plate-forme en bois a été ajouté à la maison principale. Des panneaux solaires alimentent en électricité les fontaines et cours d'eau de la propriété. Des escaliers extérieurs ont été ajoutés à la maison et à une maison d'hôtes. Alberto Kalach a adopté une approche délibérément légère et déclare : « Pour le projet de l'hacienda Tzalancab, j'ai essayé de laisser les choses le plus possible en l'état. Nous avons ajouté une pergola pour profiter du toit et un seul escalier ; sinon, mon but est que les visiteurs ne puissent pas reconnaître l'intervention de l'architecte. Je vois cette intervention comme une réparation de la structure, pas comme une intrusion abusive. » Il évoque également son travail paysager en des termes similaires : « Nous sommes intervenus près de la piscine en ajoutant quelques plantes pour créer une composition paysagère. Je pense qu'une composition végétale est comme un orchestre et doit s'accorder sur des sons différents. » Il considère en quelque sorte ce projet comme une ruine qu'il a tenté de ne modifier que légèrement. « Le temps et la crasse donnent à l'architecture une dimension unique. Imaginez une peinture de Léonard de Vinci. Vous voulez la préserver le mieux possible pendant des années. Mais l'architecture tombe en ruines avec le temps et c'est un processus unique et très spécial. De voir ce que vous avez ruiné ou ce que vous ruinez avec la vie au fur et à mesure que nous vieillissons, nous les hommes, c'est la nature. »

PALINDA KANNANGARA

Frame Holiday Structure
Imaduwa, Sri Lanka, 2018
Area: 225 m²

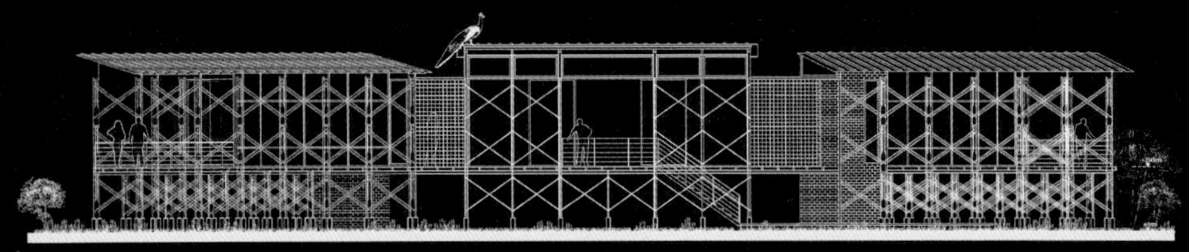

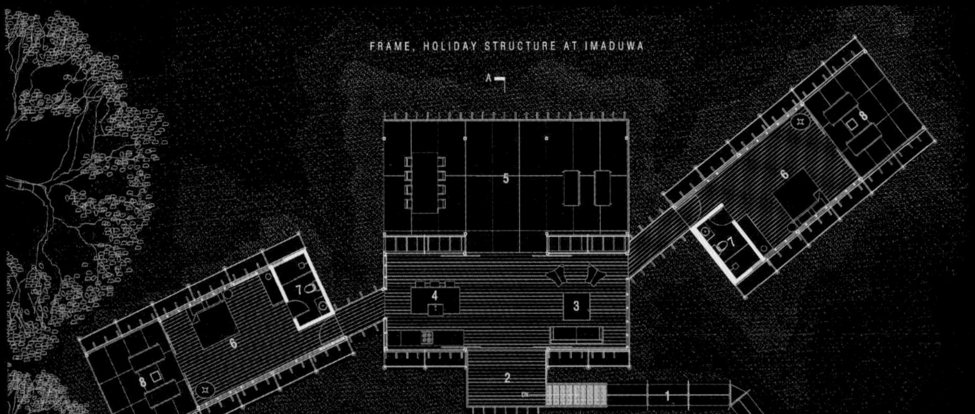

FRAME, HOLIDAY STRUCTURE AT IMADUWA

LEGEND

1 Boardwalk
2 Entrance Deck
3 Living
4 Kitchen and Dining
5 Deck
6 Bedroom
7 Bathroom
8 Balcony

FLOOR PLAN

*he extremely light structure of the house allows it
› sit entirely above the ground, with a design that is
›spired by construction scaffolding.*

his unusual house was built on a 3.2-hectare site
›ith steel scaffolding, exposed brick, and timber
oors for a budget of $40 000. It was built in a
eriod of just four months for the ethno-musician
nd jazz drummer Sumudi Suraweera. Because
ne site near the client's childhood village was
xposed to frequent flooding, the solution found
y the architect, lifting the structure up on scaf-
olding, addressed not only the frequent presence
f water, but also the limited budget available.
'here are three main platforms, a dining and
antry area, and two bedroom wings, all of which
re connected by light bridges. The structure
an, of course, be easily dismounted and moved
' required. There are few walls and those that
xist were made with lightweight Superflex dry
valls on timber frames, except for the brick toilet
valls. Adjustable glass louvers are used in the liv-
ng area. Furnishings were made with reclaimed
r leftover site materials, in close collaboration
with the client. Because the scaffolding modules
dictated the size of the areas of the house, much
less labor was required than would have been th
case for a more elaborate design.

Dieses ungewöhnliche Haus wurde auf einem
3,2 Hektar großen Grundstück mit Stahlgerüsten
sichtbaren Ziegeln und Holzböden für ein Budge
von 40 000 Dollar errichtet. Es wurde in nur
vier Monaten für den Ethnomusiker und Jazz-
schlagzeuger Sumudi Suraweera gebaut. Da der
Baugrund nahe dem Dorf, in dem der Bauherr
aufwuchs, häufig von Überschwemmungen heim
gesucht wird, fand der Architekt eine Lösung, di
nicht nur den wiederkehrenden Wassermassen,
sondern auch dem begrenzten Budget Rechnun
trägt: Er stellte das Gebäude auf ein Gerüst. Dre
Hauptplattformen – ein Ess- und Vorratsbereich
und zwei Schlaftrakte – sind durch leichte Brücken miteinander verbunden. Natürlich kann die

The scaffolding is readily apparent, framing and supporting the house in its luxuriant Sri Lanka setting.

Struktur bei Bedarf leicht demontiert und versetzt werden. Die wenigen vorhandenen Wände wurden mit Ausnahme der gemauerten Toilettenwände aus leichten Superflex-Trockenmauern auf Holzrahmen gefertigt. Im Wohnbereich werden verstellbare Glaslamellen verwendet. Das Mobiliar wurde in enger Zusammenarbeit mit dem Bauherrn aus wiedergewonnenen oder überschüssigen Materialien hergestellt. Da die Gerüstmodule die Größe der Gebäudebereiche vorgaben, war viel weniger Planungsarbeit erforderlich als bei einem aufwendigeren Entwurf.

Cette maison originale a été construite sur un terrain de 3,2 hectares en échafaudages d'acier, briques apparentes et planchers pour un budget de 40 000 dollars. Elle a été achevée en seulement quatre mois pour l'ethno-musicien et batteur de jazz Sumudi Suraweera. Comme le site, à proximité du village où le client a passé son enfance, est sujet à des inondations fréquentes, la solution imaginée par l'architecte – surélever la structure sur des échafaudages – s'est avérée correspondre au problème de l'eau, mais aussi au budget disponible. L'ensemble compte trois plates-formes principales, un espace destiné aux repas qui sert aussi de cellier, et deux ailes où se trouvent des chambres reliées par de légères passerelles. La structure peut être facilement démontée et changée d'endroit. Elle ne comporte que peu de murs et ce sont des murs secs et légers enduits de Superflex sur des cadres en bois – sauf ceux des toilettes qui sont en briques. Le salon comporte des persiennes en verre réglables. Les meubles sont faits de matériaux de récupération ou trouvés sur place, en collaboration avec le client. Les volumes des échafaudages ont dicté la taille des différentes parties de la maison, ce qui a nécessité moins de travail que s'il avait fallu les concevoir avec soin.

KRADS

Holiday Home at Lake Þingvallavatn
Southwest Iceland, 2015–20
Area: 153 m² (house), 21 m² (boathouse)

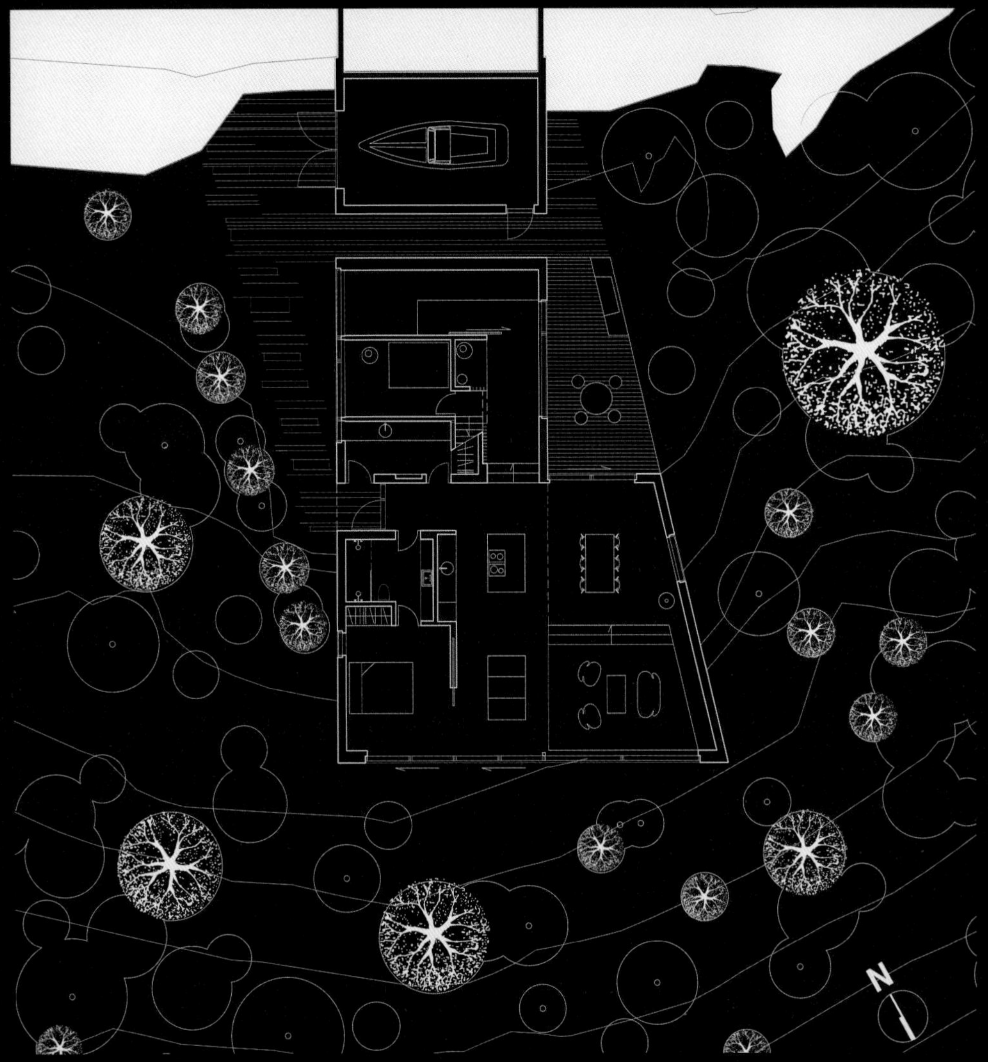

The house appears to emerge in a natural way from its site, even more so because of its green roof.

The concrete foundation of the wooden house was laid out in three staggered planes to follow the topography of the site. The accessible roof is sloped in two directions, and is covered with local grasses and moss. Built for a cost of $650 000 on a 1000-square-meter site, the house is almost surrounded by natural vegetation. By contrast the architecture is simple and pared back, giving an impression of modesty. The architects state: "Preserving the landscape as pristine as possible was a major intention in both the design process and during the construction of the house." The main room of the house offers open views of the second largest lake in Iceland and the Skjaldbreið mountain. A terrace that faces southwest provides further views of the mountains.

Das Betonfundament des Holzhauses wurde in drei gestaffelten Ebenen angelegt, um sich der Topografie des Geländes anzupassen. Das begehbare Dach ist in zwei Richtungen abgeschrägt flach und mit einheimischen Gräsern und Moos bewachsen. Das Haus, das für 650 000 Dollar auf einem 1000 Quadratmeter großen Grundstück errichtet wurde, ist fast komplett von natürlicher Vegetation umgeben. Im Gegensatz dazu gibt sich die Architektur einfach und zurückhaltend und vermittelt einen Eindruck von Bescheidenheit. „Die Landschaft so ursprünglich wie möglich zu erhalten war eine der Hauptintentionen sowohl im Entwurfsprozess als auch beim Bau des Hauses", so die Architekten. Der Hauptraum des Hauses bietet einen freien Blick auf Islands zweitgrößten See und den Berg Skjaldbreið. Eine nach Südwesten ausgerichtete Terrasse wartet mit weiteren Ausblicken auf die Berge auf.

The transparency of the house allows residents to take in the sloped and wild natural setting more fully.

Les fondations en béton de la maison en bois ont été posées en trois plans échelonnés pour épouser la topographie du terrain. Le toit praticable est incliné dans deux directions et est couvert d'herbes locales et de mousse. Construite pour 650 000 dollars sur un terrain de 1 000 mètres carrés, la maison est presque entièrement entourée de végétation sauvage. L'architecture, par contraste, est très simple et dépouillée, donnant une impression de modestie. Les architectes expliquent : « Préserver le paysage le plus possible dans son état d'origine était l'une de nos intentions principales, pendant la conception et la construction de la maison. » La pièce principale a vue sur le deuxième plus grand lac d'Islande et la montagne de Skjaldbreið. Une terrasse orientée au sud-ouest offre d'autres vues sur les montagnes.

nteriors are high and bright with wooden ceilings and kitchen elements as seen below and left.

MACKAY-LYONS SWEETAPPLE

Sunset Rock House
Nova Scotia, Canada, 2011
Area: 139 m²
Collaboration: Campbell Comeau Engineering (Engineer), Garian Construction Ltd (Builder)

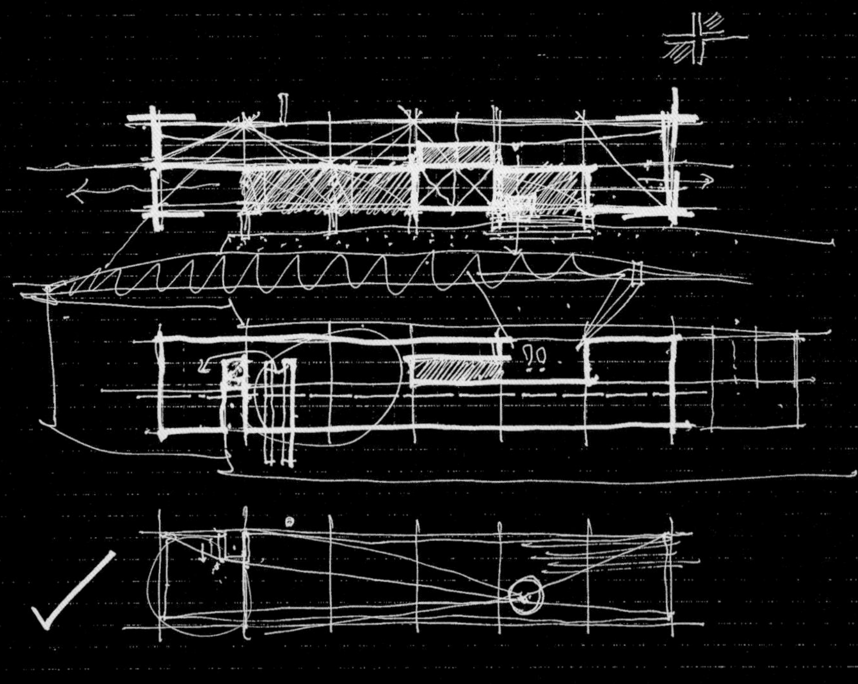

he long house angles up toward the water and s lifted above of the rocky shoreline.

his house is anchored on a rugged granite point of Nova Scotia that is washed by the Atlantic Ocean. The owner wanted "to have an intimate connection to the sea" and this design surely fulfills that wish. The long, narrow structure is mostly clad in metal aside from the windows and the covered deck at the oceanside. Barn doors can be used to close the openings in stormy weather. The house rests on a series of concrete fins that allow waves to pass under the structure when required. The beds have views of the sky through clerestory windows. The ocean can also be seen from the bathtub. The interiors of the house are white, in rder to better perceive the "power and immediacy of the ocean." The architects state: "With silver metal skin the house disappears within he blanket of fog which frequents the site. The calm sculptural nature of the house, expressed oth in its form and materials, is drawn from the vernacular and ethic of the local buildings used in the commercial fishery."

Dieses Haus wurde auf einer zerklüfteten, vom Atlantik umspülten Granitspitze in Nova Scotia verankert. Der Eigentümer wünschte sich „eine enge Verbindung zum Meer," und der Entwurf erfüllt diesen Wunsch mit Sicherheit. Abgesehen von seinen Fenstern und dem überdachten Deck zum Meer hin, ist die lange, schmale Struktur größtenteils mit Metall verkleidet. Bei stürmischem Wetter bedecken Schiebetore die Gebäudeöffnungen. Das Haus ruht auf einer Reihe von Betonflossen, die es den Wellen erlauben, notfalls unter dem Gebäude hindurchzuwogen. Von den Betten aus ist durch Oberlichter der Himmel zu sehen, die Badewanne bietet einen Meeresblick. Die Innenräume des Hauses sind weiß, um die „Kraft und Unmittelbarkeit des

Ozeans“ besser wahrnehmen zu können. „Mit seiner silbernen Metallhaut verschwindet das Haus im Nebel, wenn dieser den Ort heimsucht“, so die Architekten. „Der ruhige, skulpturale Charakter des Hauses, der sich in seiner Form wie auch in den Materialien ausdrückt, wurde von der Tradition und Ethik der Wirtschaftsgebäude der heimischen Fischerei inspiriert.“

La maison est ancrée à une pointe granitique déchiquetée de Nouvelle-Écosse, balayée par l'océan Atlantique. Le propriétaire désirait « une relation intime avec la mer » et ce projet a certainement exaucé son souhait. La structure longue et étroite est presque entièrement revêtue de métal à l'exception des fenêtres et du ponton couvert côté océan. De grandes portes de grange peuvent obstruer les ouvertures en cas de tempête. La maison est posée sur des ailerons de béton qui laissent les vagues passer en dessous au besoin. Les lits ont vue sur le ciel par des fenêtres à claire-voie. On voit aussi l'océan depuis la baignoire. L'intérieur est blanc afin de mieux percevoir la « force et l'instantanéité de l'océan ». Les architectes expliquent : « Avec son enveloppe de métal argenté, la maison disparaît sous la couverture de brume fréquente à cet endroit. Sa nature calme et sculpturale, exprimée à la fois par sa forme et par les matériaux utilisés, vient du langage et de l'esprit des bâtiments locaux utilisés pour la pêcherie commerciale. »

With its silvery metal skin, the house seems related to ships in its material presence. Its location allows the interior of the residence to be in almost direct contact with the ocean. Below: *the main plan of the residence.*

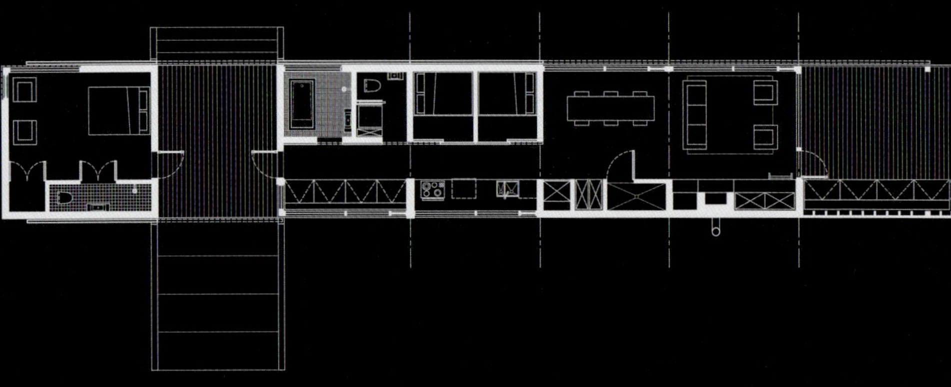

GURJIT MATHAROO

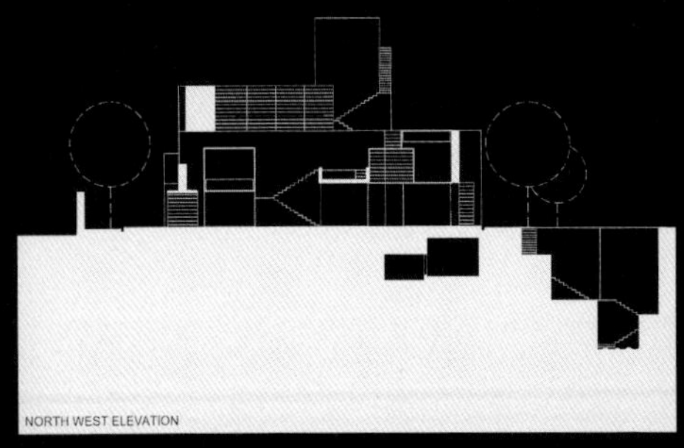

150 Steps Up to the Sea
Surat, Gujarat, India, 2017–20
Area: 1440 m^2

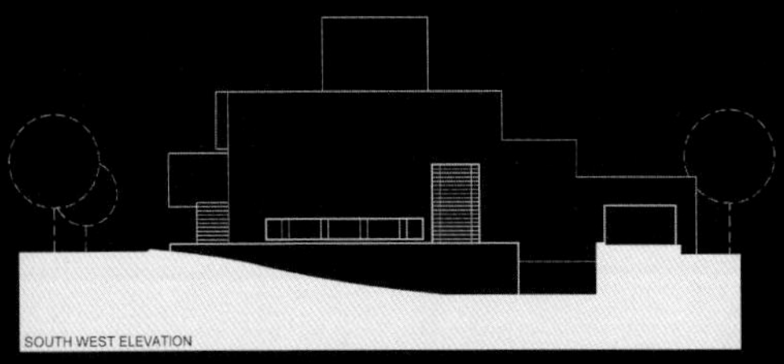

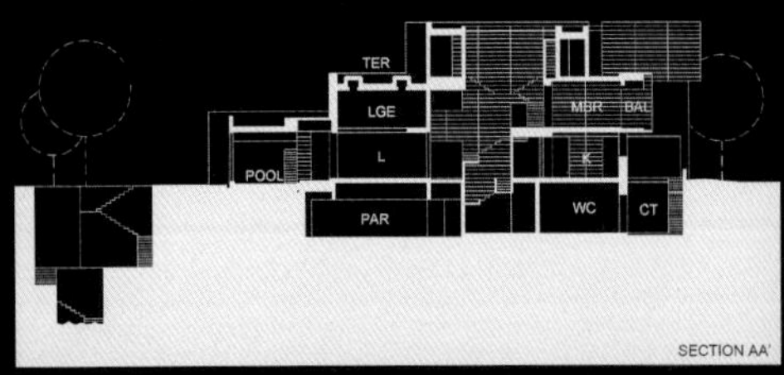

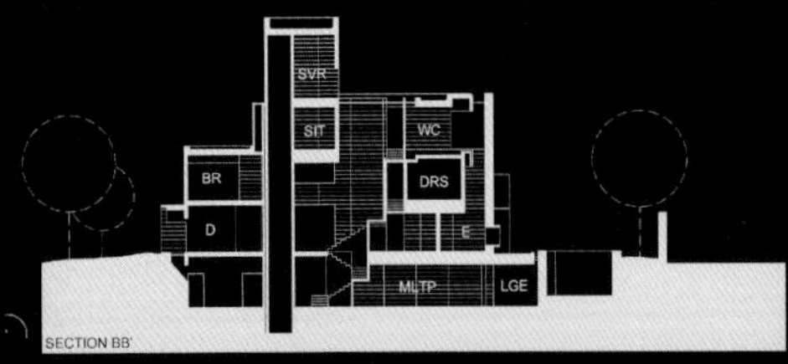

The architect took inspiration from the forms of ancient Indian step wells, but his geometric composition above all evokes a rich contemporary understanding of modern architecture.

Trade in diamonds, textiles, oil, and metals have made Surat one of the most prosperous and vibrant cities in India. It is due to be the fastest-growing city in the country up until 2035 at least. This house is located 20 kilometers from the city center in the coastal town of Dumas. Built for a couple in the jewelry business and their son, the residence provides enough elevation over palm trees to provide views of the Arabian Sea. The architect imagined creating a connection between a freshwater well found on the site and the sea as the driving idea for the design. Elements such as the entrance, kitchen, bedrooms, and ponds were designed according to the *Vastu shastra* rules of traditional Indian building. A stone base is topped by stacked, thin concrete tubes. Each tube on the upper levels contains bedrooms, with the living areas below. The living and dining areas are on a semi-open verandah at one corner of the house near the swimming pool. The first-floor master bedroom looks out on this space making it the central volume of the house. This 1280-square-meter five-story private residence was built with stone walls, reinforced-concrete columns and walls, and reinforced-concrete slabs. Flooring is in wood from Kadapa and walls are in Burmese teak. The house footprint is 380 square meters and the site area is 5780 square meters. Gurjit Matharoo explains: "Inspired by the now extinct typology of the ancient Indian step well, a long flight of steps that give access to an ever fluctuating table of water—the stair starts from the base of the well, rings along the inside and wraps around the sunlit void, connecting all of the spaces as one rises to the top—a walk 150 steps up to the sea."

Surat ist eine der wohlhabendsten Städte Indiens, die sehr schnell wächst. Dieses Haus liegt 20 Kilometer vom Stadtzentrum entfernt im Küstenort Dumas. Für ein Ehepaar und seinen Sohn erbaut, erhebt sich das Haus hoch genug über die Palmen, um einen Blick über das Arabische Meer zu bieten. Treibende Idee des Designs war die Vorstellung des Architekten, eine Verbindung zwischen einem auf dem Grundstück entdeckten Süßwasserbrunnen und dem Meer zu schaffen. Elemente wie Eingang, Küche, Schlafzimmer und Teiche wurden gemäß der *Vastu-Shastra*-Regeln der traditionell indischen Bauweise entworfen. Ein Steinsockel wird von gestapelten dünnen Betonröhren gekrönt. Jede Röhre der oberen Etagen enthält Schlafzimmer mit darunterliegenden Wohnbereichen. Wohn- und Essbereiche befinden sich auf einer halboffenen Veranda in einer Ecke des Gebäudes in der Nähe des Pools. Das Hauptschlafzimmer im ersten Stock blickt auf diesen Platz und macht ihn somit zum zentralen Platz des Hauses. Dieses fünfstöckige Privathaus mit 1280 Quadratmetern wurde mit Steinmauern, Stahlbetonsäulen und -wänden sowie Stahlbetonplatten errichtet. Die Fußböden sind aus Kadapa-Holz und die Wände aus burmesischem Teakholz. Das Haus hat eine Grundfläche von 380 Quadratmetern, das Grundstück misst 5780 Quadratmeter. Gurjit erklärt: „Inspiriert von der heute nicht mehr verwendeten Typologie des altindischen Stufenbrunnens, einer langen Treppe, die den Zugang zu einem ständig schwankenden Wasserspiegel ermöglichte, beginnt die Treppe an der Brunnenbasis, führt an der Innenseite entlang und wickelt sich um die sonnenbeschienene Leere, um alle Räume zu verbinden, während man nach oben steigt – ein Spaziergang 150 Stufen hinauf zum Meer."

Contrasting concrete and dark stone are used in alternation, animating the surface of the house which is articulated around a stepped form. Inside, the same dark and light volumes appear with large glazed surfaces allowing views of the garden.

Below: plans of the house with its complex interlocking, rectilinear volumes.

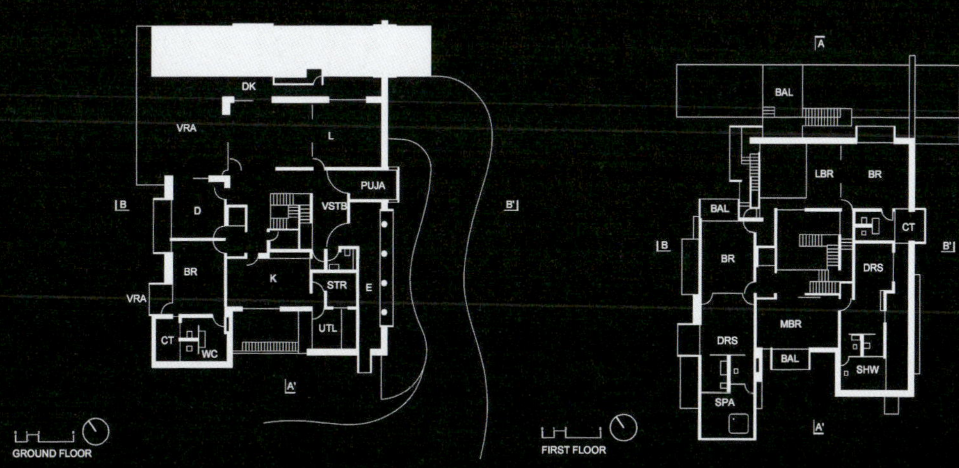

he complex central stairway brings to mind the ork of the Dutch graphic artist M.C. Escher. Above: *bathroom where concrete dominates, with a con-rolled presence of natural light.*

.e commerce des diamants, des étoffes, du étrole et des métaux ont fait de Surat l'une des illes les plus prospères et les plus animées l'Inde. Elle devrait être celle à la croissance a plus rapide du pays en 2035. La maison est ituée à 20 kilomètres du centre-ville, dans la ité de Dumas. Construite pour un couple de ijoutiers et leur fils, la résidence est à une auteur suffisante au-dessus des palmiers pour voir vue sur la mer. L'architecte a imaginé accorder un puits d'eau douce découvert sur e terrain à la mer et en a fait l'idée motrice du oncept. L'entrée, la cuisine, les chambres et les assins ont été conçus selon les préceptes de ons-truction traditionnelle *(Vastu shastra)*. Une ase de pierre est surmontée de tubes empilés n béton fin dont chacun de ceux des étages upérieurs contient des chambres, tandis que es espaces de vie sont placés en dessous. Le salon et l'espace destiné aux repas occupent une véranda semi-ouverte dans un angle, à côté de la piscine. La chambre au premier niveau donne sur cet espace qui constitue le volume central. La résidence à cinq niveaux de 1280 mètres carrés présente des murs de pierre, des colonnes et des dalles de béton armé. Le sol est en bois de Kadapa et les murs en teck birman. L'empreinte au sol de la maison est de 380 mètres carrés tandis que la surface du terrain est de 5780 mètres carrés. Gurjit explique : « Inspiré par la typologie aujourd'hui disparue des anciens puits à degrés indiens où une longue volée de marches donne accès à une nappe phréatique au niveau toujours fluctuant, l'escalier de la maison part du fond du puits, monte en colimaçon à l'intérieur et s'enroule autour du vide ensoleillé, traversant les différents espaces au fur et à mesure de l'ascension – 150 marches qui montent vers la mer. »

MCFARLANE BIGGAR

Bowen Island House
Bowen Island, British Columbia, Canada, 2016–19
Area: 272 m²

The house juts out from its sloped site, with a cantilevered deck facing the water. The deck is seen in a closer view on the next double page.

The architects call this house "a contemporary version of a cabin in the woods." Built on a rugged 3.24-hectare site on the northern coast of Bowen Island, which is part of metropolitan Vancouver, the two-level structure is a retreat for a young couple and their two children seeking refuge from their busy city life. The rectangular structure is set perpendicular to the coastline to help diminish its presence from the water and allowing it to sit tightly between the intimate flora and the ever-changing presence of ocean, mountains, and sky. The remote site prioritized design solutions focused on formal economy and simple details, ensuring construction had minimal disruption to the landscape. Able to function entirely off the grid when necessary with independent sources for heat and electricity, the modest scale of the house further minimizes its environmental footprint. Holistically integrated throughout, the simple tectonic language and spatial clarity resonate with the surrounding coastal landscape, creating memorable architecture deeply rooted in its place.

Für die Architekten ist dieses Haus „eine zeitgenössische Version einer Waldhütte". Das zweistöckige Gebäude wurde auf einem 3,24 Hektar großen, zerklüfteten Grundstück an der Nordküste von Bowen Island im Großraum Vancouver errichtet. Es dient als Rückzugsort für ein junges Paar und seine beiden Kinder, die sich dem hektischen Stadtleben entziehen wollen. Das rechteckige Haus steht im rechten Winkel zur Küstenlinie, damit es von der Seeseite aus nicht leicht zu entdecken ist und eine enge Beziehung sowohl zur dichtwüchsigen Flora als auch zur sich ständig verändernden Präsenz von Meer, Bergen und Himmel knüpfen kann. Dem abgelegenen Standort entsprechend zeigt das Design

ɜeen from the entrance side the house appears to ɘe quite narrow and is marked by its asymmetric slab ɔof with emerging skylights.

ɘine reduzierte Formsprache und schlichte Details, so dass sein Bau nur minimal in die ɹandschaft eingreifen musste. Die bescheidene Größe des Hauses, das bei Bedarf dank eigener Wärme- und Stromquellen völlig netzunabhängig ist, trägt zur Minimierung seines ökologischen Fußabdrucks bei. Die durchgehend präsente einfache tektonische Sprache und räumliche Klarheit stehen im Einklang mit der Küstenlandschaft und schaffen eine denkwürdige, eng mit ihrem Standort verwurzelte Architektur.

Les architectes définissent la maison comme « une version contemporaine de cabane dans les bois ». Construit sur un terrain escarpé de ,24 hectares sur la côte nord de l'île Bowen qui fait partie de la métropole de Vancouver, le bâtiment à deux niveaux offre une retraite à un jeune couple et leurs deux enfants qui cherchaient un refuge à l'écart de leur vie citadine. La structure rectangulaire a été placée perpendiculairement à la côte afin d'effacer sa présence face à la mer ce qui a permis de la nicher étroitement parmi la flore et le paysage toujours changeant de l'océan des montagnes et du ciel. Du fait de son emplacement isolé, la conception a mis l'accent sur l'économie formelle et des détails simples pour garantir une perturbation minimale du paysage. La maison peut fonctionner entièrement sans être raccordée au réseau électrique si nécessaire et possède des sources de chaleur et d'électricité indépendantes. Ses dimensions modestes contribuent également à réduire son empreinte environnementale. Parfaitement intégrée de manière holistique, le langage tectonique simple et la clarté de l'espace font écho au paysage côtier environnant, et créent une architecture remarquable, profondément ancrée au lieu.

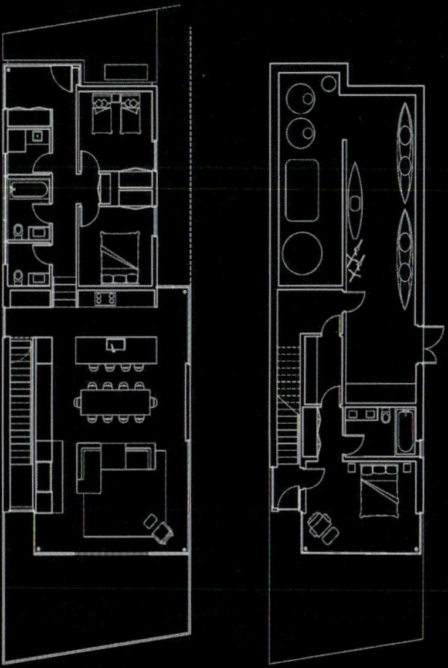

Opposite: the white kitchen and dining area, with the wood-clad ceiling visible. Above: a bedroom and plans of the house. Below: the living room with the deck and the view of the water beyond.

MCLEOD BOVELL

Blackcliff House
West Vancouver, British Columbia, Canada, 2016–19
Area: 996 m²
Collaboration: Sandy Wang

The house provides a stable platform inscribed into the rough granite cliff face seen on the right page. Its volumes are angular and calculated to provide views and natural light for residents. Below: *plans and section drawings of the house.*

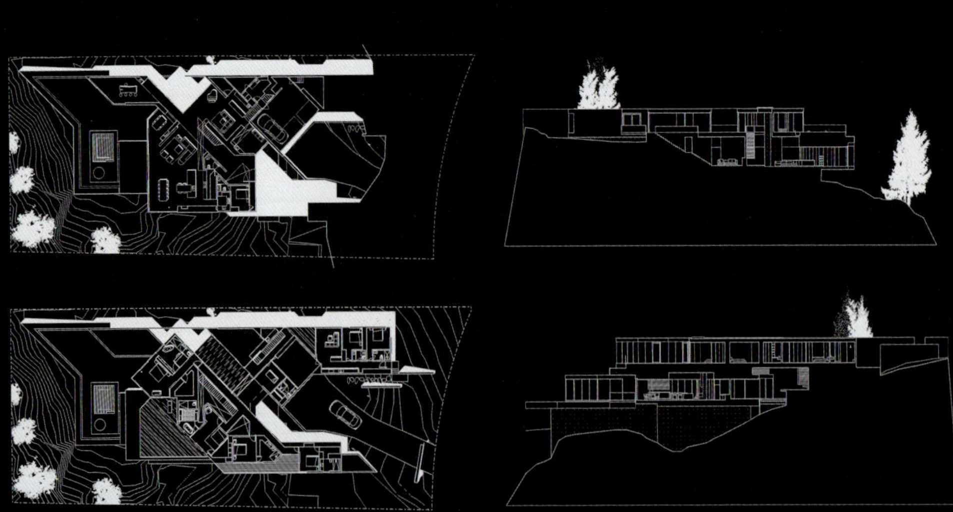

This residence was built on a granite outcropping nearly 43 meters above the shoreline. The client sought a “gathering place for current and future generations while still being able to accommodate a smaller family unit.” The main and upper floors are directed to the southwest and to the west, with a void between them in the middle of the site. The upper floor centers on a more intimate family sleeping area that is connected to the larger family units by a shared outdoor terrace. The living spaces are on the main floor and include a painting room, the entrance foyer, family room, office, and tearoom with a courtyard that brings light to interior spaces. According to the architects: “The spatial experience of the house is both familiar and slightly disorienting, striving to balance the relationship between the regular orientation of the steeply sloping ground and the off-axis orientation of the light and views to create essential and intimate spaces at the core which have a strong connection to the outdoor environment.”

Dieses Haus wurde auf einem Granitfelsen knapp 43 Meter oberhalb der Küste errichtet. Der Bauherr wünschte sich einen „Treffpunkt für die jetzigen und künftigen Generationen, der gleichzeitig Platz für eine kleinere Familie bieten sollte“. Das Haupt- und das Obergeschoss sind nach Südwesten und Westen ausgerichtet mit einer Lücke dazwischen in der Mitte des Grundstücks. Die obere Etage beherbergt einen intimen Schlafbereich für die Familie, den eine gemeinsame Außenterrasse mit den größeren Familienräumen verbindet. Die Wohnbereiche liegen im Hauptgeschoss und umfassen ein Malzimmer, das Eingangsfoyer, ein Familienzimmer, ein Büro sowie eine Teestube mit Innenhof, der Licht in

'he deck and pool extend from the living spaces /here sliding glass walls allow for a direct contact /ith the exterior when weather allows.

ie Innenräume lässt. „Die Raumerfahrung des lauses weckt das Gefühl von Vertrautheit und st gleichzeitig leicht desorientierend", so die rchitekten. „Sie will die Beziehung zwischen der egelmäßigen Ausrichtung des steil abfallenden ieländes und der außermittigen Ausrichtung des ichts und der Ausblicke ausbalancieren, um im ern essenzielle und intime Räume mit starker 'erbindung zur Außenumgebung zu schaffen."

a résidence a été construite sur un affleurement ranitique à presque 43 mètres au-dessus du ivage. Le client cherchait un « lieu de rassemblement des générations actuelles et futures ui soit à même de loger une petite cellule familiale ». L'étage principal et l'étage supérieur sont rientés au sud-ouest et à l'ouest et séparés par n vide au centre du terrain. L'étage supérieur est entré sur un espace de couchage familial plus intime, relié aux unités familiales plus grandes par une terrasse commune. Les lieux de vie sont situés au niveau principal et comprennent une salle de peinture, le hall d'entrée, la pièce familiale, un bureau et un salon de thé avec une cour qui fait entrer la lumière. Selon les architectes : « Le ressenti de l'espace est à la fois familier et légèrement déroutant, s'efforçant d'équilibrer le rapport entre l'orientation du terrain en pente raide et l'orientation désaxée de la lumière et des vues afin de créer des espaces essentiels et intimistes au centre, étroitement liés au décor extérieur. »

MAURICIO CEBALLOS X ARCHITECTS

Mague House
Malinalco, Mexico, 2019–20
Area: 270 m²

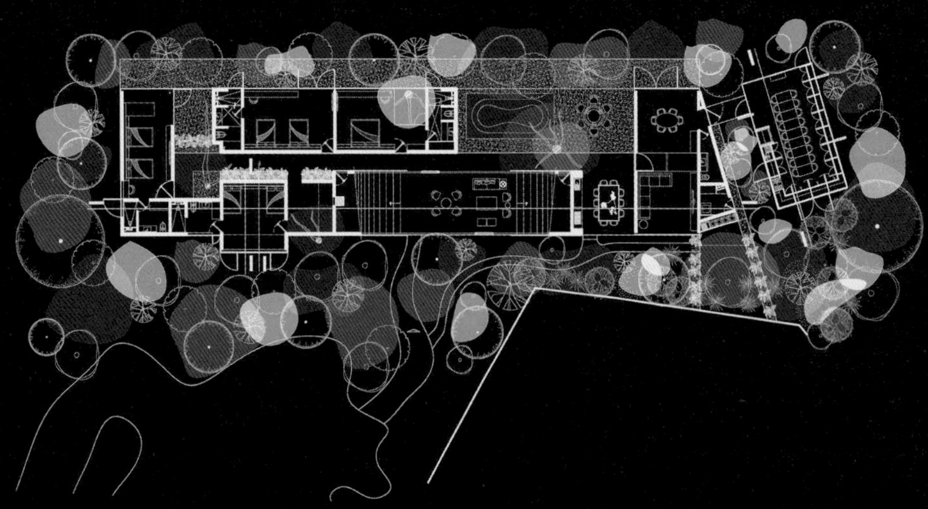

The architects use wooden canopies and walls to delineate the exterior spaces seen in these images near a pool.

Located in south-central Mexico, Malinalco is well-known as a center of Aztec culture, with many monuments located in the Cuauhtinchan Archeological Zone. The architects state: "We approached the project by asking ourselves the following questions: How to create a construction with contemporary language within a pre-Hispanic context, which manages to merge with the natural and cultural environment, respecting 100% the existing vegetation? How to develop a flexible and timeless home? How to develop a construction that mimics nature?" Built for a cost of $365 000, the house was sited to preserve not only existing trees, but also their roots and branches. The architects used locally sourced wood and stone for the structure as well as chukum, a traditional limestone-based stucco mixed with resin from chukum *(Havardia albicans)* trees, a species endemic to the Yucatan region of Mexico. Flexible multifunctional spaces are an important part of the design. The main floor includes four bedrooms, a living area, a studio, TV room, and a nearly separate angled kitchen and dining area. The architects insist on the close connection of the design to local history and culture: "The project makes reference to its historic site in several ways: the pyramid is reinterpreted in the main exterior space, built with blocks of wood; the carved monolithic stone that functions as a bonfire represents Mexican food culture; 'Molcajete' is used as a mortar; and the directed views to the aqueduct that limits the site create a harmonious combination that functions as a single whole."

Section drawings reveal the long, low form of the house which was carefully inscribed into the site to avoid cutting existing trees and their roots.

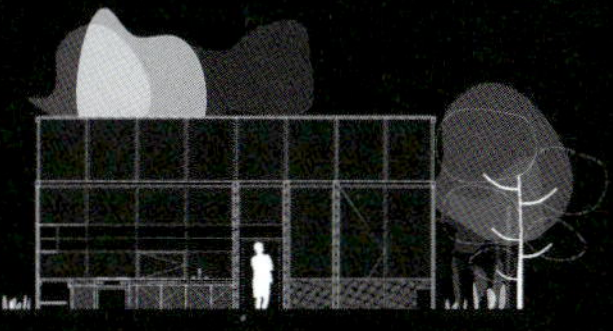

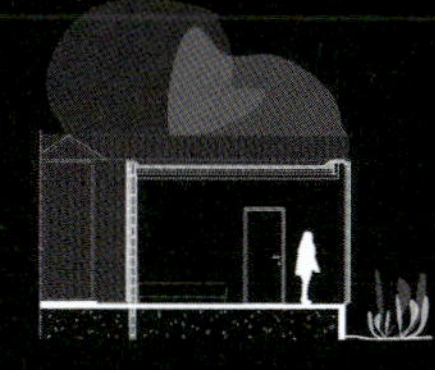

The dense vegetation on the site is present from almost every angle. A covered exterior seating area and opposite the long wooden table of the glass kitchen still offers broadly glazed views of the exterior.

Malinalco liegt im südlichen Zentralmexiko und ist als Zentrum der aztekischen Kultur bekannt mit zahlreichen Monumenten in der archäologischen Zone Cuauhtinchan. „Wir näherten uns dem Projekt mit folgenden Fragen: Wie kreiert man zeitgenössisch in einem prähispanischen Kontext ein Bauwerk, das mit der natürlichen und kulturellen Umgebung verschmilzt und die vorhandene Vegetation zu 100 Prozent respektiert? Wie entwickelt man ein flexibles und zeitloses Zuhause? Wie schafft man eine Konstruktion, die die Natur nachahmt?“ Das Haus, dessen Baukosten sich auf 365 000 Dollar beliefen, wurde so platziert, dass nicht nur die vorhandenen Bäume, sondern auch ihre Wurzeln und Äste erhalten blieben. Die Architekten verwendeten für die Konstruktion Holz und Stein aus der Region sowie Chukum, einen traditionellen Putz auf Kalksteinbasis, (*Havardia albicans*), einer in der mexikanischen Region Yucatán beheimateten Baumart. Flexible, multifunktionale Räume sind ein wichtiger Bestandteil des Entwurfs. Im Hauptgeschoss befinden sich vier Schlafzimmer, ein Wohnbereich, ein Studio, ein TV-Raum und eine fast separate Küche mit Essbereich. Die Architekten betonen die enge Verbindung des Designs mit der lokalen Geschichte und Kultur: „Das Projekt bezieht sich in mehrfacher Hinsicht auf seinen historischen Standort: Die Pyramide wird mit Holzblöcken im Hauptaußenbereich neu interpretiert; der als Feuerstelle fungierende behauene Monolith steht für die mexikanische Esskultur; eine ‚Molcajete‘ wird als Mörtel verwendet, und der Blick auf das Aquädukt, das den Ort begrenzt, schafft eine harmonische Kombination, die als abgeschlossenes Ganzes wirkt.“

ans le centre-sud du Mexique, Malinalco est
n centre de la culture aztèque bien connu dont
eaucoup de monuments sont situés dans la
one archéologique de Cuauhtinchan. Les archiectes expliquent : « Nous avons approché le
rojet en nous posant les questions suivantes :
omment construire dans un langage contem-
orain au sein d'un contexte préhispanique et
éussir à fusionner avec l'environnement natu-
el et culturel tout en respectant la végétation
éjà présente à 100 % ? Comment créer une
naison modulable et intemporelle ? Comment
onstruire en imitant la nature ? » Bâtie pour un
oût de 365 000 dollars, la maison a été placée
le manière à préserver les arbres existants, mais
ussi leurs racines et leurs branches. Les archiectes ont utilisé du bois et de la pierre d'origine
ocale pour la structure, ainsi que du chukum, un
nduit traditionnel à base de calcaire mélangé
à de la résine de chukum (*Havardia albicans*), un arbre endémique dans la région du Yucatan. Les espaces modulables multifonctionnels sont un élément important du concept. Le niveau principal comprend quatre chambres, un salon, un studio, une salle télé ainsi qu'une cuisine et un coin repas d'angle presque séparés. Les architectes insistent sur le lien étroit avec l'histoire et la culture locales : « Le projet fait référence au site historique de plusieurs manières : la pyramide est réinterprétée en blocs de bois dans le principal espace extérieur ; la pierre taillée monolithique qui sert au feu représente la culture gastronomique mexicaine ; un « molcajete » est utilisé comme mortier et les vues orientées vers l'aqueduc qui délimite le terrain forment un ensemble harmonieux qui fonctionne comme un seul tout. »

MIA DESIGN STUDIO

Villa Tan Dinh
District 3, Ho Chi Minh City, Vietnam, 2020
Area: 538 m²

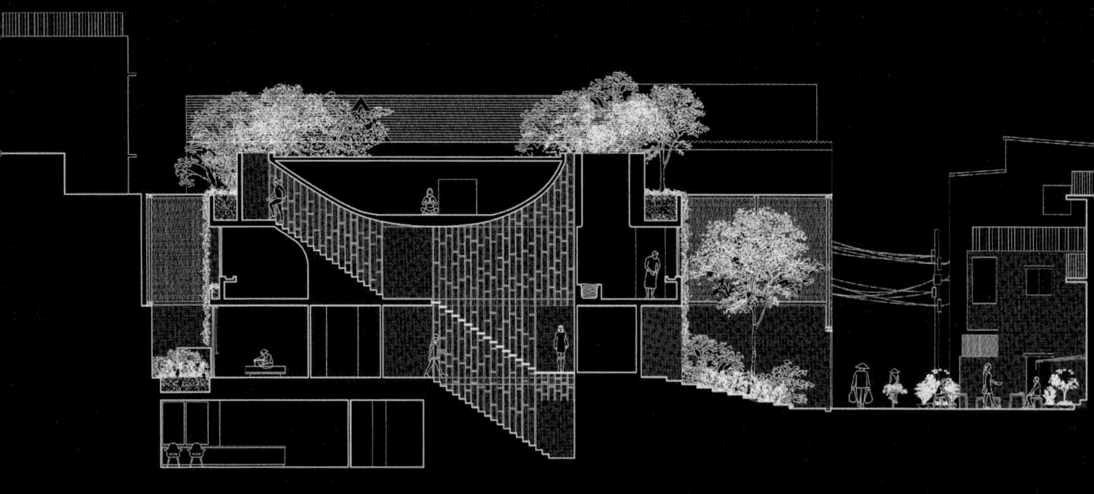

Hanging vines, a dark pool, and covered exterior spaces provide shading and some protection from the heat. Opposite: *the house stands out in its dense urban environment precisely because of its extensive presence of vegetation.*

Located near the dense center of Ho Chi Minh City, near the Tan Dinh Market and a church of the same name, this house was designed to meet the specific needs of the owner, but no more. "The principal concept," say the architects, was "to create a living space that hovers above a mini-garden, giving you the feeling of walking on bridges." Steel nets were provided to allow liana-type plants to fully cover the structure over time. Rolling shutters make a clear separation between interior and exterior. Again, according to the architects, the shape of the house "could be seen as a simple box if we look at it from outside but, from the inside, it contains many layers of space as well as alternation between light and dark, intertwined with the raw materials—concrete and stone." The kitchen is below grade, while the ground floor includes the dining and living areas, as well as a bedroom, and a terrace and pond. Another bathroom and a terrace are on the next floor up. The narrow top floor has another terrace, a barbecue area, and an altar.

Das im dicht bebauten Zentrum von Ho-Chi-Minh-Stadt nahe dem Tan-Dinh-Markt und der gleichnamigen Kirche stehende Haus wurde entworfen, um die spezifischen Bedürfnisse des Eigentümers zu erfüllen, mehr aber auch nicht. „Das Hauptkonzept", so die Architekten, „bestand darin, einen über einem Minigarten schwebenden Wohnraum zu schaffen, der einem das Gefühl vermittelt, über Brücken zu gehen." Stahlnetze wurden angebracht, um von lianenartigen Pflanzen mit der Zeit vollständig überrankt zu werden. Rollläden sorgen für eine klare Trennung zwischen innen und außen. Den Architekten zufolge könnte die Form des Hauses „von außen betrachtet als einfache Kiste erscheinen, das

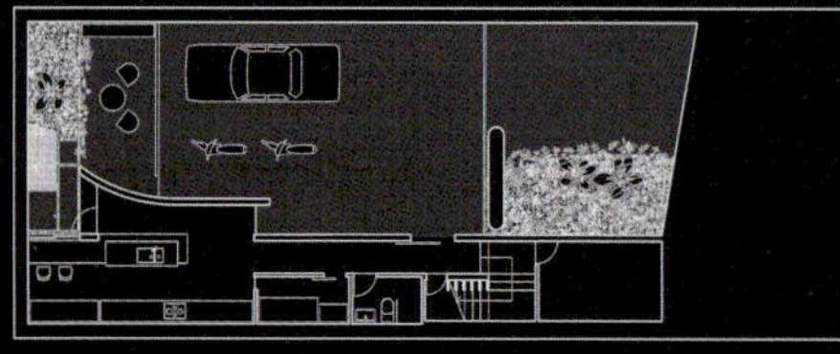

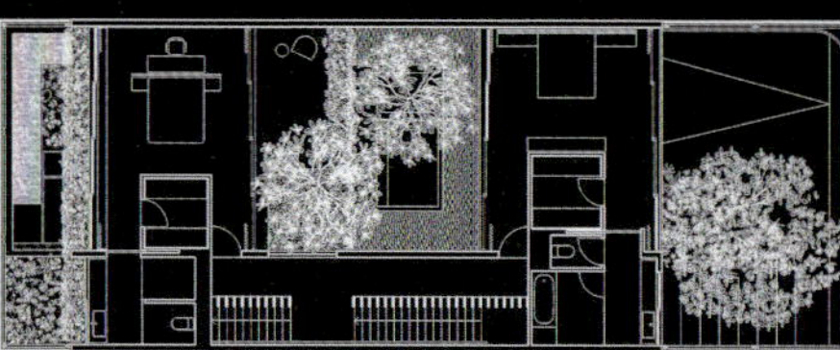

Above: *a wooden stairway and plans of the house.*
Below: *a bedroom with a shaded exterior terrace.*

The architects emphasize the alternation between light and dark and the contrasting materials used in their design. Where dark spaces are concerned, natural light is always visible.

Innere aber offenbart viele Raumschichten sowie einen Wechsel zwischen Hell und Dunkel, der mit den rohen Materialien Beton und Stein verwoben ist“. Die Küche liegt im Untergeschoss, während sich im Erdgeschoss der Ess- und Wohnbereich sowie ein Schlafzimmer, eine Terrasse und ein Teich befinden. Ein weiteres Badezimmer und eine Terrasse sind auf der nächsthöheren Etage untergebracht, das schmale Dachgeschoss birgt eine weitere Terrasse, einen Grillplatz und einen Altar.

Proche du centre dense d'Hô Chi Minh-Ville, du marché Tan Dinh et d'une église du même nom, la maison a été conçue pour répondre aux besoins spécifiques de son propriétaire, mais rien de plus. « Le concept principal », expliquent les architectes, consistait à « créer un lieu de vie qui flotte au-dessus d'un mini-jardin pour donner l'impression de marcher sur des ponts ». Des filets en acier ont été installés pour permettre à des plantes de type lianes de recouvrir entièrement la structure avec le temps. Des volets roulants créent une séparation nette entre l'intérieur et l'extérieur. Là encore, selon les architectes, la forme de la maison « pourrait être vue comme un simple cube de l'extérieur, mais de l'intérieur, elle présente plusieurs couches d'espace et une alternance de clair et de sombre conjuguée avec les matériaux bruts – béton et pierre ». La cuisine est au sous-sol tandis que le rez-de-chaussée accueille les espaces destinés aux repas et au séjour, ainsi qu'une chambre, une terrasse et un bassin. Une autre salle de bains et une terrasse se trouvent à l'étage au-dessus. Le dernier niveau, étroit, se compose d'une autre terrasse, d'un espace barbecue et d'un autel.

MILLER HULL

Loom House
Bainbridge Island, Washington, USA, 2018–19
Area: 297 m²
Collaboration: Charlie Hellstern Interior Design, Clark Construction, Anne James Landscape Architecture

Although the house is fairly large taken as a whole, it projects a modest presence along the lake shore, emerging from the trees. Opposite: *the entry bridge to the house.*

Based on an existing 186-square-meter house built in 1968 as well as a small guest pavilion (added later), this residence made use of the primary structure and exterior cladding of its predecessor. The guesthouse was transformed into an office and art studio. New wood used in the house was either salvaged or FSC-certified. The floor plan of the main house was modified to make it more open and to include a formal entrance instead of the sliding glass doors previously used. That entrance is now reached by crossing over a new wood-covered steel bridge. Salvaged steel from an old ship was used for the new front door. The old concrete walkways were reused for retaining walls as part of the new project. Even some of the furniture was conceived in this spirit with FSC-certified wood and materials such as wool, organic latex, or down feathers used instead of petroleum-related substances.

The transport of construction materials and the use of project waste for salvaging or landfills was also carefully monitored. *Dwell* magazine called the project: “The most ecologically ambitious home renovation on the planet.” The house was designed to the standards of the Living Building Challenge, administered by the Seattle-based International Living Future Institute (ILFI).

Auf der Grundlage eines bestehenden, 1968 errichteten, 186 Quadratmeter großen Hauses und eines kleinen, später hinzugefügten Gästepavillons wurden für dieses Wohnhaus die Grundstruktur und Außenverkleidung des Vorgängerbaus übernommen. Das Gästehaus wurde in ein Büro und Kunstatelier umgewandelt. Das neue, im Haus verwendete Holz ist zum Teil wiederverwendet, zum Teil FSC-zertifiziert. Der Grundriss des Haupthauses wurde geändert, um es offener zu gestalten und anstelle der früheren Glasschiebetüren einen formellen Eingang hinzuzufügen. Die neue Eingangstür, die über eine neue holzverkleidete Stahlbrücke zu erreichen ist, besteht aus dem Stahl eines alten Schiffes. Die alten Betonstege fanden als Stützmauern Wiederverwendung. Selbst ein Teil der Möbel wurde in diesem Sinne konzipiert: FSC-zertifiziertes Holz und Materialien wie Wolle, organischer Latex oder Daunenfedern wurden anstelle von erdölhaltigen Stoffen verwendet. Auch der Transport der Baumaterialien und die Nutzung von Projektabfällen zur Wiederverwertung oder Entsorgung wurden sorgfältig überwacht. Die Zeitschrift *Dwell* nannte das Projekt „die ökologisch ehrgeizigste Hausrenovierung des Planeten". Das Haus wurde nach den Standards der Living Building Challenge des International Living Future Institute (ILFI) in Seattle entworfen.

Inside, the generously glazed walls and skylights bring ample natural light (as well as views) into the house.

Basée sur une maison existante de 186 mètres carrés construite en 1968 et un petit pavillon d'hôtes (ajouté ultérieurement), la résidence en réutilise la structure d'origine et le revêtement extérieur. La maison d'hôtes a été transformée en bureau et studio artistique. Le nouveau bois utilisé était soit récupéré, soit certifié FSC. Le plan au sol de la maison principale a été modifié pour l'ouvrir davantage et y inclure une véritable entrée à la place des portes vitrées coulissantes précédentes. On y accède désormais par une passerelle en acier couverte de bois. La nouvelle porte de devant est en acier récupéré sur un navire. Les anciens sentiers en béton ont été réutilisés pour les murs de soutènement du nouveau projet. Certains éléments du mobilier ont également été conçus dans cet esprit en bois certifié FSC et matériaux tels que de la laine, du latex bio ou du duvet au lieu de produits dérivés du pétrole. Le transport des matériaux de construction et l'utilisation des déchets, récupérés ou enfouis, ont également fait l'objet d'un suivi rigoureux. Le magazine *Dwell* a qualifié le projet de « rénovation la plus écologiquement ambitieuse de notre planète ». La maison a été conçue selon les normes du programme Living Building Challenge, géré par l'International Living Future Institute (ILFI) basé à Seattle.

Outdoor decks under the shade of the trees communicate directly with the interior when weather permits.

MWWORKS

Whidbey Farm Retreat
Whidbey Island, Washington, USA, 2015–19
Area: 449 m²
Collaboration: PCS Structural Solutions (Structural Engineer), Kenneth Philp Landscape Architects, Dovetail General Contractors

This house was built for a local family on the site of their existing farm. It is located at the edge of a densely forested hill and is intended to remain discreet vis-à-vis neighboring old agricultural buildings. The house has a "living pavilion" marked by views of the site and a rugged stone fireplace. It combines the living, kitchen, and dining areas. Protection of existing Douglas fir trees on the site was one priority of the construction. A second, perpendicular volume contains the main bedroom spaces, while a distinct rectangular structure houses another living space with bunk beds. The architects explain: "With a palette of naturally weathered woods, concrete, locally quarried stone walls, deep oak window jambs, soft plaster walls, and black steel accents, the house strives to be warm and rustic yet simple, clean, and open—a house that honors both the timelessness of the forest and agricultural heritage of the site. Whidbey Farm Retreat is designed for longevity and low maintenance, reducing the life cycle cost of the house for the owners." The wood siding of the house is in stained clear Western red cedar. The decks are hardwood. The cabinetry inside consists primarily of custom teak, countertops are in textured black granite, while floors are in custom-colored concrete. The wood ceilings are in stained Western red cedar.

Dieses Haus wurde für eine Familie auf dem Gelände ihres Bauernhofs gebaut. Es befindet sich am Rande eines bewaldeten Hügels und soll gegenüber den benachbarten alten landwirtschaftlichen Gebäuden nicht auffallen. Es verfügt über einen „Wohnpavillon", der durch die Aussicht auf das Gelände und einen robusten Steinkamin geprägt ist. In ihm vereinen sich die

Above: *the kitchen and dining area.* Opposite: *the open kitchen seen from the opposite side with the living area in the foreground. Wood ceilings complement the high windows to generate a feeling of intimate connection to the natural setting.*

Bereiche Wohnen, Küche und Essen. Der Schutz alter Douglasien war eine der Prioritäten bei der Planung. Ein zweites, rechtwinkliges Gebäudeelement beherbergt die Hauptschlafräume, während sich in einem weiteren rechteckigen Baukörper ein Wohnbereich mit Etagenbetten befindet. „Mit natürlich verwittertem Holz, Beton, Wänden aus heimischem Stein, tiefliegenden Eichenholzfenstern, leichten Gipswänden und schwarzen Stahlakzenten möchte das Haus warm und rustikal und doch einfach, klar und offen sein", so die Architekten. „Ein Haus, das sowohl die Zeitlosigkeit des Waldes als auch das landwirtschaftliche Erbe des Ortes ehrt. Das Design des Hauses ist auf Langlebigkeit und geringen Wartungsaufwand ausgelegt, um die Lebenszykluskosten des Hauses zu senken." Die Verkleidung und die Decken bestehen aus dem gebeizten hellen Holz des Riesen-Lebensbaums. Für die Holzdecks wurde Ipe-Holz verwendet. Die Innenschränke sind vorwiegend aus Teakholz, die Arbeitsplatten aus schwarzem, strukturiertem Granit und die Böden aus farbigem Beton.

La maison a été construite pour une famille de la région sur le terrain de leur ferme. Elle est située à proximité d'une colline boisée et a été conçue pour rester discrète par rapport aux bâtiments voisins plus anciens. Elle comprend un « pavillon de vie » qui offre des vues du site et possède un foyer en pierre grossièrement taillée. Il associe les espaces salon, cuisine et salle à manger. La protection des pins de Douglas présents sur place était l'une des priorités. Un second volume perpendiculaire abrite les chambres et une structure rectangulaire séparée contient un autre espace de vie avec des lits superposés. Les architectes expliquent qu'« avec une gamme

de bois naturellement patiné, de béton, de murs de pierres extraites localement, de montants de fenêtres en chêne profond, de parois en crépi doux et de notes d'acier noir, la maison s'efforce d'être chaleureuse et rustique, mais simple, propre et ouverte – une maison qui rend hommage à l'intemporalité de la forêt et au patrimoine agricole du site. Whidbey Farm Retreat a été conçue pour durer sans nécessiter beaucoup d'entretien, de manière à réduire le coût de son cycle de vie pour ses propriétaires ». La maison présente un bardage en cèdre rouge. Les pontons sont en bois d'ipé. Les boiseries intérieures sont en teck sur mesure, les placards en granite noir texturé et les sols en béton teint spécialement. Les plafonds en bois sont en cèdre rouge teint.

NEW MATERIAL RESEARCH LABORATORY (SHINSOKEN)

Private Residence Ukitsubo (The Floating Inner Garden)
New York, USA, 2018
Area: 700 m²
Collaboration: Yun Architecture (Associate Architect), Xhema (Construction), Mizusawa Komuten, Ishimaru, Tagawa Shikkui Lab (Tea Room, Furniture and Plaster)

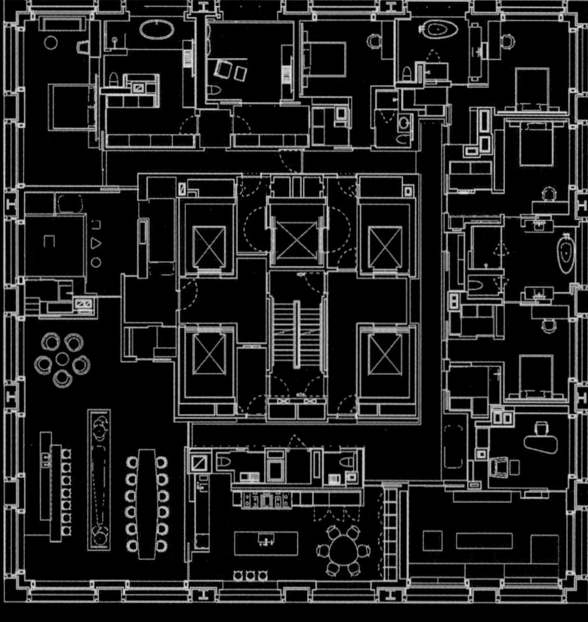

Hand hammered metal was used for kitchen surfaces. A table in Towada stone and caned chairs were designed by the New Material Research Laboratory.

This apartment is in one of the tallest residential buildings in the world in Manhattan. The plan of the apartment is square, corresponding to the exterior shape of the building of which it occupies an entire floor. The geometric rigidity implied by the plan is contrasted with the lightness and refinement imagined by Hiroshi Sugimoto. Materials from Japan such as salvaged 1,000-year-old wood, centuries-old, recycled stone slabs, handmade ceramic tiles, and original Shikkui plaster grace the interior, but the overall atmosphere is decidedly contemporary. The owners of the apartment originally discussed designing a tearoom with Sugimoto since he has had considerable experience in that area, but they eventually asked him to design the entire large apartment. The project is called *Ukitsubo*, which means "floating inner garden," a reference to the "The Tale of Genji." Because it proved to be impossible to create a real garden inside the tower, Sugimoto opted for two bonsai trees in a rectangular space in the dining room separated by a 3.2-meter-long slab of Komatsu stone. The black, square tiles used in the hallway of the apartment are handmade clay floor tiles produced by a ceramist from Nara and many other features of the design are distinctly and carefully related to Japanese architectural and decorative traditions.

\n alcove with a photo by Hiroshi Sugimoto
ɪnd a stone from a Japanese garden is set next
o a family room.*

Dieses Apartment liegt in Manhattan in einem ler höchsten Wohngebäude der Welt. Der ɿuadratische Grundriss entspricht der äußeren Form des Gebäudes, in dem die Wohnung eine ɡanze Etage einnimmt. Seine geometrische Strenge steht im Gegensatz zur von Sugimoto ɛrdachten Leichtigkeit und Raffinesse. Materialien aus Japan wie wiederverwendetes 000 Jahre altes Holz, jahrhundertealte, recycelte Steinplatten, handgefertigte Keramikfliesen und originaler Shikkui-Putz zieren die Innenräume, loch die Gesamtatmosphäre ist entschieden zeitgenössisch. Anfangs baten die Wohnungseigentümer Sugimoto nur um die Gestaltung einer Teestube, da der Architekt über beträchtliche Erfahrung in diesem Bereich verfügt, schließlich jedoch um Gestaltung des gesamten Apartments. Der Projektname *Ukitsubo* bedeutet so viel wie „schwebender innerer Garten", eine Anspielung auf „Die Geschichte vom Prinzen Genji". Da im Inneren des Gebäudes kein echter Garten angelegt werden konnte, entschied sich Sugimoto für zwei Bonsais, die in einem rechteckigen Bereich des Esszimmers durch eine 3,2 m lange Komatsu-Steinplatte voneinander getrennt sind. Die schwarzen quadratischen Fliesen im Flur sind handgefertigte Tondachziegel, gefertigt von einem Keramiker aus Nara, und auch viele weitere handverlesene Designelemente beziehen sich eindeutig auf japanische Architektur- und Dekorationstraditionen.

Traditional tatami mats, light-colored materials and a window screen evoke Japanese culture, no matter he Midtown Manhattan location of this apartment.

Opposite: *a shower finished with Komatsu stone.*

'appartement se trouve dans l'un des immeubles ésidentiels les plus hauts du monde, à Manhattan. Son plan est carré et correspond à la forme extérieure du bâtiment, dont il occupe un étage entier. La rigueur géométrique imposée par le plan contraste avec la légèreté et e raffinement imaginés par Hiroshi Sugimoto. Des matériaux japonais, notamment du bois de écupération vieux de 1 000 ans, des pierres plates recyclées vieilles de plusieurs siècles, des carreaux de céramique faits main et du plâtre shikkui original donnent une certaine grâce à 'intérieur même si son caractère est résolument contemporain. Les propriétaires avaient d'abord parlé de créer une maison de thé avec Sugimoto, car il possède une grande expérience dans ce domaine. Ils lui ont finalement demandé de concevoir la totalité de leur grand appartement. Le projet porte le nom d'*Ukitsubo*, qui signifie « jardin intérieur flottant », en référence au conte de Genji. Il s'est cependant avéré impossible de créer un véritable jardin dans la tour, Sugimoto a donc choisi de simplement placer deux bonsaïs dans un espace rectangulaire de la salle à manger, séparés par une dalle de pierre komatsu de 3,2 mètres de long. Les carreaux noirs en argile de l'entrée sont faits main par un céramiste de Nara et de nombreux éléments rappellent clairement et discrètement les traditions architecturales et ornementales japonaises.

NO ARCHITECTURE

The Flower House
Egremont, Massachusetts, USA, 2015–20
Area: 336 m²
Collaboration: Quadresign/David Haust (General Contractor), Madden & Baughman Engineering, Inc./Jerome Madden (Structural Engineer), Patrick Cullina Horticultural Design

An aerial image shows the six interlocking elements of the house forming a hexagonal central garden.

This unusual residence is made up of six interlocking timber canopies that form a continuous loop. Set on a stepped concrete slab, the pavilions are "optimized for passive heating and cooling, solar access and natural ventilation." The position of these elements creates an open, central hexagonal courtyard. The structure is partly dug into its hillside site, improving its thermal insulation. This hillside location allows for privacy at the upper end where the bedrooms are located: these receive natural light from clerestory windows. The public areas of the house have full-height glazing. The architect states: "Since the built form not only responds to the topography, but also embeds literally into the land, the resulting profile respectfully alters its context, and, from a distance, reflects the undulating mountains along the horizon." Built for a cost of $2.4 million using concrete, Douglas fir, white oak, glass, stone, tile, and galvalume (zinc, aluminum, and silicon protective coating), the house does indeed bring to mind the "flower" of its name.

Dieses ungewöhnliche Wohnhaus besteht aus sechs ineinandergreifenden Holzbaldachinen, die einen geschlossenen Ring bilden. Die Pavillons stehen auf einer gestuften Betonplatte und wurden „für passives Heizen und Kühlen, Sonneneinstrahlung und natürliche Belüftung optimiert". Durch die Anordnung dieser Elemente entsteht ein offener zentraler sechseckiger Innenhof. Die Struktur ist teilweise in den Hang eingegraben, was die Wärmedämmung verbessert. Die Hanglage gewährleistet dem oberen Bereich mit den Schlafzimmern Privatsphäre: Hier fällt natürliches Licht durch Oberlichter ein. Die Gemeinschaftsbereiche des Hauses sind vollflächig verglast. „Da die errichtete Form nicht nur auf die Topografie

'he fully glazed volume appears to sit lightly on the atural site, contrasting with the roughness of the nmediate terrain and its shrubs.

eagiert, sondern auch buchstäblich in das Land ingebettet ist, verändert das entstandene Profil espektvoll dessen Kontext und spiegelt, von Veitem betrachtet, die wellenförmigen Berge entang des Horizonts wider", erklärt der Architekt. Das für 2,4 Mio. Dollar errichtete Haus wurde aus Beton, Douglasienfichte, Weißeiche, Glas, Stein, Fliesen und Galvalume (einer Schutzbeschichtung aus Zink, Aluminium und Silizium) gebaut und ähnelt tatsächlich der „Blume" in seinem Namen.

Cette résidence originale est constituée de six uvents en bois emboîtés les uns dans les autres pour former une boucle ininterrompue. Posés sur ne dalle de béton à degrés, les pavillons sont optimisés pour le chauffage et le refroidissement passifs, l'apport solaire et la ventilation naturelle ». La position des différents éléments

La structure est partiellement enterrée dans le versant de la colline pour une meilleure isolation thermique. Cet emplacement à flanc de coteau permet plus d'intimité à l'extrémité supérieure où se trouvent les chambres : la lumière naturelle y pénètre par des fenêtres à claire-voie. Les parties communes sont vitrées sur toute leur hauteur. L'architecte explique que « comme la forme de la construction, en plus de correspondre à la topographie du site, est littéralement enfoncée dans la terre, le profil qui en résulte modifie respectueusement le décor et reflète de loin les ondulations des montagnes à l'horizon ». Construite pour 2,4 millions de dollars en béton, pin de Douglas, chêne blanc, verre, pierre, tuiles et galvalume (revêtement de protection en zinc, aluminium et silicone), la maison fait effectivement penser à la « fleur » qui lui donne son nom.

Above: *the kitchen and dining space.*
Opposite*: bathroom with a rectangular wooden tub.*

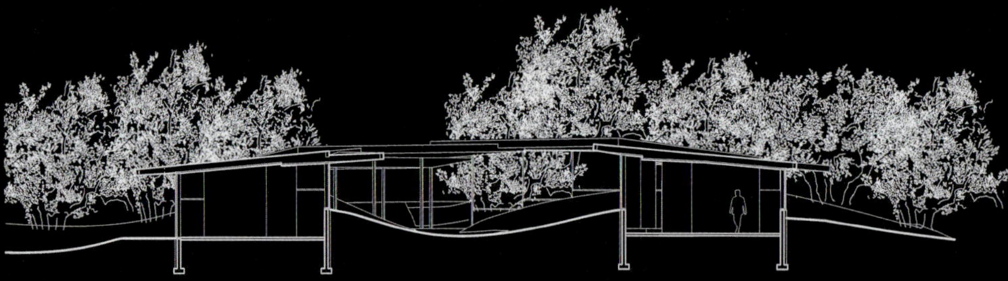

OLSON KUNDIG

Tofino Beach House
Tofino, British Columbia, Canada, 2013–16
Area: 232 m^2
Collaboration: Spearhead (Structure Prefabrication and Front Door)

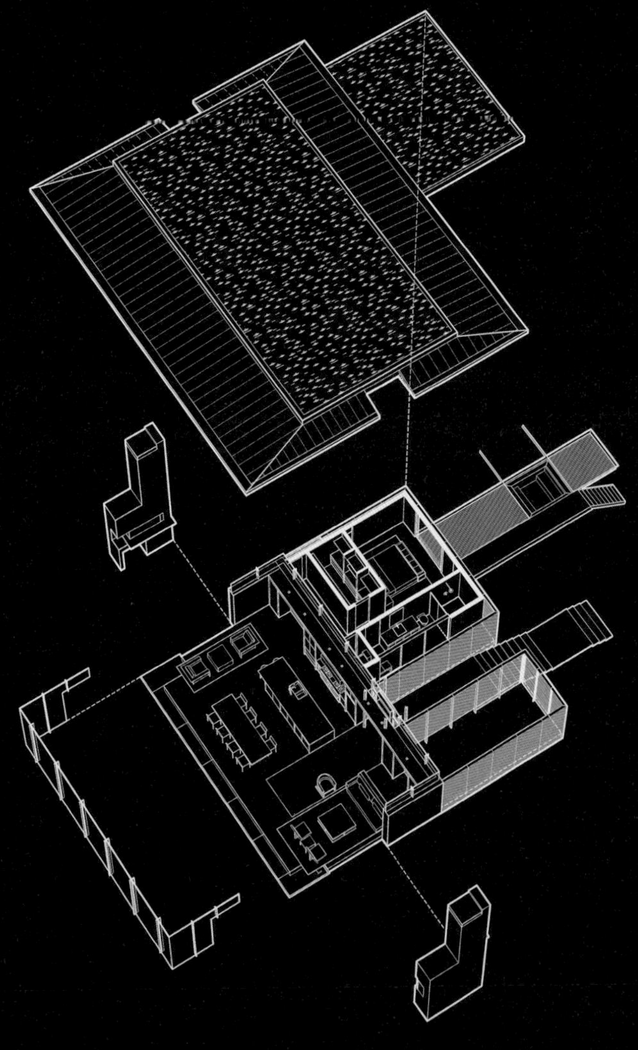

The house glows from within at nightfall.
Right page, *the entrance with its horizontal wooden slats leading to the open views provided by the design.*

Made up essentially of one room, this house faces the ocean on the south side and a forest on the other. As the architect states, the emphasis is on "feeling connected to the ocean and the surrounding woods." Glass walls provide open views of both perspectives. Fireplaces "on either end anchor the space and provide a feeling of refuge." The architect Jim Olson created spaces specifically for the owner's paintings by Sam Francis and Diego Singh, hanging on these solid concrete fireplaces. An unusual aspect of the design is a glass floor around the perimeter of the main room in an area that is cantilevered over the forest floor. The house features walnut casework, tight knot cedar ceilings, concrete floors with radiant heating, teak panelling (bedroom), and custom furniture by Jim Olson throughout.

Dieses Haus besteht im Wesentlichen aus einem einzigen Raum und ist auf der Südseite zum Meer und auf der anderen Seite zum Wald hin ausgerichtet. Laut dem Architekten liegt der Schwerpunkt auf „dem Gefühl der Verbundenheit mit dem Ozean und den umliegenden Wäldern". Glaswände ermöglichen Ausblicke in beide Richtungen. Kamine „an beiden Enden verankern den Raum und wecken ein Gefühl der Zuflucht". An diesen massiven Betonkaminen hängen Gemälde des Eigentümers von Sam Francis und Diego Singh, für die Architekt Jim Olson eigens Platz schuf. Ein ungewöhnlicher Aspekt des Designs ist ein Glasboden, der an einer Stelle des Hauptraums über den Waldboden hinausragt. Das Haus ist mit Nussbaumtäfelung, Decken aus Zedernholz, Betonböden mit Fußbodenheizung, Teakholzverkleidung (Schlafzimmer) und maßgefertigten Möbeln von Jim Olson ausgestattet.

Above: *The full-height glazing almost gives the impression that the house has no walls. A painting by the Argentine artist Diego Singh hangs on the concrete fireplace seen here.*

Opposite: *On the opposite side of the room another symmetrical fireplace offers space for a painting by Sam Francis, which provides a colorful and exuberant counterpoint to the carefully defined architecture.* Below: *a floor plan of the house.*

Formée pour l'essentiel d'une pièce, la maison fait face à l'océan du côté sud et à une forêt de l'autre côté. Selon les mots de l'architecte, l'accent est mis sur le « sentiment associé à l'océan et aux bois environnants ». Des parois vitrées offrent des vues dégagées sur les deux perspectives. Des cheminées « délimitent l'espace de chaque côté et donnent un sentiment de refuge ». L'architecte Jim Olson a créé des espaces spécifiques pour les peintures du propriétaire réalisées par Sam Francis et Diego Singh, accrochées au-dessus des cheminées en béton. Le concept ne manque pas d'originalité, comme le plancher de verre qui entoure la pièce principale et forme une zone en porte-à-faux par rapport au sol de la forêt. La maison possède également des meubles en noyer, des plafonds en cèdre à nœuds solides, des sols en béton au chauffage par rayonnement, des panneaux de teck (chambre) et des meubles sur mesure de Jim Olson.

1. Living Room
2. Kitchen/Dining
3. Bedroom
4. Closet
5. Green Roof
6. Hot Tub

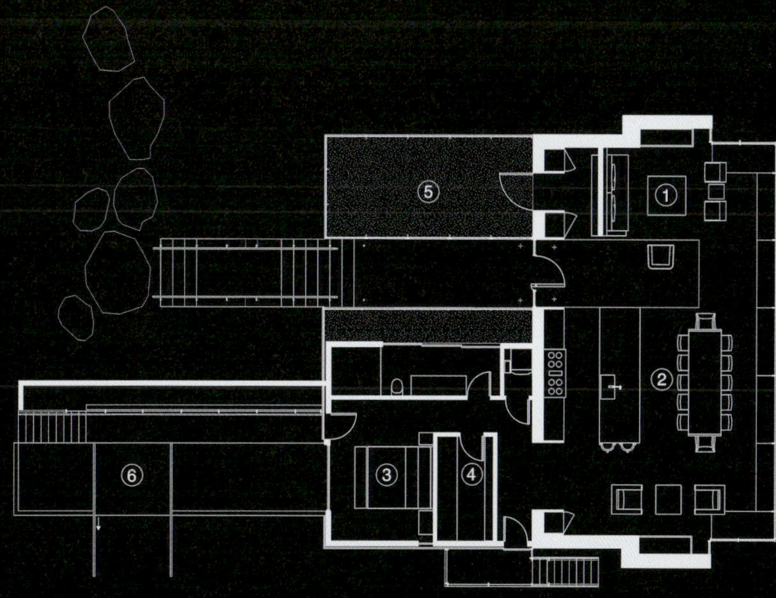

PATALANO ARQUITETURA AND MAREINES ARQUITETURA

Punta Cana House
Punta Cana, Dominican Republic, 2016–18
Area: 2000 m²

he wave-like or organic plan of the house ives rise to this succession of angled forms at he edge of the house.

he Punta Cana House was the first design arried forward by Mareines and Patalano outside of Brazil. They used ideas first developed or the Wave House (Rio de Janeiro, 2016), understanding the tropical beach house as a neans to enhance contact with nature, not to eparate its users from it." At the center of the lesign, an organically shaped double-curved lulam roof supported by steel columns that overs a 650-square-meter verandah runs from he entrance to the beach. The verandah forms kind of "canyon" according to the architects hat contains an enclosed cylindrical family oom. The covered deck also separates the northern element of the design that contains six edroom suites from the southern, public areas of the residence. The air-conditioned dining oom, kitchen, game room, gym, and service ooms are located in this southern part of the single-story house. Concrete was used for the structure, in part with the intention to firmly anchor the verandah roof, even in hurricane conditions. The steel columns and glulam roof structure elements were fabricated in France and the curved window glass and frames were made in Spain.

Luxuriant vegetation faces a largely covered outdoor dining table made from a large tree trunk.

Das Punta Cana House war der erste Entwurf, den Mareines und Patalano außerhalb Brasiliens verwirklichten. Sie griffen auf für das Wave House (Rio de Janeiro, 2016) entwickelte Ideen zurück, wobei sie „das tropische Strandhaus als Mittel zur Verbindung mit der Natur und nicht zur Trennung seiner Bewohner von ihr verstanden". Das Zentrum des Entwurfs bildet ein organisch geformtes, doppelt gekrümmtes Leimholzdach, das von Stahlstützen getragen wird und eine 650 Quadratmeter große Veranda überspannt, die vom Eingang bis zum Strand führt. Die Veranda bildet eine Art „Schlucht", in der sich ein geschlossener zylindrischer Familienraum befindet. Das überdachte Deck trennt auch den nördlichen Gebäudeteil mit seinen sechs Schlafsuiten von den südlichen, gemeinschaftlichen Bereichen des Wohnhauses. In diesem südlichen Teil des einstöckigen Baus liegen das klimatisierte Esszimmer, die Küche, das Spielzimmer, der Fitnessraum und die Wirtschaftsräume. Für die Struktur wurde Beton verwendet, u. a. um das Verandadach auch bei Hurrikans fest zu verankern. Die Stahlstützen und die Elemente der Dachkonstruktion aus Brettschichtholz wurden in Frankreich, die gebogenen Fensterscheiben und -rahmen in Spanien gefertigt.

)pposite: *the firmly anchored glulam verandah tructure defines the house and allows for generous pen views of the water.*

A bedroom where wood in particular in the ceiling designs is a unifying element.

a maison de Punta Cana est le premier projet éalisé hors du Brésil de Mareines et Patalano. s ont repris des idées déjà développées pour a Maison de la vague (Rio de Janeiro, 2016), voyant la maison de plage tropicale comme n moyen d'intensifier les contacts avec la nature, as d'en séparer les habitants ». Au centre du oncept, un toit en lamellé-collé de forme orga-ique à double courbure, porté par des colonnes n acier, recouvre une véranda de 650 mètres arrés qui va de l'entrée à la plage. La véranda orme une sorte de « canyon », selon les termes es architectes, et abrite une pièce familiale ylindrique close. Le ponton couvert sépare élément nord qui contient six suites et l'élément ud avec les parties communes de la résidence. a salle à manger climatisée, la cuisine, la salle e jeux, la salle de sport et les locaux techniques se trouvent dans cette partie sud de la maison à un seul étage. Le béton a été choisi, notamment dans le but d'ancrer solidement le toit de la véranda même en cas d'ouragan. Les colonnes en acier et les éléments structuraux en lamellé-collé du toit ont été fabriqués en France, tandis que les vitres incurvées et les cadres viennent d'Espagne.

PABLO SARIC + WINCKLER ARQUITECTOS

SS House
Huentelauquen, Chile, 2019–20
Area: 128 m²

In its exposed shoreline setting the house contrasts a dark, almost fully closed entrance-side façade with the much more open Pacific Ocean side.

'he relatively simple design is a contrast ›etween open and closed surfaces, and between ›lack and white.

'he SS House is located 270 kilometers north ›f Santiago. It was built on a 5000-square-meter ;ite set back 85 meters from the coastline. The ow (2.3-meter) interior ceiling height was magined in order to accentuate the horizontal-ty of the house. The main volume is 22.8 meters ong and 5.5 meters wide. The private areas are at either end, freeing the center for the public spaces. Glazed façades integrate the living oom, dining room, and kitchen with the west errace and the central interior sand patio. Cross ventilation allows the regulation of the nterior temperature of the house. The structure was prefabricated in Santiago and transported o the site in the form of nine modules that were assembled using a small truck crane. A small n situ concrete base supports the modules. Although it is off grid, the house has solar pan-els and uses gray water to irrigate surrounding native vegetation. The house was built for a cost of $130 000.

Das SS House steht 270 Kilometer nördlich von Santiago auf einem 5000 Quadratmeter großen Grundstück 85 Meter von der Küstenlinie ent-fernt. Die niedrige Deckeninnenhöhe (2,3 Meter) wurde gewählt, um die Horizontalität des Hauses zu betonen. Das Hauptgebäude ist 22,8 Meter lang und 5,5 Meter breit. Die privaten Bereiche befinden sich an beiden Enden, sodass die Mitte den gemeinschaftlichen Räumen zur Verfügung steht. Verglaste Fassaden verbinden Wohn-zimmer, Esszimmer und Küche mit der West-terrasse sowie dem zentralen, sandbedeckten Patio. Die Querlüftung ermöglicht die Regulierung der Innentemperatur. Die in Santiago vorge-fertigte Grundstruktur wurde in neun Modulen angeliefert und mittels eines kleinen Mobilkrans

sheltered seating area is placed directly in he sand, surrounded on three sides by blackened vood forms of the house.

usammengesetzt. Ein dünnes Fundament aus Ortbeton stützt die Module. Das Haus ist nicht ans Stromnetz angeschlossen, verfügt aber über Solarpaneele und nutzt Grauwasser zur Bewässerung der umliegenden einheimischen Vegetation. Die Kosten für den Bau des Hauses beliefen sich auf 130 000 Dollar.

La Maison SS se trouve à 270 kilomètres au nord de Santiago. Elle a été construite sur un terrain de 5000 mètres carrés à 85 mètres en retrait du littoral. La faible (2,3 mètres) hauteur sous plafond de l'intérieur vise à accentuer l'horizontalité de la maison. Le volume principal est long de 22,8 mètres et large de 5,5 mètres. Les parties privées en occupent les deux extrémités et libèrent le centre pour les parties communes. Des façades vitrées intègrent le salon, la salle à manger et la cuisine à la terrasse ouest et le patio sableux au centre. La ventilation croisée permet de réguler la température intérieure. La structure de la maison a été préfabriquée à Santiago et transportée jusqu'au site sous forme de neuf modules qui ont été assemblés à l'aide d'un petit camion-grue. Une base en béton *in situ* de petites dimensions porte les modules. Bien qu'elle ne soit pas raccordée au réseau électrique, la maison est équipée de panneaux solaires et utilise les eaux grises pour irriguer la végétation environnante. La construction a coûté 130 000 dollars.

SAUNDERS ARCHITECTURE

Villa Grieg
Bergen, Norway, 2016–18
Area: 286 m²
Collaboration: Pedro Léger Pereira, Attila Béres, Pål Storsveen

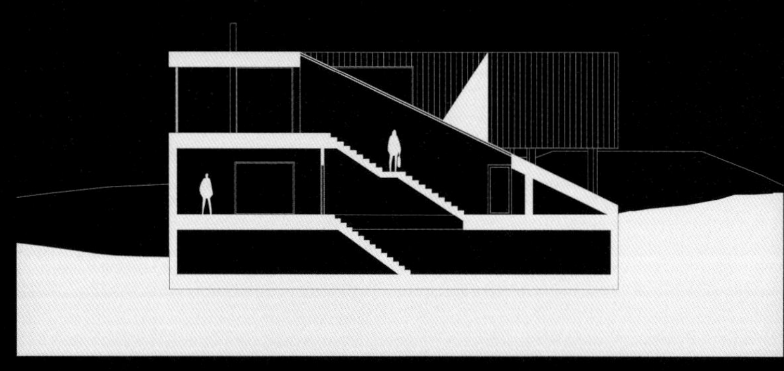

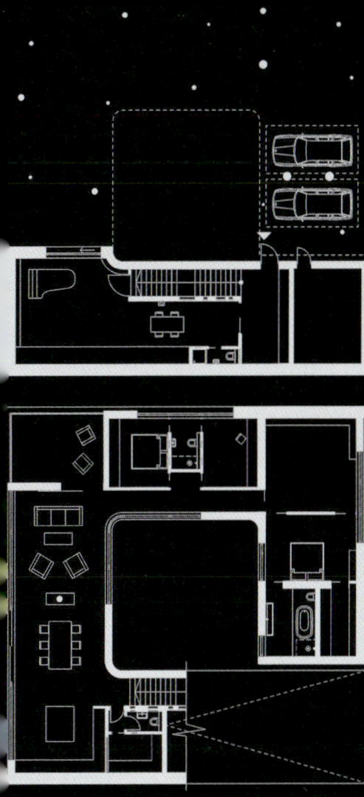

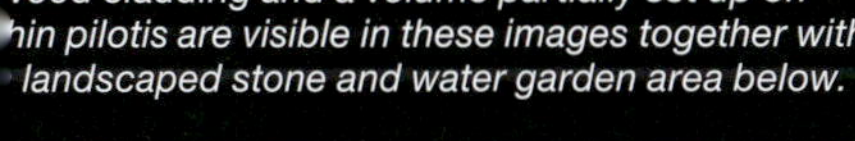

Vood cladding and a volume partially set up on hin pilotis are visible in these images together with landscaped stone and water garden area below.

Villa Grieg overlooks Lake Nordås, which is 5 minutes south of Bergen. The views from the house are intentionally focused on the lake. The house includes an integrated recording studio for the owner, musician Alexander Grieg. Saunders used some ideas incorporated into his own Villa S, such as an elevated family space, an open living area, and a clear separation from the workspace. The scheme also revolves around protecting trees that existed on the side. A storage area and the music studio are located on the ground floor, where the entrance and staircase are also placed. Above, the main living area has a horizontal glass wall. There are also two bedrooms in this section of the house, which is elevated on pilotis. The full-height glazing in the living area slides open to form an open balcony facing west. The daughter of the owners has a bedroom facing an open courtyard, and there is a guest bedroom as well. Landscape interventions on the site were kept to a minimum. The architects explain: "Rather than any grading of the site, the steel-framed building adapts to the undulations of the existing topography and the character of the hillside itself."

Die Villa Grieg überblickt den Nordås-See, der 15 Minuten südlich von Bergen liegt. Ihr Ausblick ist bewusst auf den See gerichtet. Das Haus umfasst ein Aufnahmestudio für den Eigentümer, den Musiker Alexander Grieg. Saunders übernahm einige Ideen von seiner eigenen Villa S, wie z. B. einen erhöht gelegenen Familienbereich, einen offenen Wohnbereich und eine klare Trennung zum Arbeitsbereich. Der Entwurf berücksichtigt auch den Schutz des vorhandenen Baumbestands. Ein Lagerraum und das Musikstudio liegen im Erdgeschoss, wo sich auch Eingang und Treppe befinden. Der Hauptwohnbereich im

The house appears to rise up in a natural way, sitting largely above the ground so as not to disturb the natural beauty of the site.

Stockwerk darüber ist mit einer horizontalen Glaswand versehen. In diesem auf Pilotis stehenden Gebäudeteil liegen auch zwei Schlafzimmer. Die raumhohe Verglasung des Wohnbereichs lässt sich zu einem offenen Balkon nach Westen hin öffnen. Das Schlafzimmer der Tochter des Eigentümers blickt auf einen offenen Innenhof; auch ein Gästezimmer ist vorhanden. Die Eingriffe in die Landschaft wurden auf ein Minimum beschränkt. „Anstatt das Gelände zu planieren, passt sich das Stahlrahmenhaus der wellenförmigen Topografie und der Hangsituation an", so die Architekten.

La Villa Grieg surplombe le lac Nordås, à 15 minutes au sud de Bergen. Les vues depuis la maison privilégient délibérément le lac. Elle comprend un studio d'enregistrement pour son propriétaire, le musicien Alexander Grieg. Saunders a repris certaines des idées qu'il a intégrées à sa maison personnelle, la Villa S, notamment un espace familial surélevé, un salon ouvert et une séparation nette de l'espace de travail. Le concept s'enroule autour d'arbres protecteurs présents sur le site avant la construction. Un espace de rangement et le studio sont situés au rez-de-chaussée ainsi que l'entrée et l'escalier. Au-dessus, le principal lieu de vie présente une paroi vitrée horizontale. Cette partie de la maison surélevée sur des pilotis compte aussi deux chambres. La vitre sur toute la hauteur du salon s'ouvre en coulissant pour former un balcon ouvert face à l'ouest. La chambre de la fille des propriétaires fait face à une cour ouverte, ainsi qu'une chambre d'amis. Les interventions paysagères ont été réduites au minimum, car les architectes expliquent que « plutôt que de rehausser le site, le bâtiment à charpente en acier s'adapte aux ondulations de la topographie et au caractère de la colline ».

From this side view, the slope can be seen to be negotiated by anchoring the volume of the house on the lower side. Within, simple and open spaces allow for generous views of the natural landscape.

FRAN SILVESTRE

House of Sand
Valencia, Spain, 2018–20
Area: 313 m²
Collaboration: Maria Masià, Fran Ayala

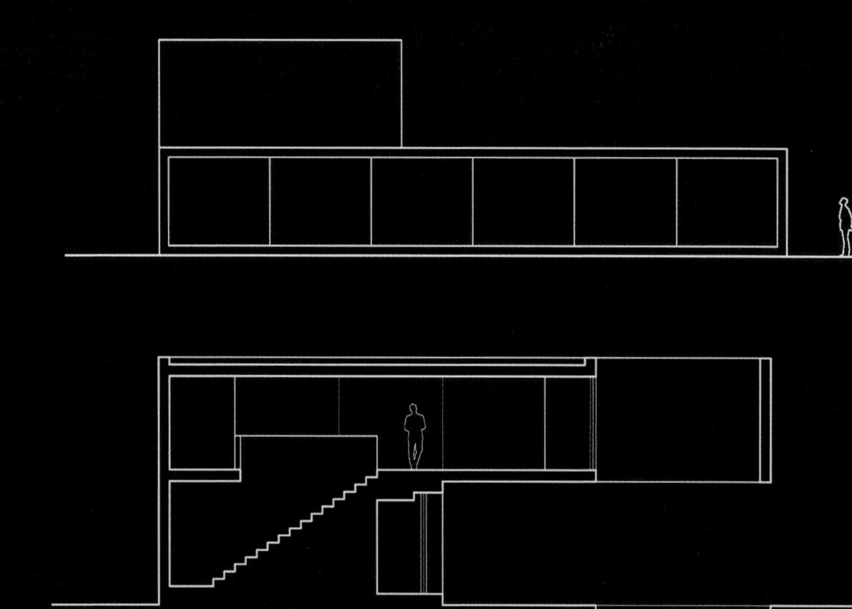

The houses of Fran Silvestre are most frequently characterized by strong, minimal white forms and such elements as the unexpected cantilever and stacked volumes seen here.

This house is located near the seashore, where there is a large sand dune. The plan consists of two perpendicular volumes. The public areas are on the upper level to allow for views of the Mediterranean. This implies that the private spaces, in particular the four bedrooms, are at the same level as the entrance, open to a swimming pool and garden. The upper floor is cantilevered over the lower one and a staircase connects the two at the point where the two meet. There is an interesting contrast between the name of this house and its concrete reality, which is formed in the context of strict, white rectilinear volumes. The sand is, of course, not related to the shape of the house, but to its setting. Silvestre masters the art of using a strictly minimal architectural vocabulary and essentially rectilinear forms to create houses that are full

Dieses Haus befindet sich in Küstennähe nahe einer großen Sanddüne. Der Grundriss weist zwei rechtwinklig zueinander stehende Elemente auf. Die Gemeinschaftsbereiche liegen auf der oberen Ebene, um einen Ausblick auf das Mittelmeer zu ermöglichen. Die privaten Räume, insbesondere die vier Schlafzimmer, die zum Pool und zum Garten hinausführen, sind auf der gleichen Ebene wie der Eingang angesiedelt. Das obere Stockwerk ragt über das untere hinaus, und dort wo sie aufeinanderliegen, verbindet sie eine Treppe. Ein interessanter Kontrast liegt in dem Namen dieses Hauses und seiner Realität aus Beton, der sich in strengen, weißen, geradlinigen Räumen ausdrückt. Der Sand hat natürlich nichts mit der Form des Hauses zu tun, sondern mit seiner Umgebung. Silvestre beherrscht die Kunst, ein strikt minimales architektonisches

'he interiors of the house are also minimalist, yet 1ey form sculptural volumes where light and views rovide a sense of variety and complexity.

'ormen zu verwenden, um Häuser voller Licht ınd Leben zu erschaffen.

.a maison est construite près de la côte où e trouve une grande dune de sable. Le plan onsiste en deux volumes perpendiculaires. Les ›ièces communes sont à l'étage pour pouvoir ›rofiter des vues sur la Méditerranée, de sorte jue les parties privées, et notamment les quare chambres, se trouvent au même niveau que entrée ouverte sur la piscine et le jardin. L'étage st placé en porte-à-faux par rapport à celui l'en dessous et un escalier relie les deux à leur ›oint d'intersection. Le contraste est intéressant ntre le nom de la maison et sa réalité en béton utour de volumes blancs rigoureusement recilignes. Le sable ne fait bien sûr pas référence la forme de la maison, mais au cadre environant. Silvestre maîtrise l'art d'un vocabulaire architectural rigoureusement minimal et des formes majoritairement rectilignes pour créer des maisons pleines de lumière et de vie.

GEORGE SINAS

Xerolithi
Serfios Island, Cyclades, Greece, 2017–18
Area: 180 m² (plus 65 m² basement)

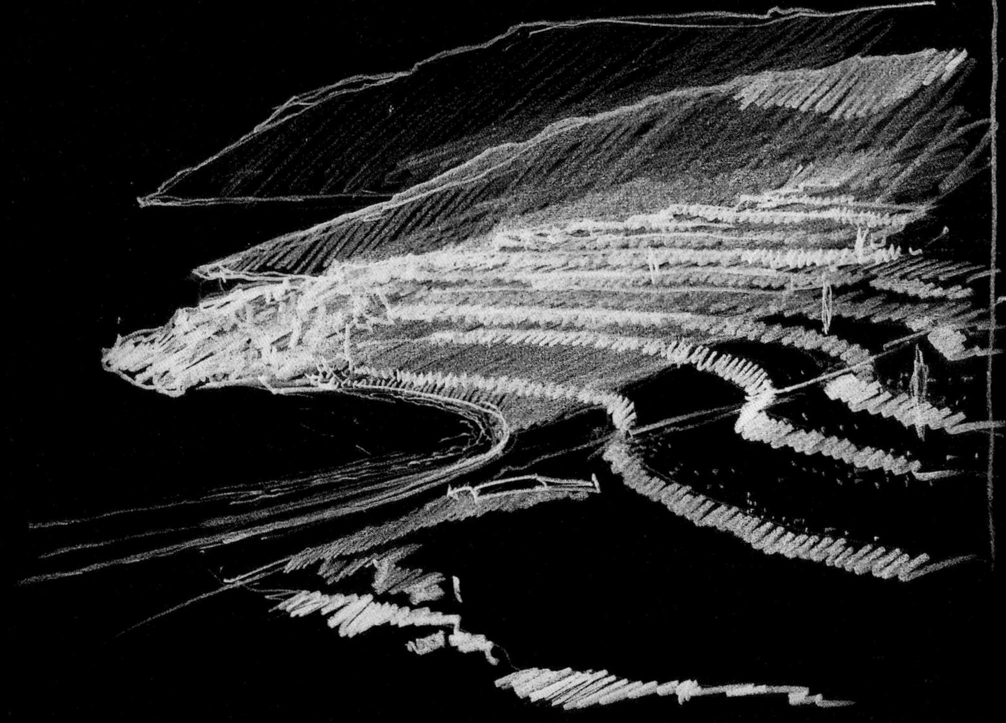

The undulating planted roof of the house allows it to almost disappear into its natural setting entirely.

Serfios is an island in the Aegean Sea with a population of 1500 people, located about 200 kilometers southeast of Athens. The architect explains: “The main focus of the design was to create a house that blends into its natural environment. An environment comprised of steep dirt and gravel slopes, dressed with scattered wild thorny bushes, and beautiful large rock formations.” Old stone retaining walls called *xerolithies* (whence the name of the house) also existed on the site. Instead of using the “white box” typology that is typical of the Greek islands, Sinas decided instead to use the *xerolithies* with their curving forms as his main source of inspiration. A traditional wooden pergola follows the curves of the plan, “like vertebrae of a long spinal cord.” The roof of the house is covered with earth and vegetation, making it “almost invisible” from above. The doors and windows “are wooden and simple with a light olive color and the main exterior walls are stone with no joint mortar. Both these decisions follow the traditional style and technique,” again according to Sinas. The main house has an area of 115 square meters including the living space, dining area, an open kitchen, and the master bedroom. There is also a 65-square-meter guesthouse with two separate bedrooms, and a 65-square-meter basement.

*'he stone used for the house also is in harmony
/ith the brown coloration of the site—again making
 blend into the hillside.*

Serfios ist eine Insel in der Ägäis mit 1500 Einvohnern, etwa 200 Kilometer südöstlich von \then gelegen. „Das Hauptaugenmerk des Entvurfs lag darauf, ein Haus zu schaffen, das sich ı seine natürliche Umgebung einfügt", erklärt er Architekt. „Eine Umgebung, die aus steilen Erd- und Schotterhängen besteht, hier und dort nit wildem Dornengestrüpp und wunderschönen ıroßen Felsformationen geschmückt." Auf dem Grundstück befanden sich auch alte Steinnauern, sogenannte *xerolithia* (daher der Name les Hauses). Anstelle auf die für die griechischen nseln typische Typologie des „weißen Kubus" :urückzugreifen, nutzte Sinas die Xerolithen mit ıren geschwungenen Formen als Hauptinspiationsquelle. Eine traditionelle hölzerne Pergola olgt den Kurven des Grundrisses, „wie die Wirbel eines langen Rückgrats". Erde und Vegetation edecken das Hausdach und machen es so von oben „fast unsichtbar". Türen und Fenster „sind schlicht und aus Holz in einem hellen Olivton, die Hauptaußenwände sind aus Stein ohne Fugenmörtel. Beides folgt dem traditionellen Stil und der traditionellen Technik", so Sinas weiter. Das Haupthaus mit Wohnbereich, Essbereich, offener Küche und Hauptschlafzimmer umfasst 115 Quadratmeter. Ferner wurde ein 65 Quadratmeter großes Gästehaus mit zwei separaten Schlafzimmern und einem 65 Quadratmeter großen Untergeschoss errichtet.

Stone walls and a wooden canopy shelter an outdoor dining area (above). The climate and lifestyle of the residents correspond to a maximized use of outdoor spaces which must in general be protected from full sun in the warm months of summer.

Serifos est une île de la mer Égée peuplée de 1500 habitants, à environ 200 kilomètres au sud-est d'Athènes. L'architecte explique que « la priorité était de créer une maison qui se fonde dans le décor naturel. Un décor de poussière et de pentes caillouteuses escarpées, habillées de buissons épineux disséminés et de superbes et imposantes formations rocheuses ». On y a aussi trouvé d'anciens murs de soutènement en pierre appelés *xerolithes* (d'où le nom de la maison). Au lieu de reprendre la typologie du « cube blanc » caractéristique des îles grecques, Sinas a décidé de faire des *xerolithes* et de leurs courbes sa source d'inspiration. Une pergola en bois traditionnelle suit les courbes du plan « comme les vertèbres d'une longue colonne vertébrale ». Le toit de la maison est recouvert de terre et de végétation qui le rendent « presque invisible » vu d'en haut. Les portes et les fenêtres « sont en bois et très simples, d'une couleur olive clair, tandis que les principaux murs extérieurs sont en pierre sans mortier. Ces choix sont conformes au style et à la technique traditionnels », toujours d'après Sinas. La maison principale a une surface de 115 mètres carrés et comprend un espace salon, un espace pour les repas, une cuisine ouverte et la chambre principale. L'ensemble compte encore une maison d'hôtes de 65 mètres carrés à deux chambres et un sous-sol de 65 mètres carrés.

Interiors have round wooden beam ceilings.
Opposite: *the dining and living space.*
Above: *the kitchen.* Below: *a shower.*

SO – IL

Duravcevic-Ben Ari House
Long Island, New York, USA, 2016–19
Area: 600 m²
Collaboration: Carl Shenton of
Shenton Architects

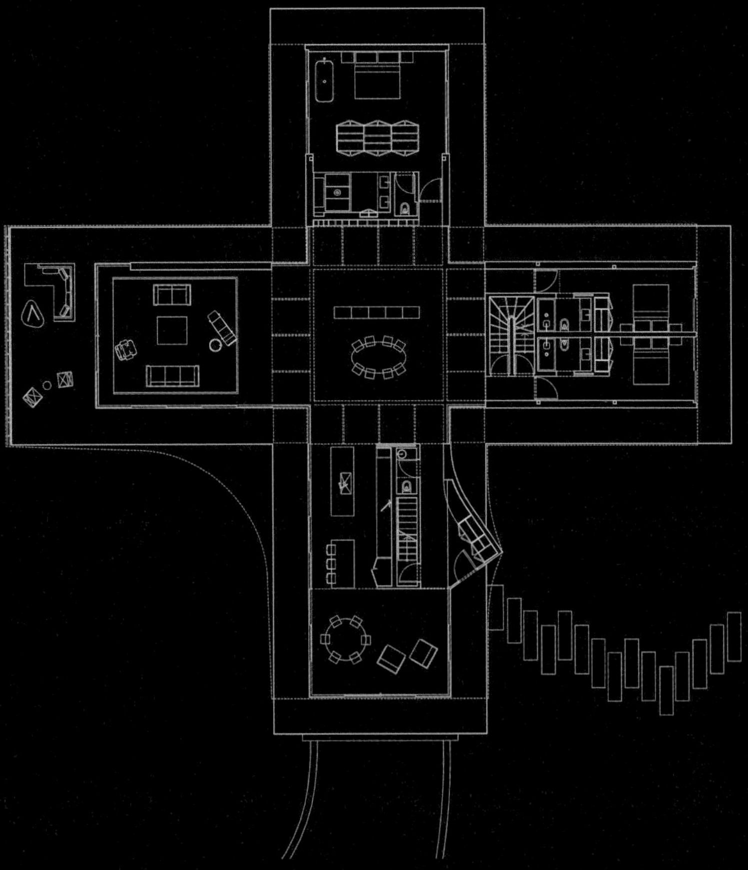

Silver-gray tones dominate because of the corrugated steel siding and zinc roofs of the house.

Set on an eight-hectare site overlooking Long sland Sound in the North Fork area, the Duravcevic-Ben Ari House takes the shape of a "simple cruciform of gable volumes" that take n a number of views. Each of the quadrants of the house has a different function, with the private, bedroom areas in the highest, most wooded segment of the residence site. The living areas face a slope that descends to the water. Corrugated stainless steel is used for cladding, and the roof is in zinc. The center of the composition is occupied by the dining area and library. The overhanging roof shelters a continuous porch around the house with a curved segment sheltering an outdoor living space. A roof terrace between the four gables offers yet another outdoor space. Interior design of the house is by the Duravcevic brothers, and the landscaping is he work of Patrick Cullina.

Das Duravcevic-Ben Ari House liegt auf einem acht Hektar großen Grundstück mit Blick auf den Long Island Sound in der Region North Fork. Es hat die Form eines „schlichten Kreuzes aus Giebeln", die eine Reihe von Ausblicken bieten. Jeder der Quadranten des Hauses hat eine andere Funktion, wobei sich die privaten Schlafbereiche auf dem höchstgelegenen, baumreichsten Grundstücksteil befinden. Die Wohnbereiche blicken auf einen zum Wasser hin abfallenden Hang. Die Hausverkleidung ist aus gewelltem Edelstahl, das Dach aus Zink. Die Mitte der Anlage wurde dem Essbereich und der Bibliothek vorbehalten. Das überhängende Dach schützt eine umlaufende Veranda rund um das Haus, wobei ein gebogenes Segment einen Außenwohnbereich überdacht. Eine Dachterrasse zwischen den vier Giebeln schafft einen weiteren Außenbereich. Während die Gebrüder Duravcevic das Innendesign

'he house sits on a platform but its curving walls and ɔof envelope both interior and exterior spaces, such s the outdoor terrace areas seen on the next spread.

estalteten, wurde Patrick Cullina für die Landchaftsgestaltung verpflichtet.

Construite sur un terrain de huit hectares qui lomine le détroit de Long Island dans le North 'ork, la maison Duravcevic-Ben Ari a une forme simplement cruciforme de volumes à pignons » ux vues multiples. Chacun des quadrants de a maison a une fonction différente, les parties rivées et les chambres sont situées dans la ection supérieure la plus boisée. Les lieux de vie ont face à une pente qui descend vers l'eau. Les nurs ont un parement en acier inoxydable ondulé t le toit est en zinc. Le centre de la composition st occupé par l'espace destiné aux repas et a bibliothèque. Le toit en surplomb abrite un orche qui fait le tour de la maison dont un segnent incurvé constitue un salon extérieur. Une errasse sur le toit entre les quatre pignons offre un autre espace extérieur. L'intérieur a été aménagé par les frères Duravcevic et l'aménagement paysager est l'œuvre de Patrick Cullina.

TETRO

Inclined Slab House
Nova Lima, Brazil, 2015–21
Area: 200 m²

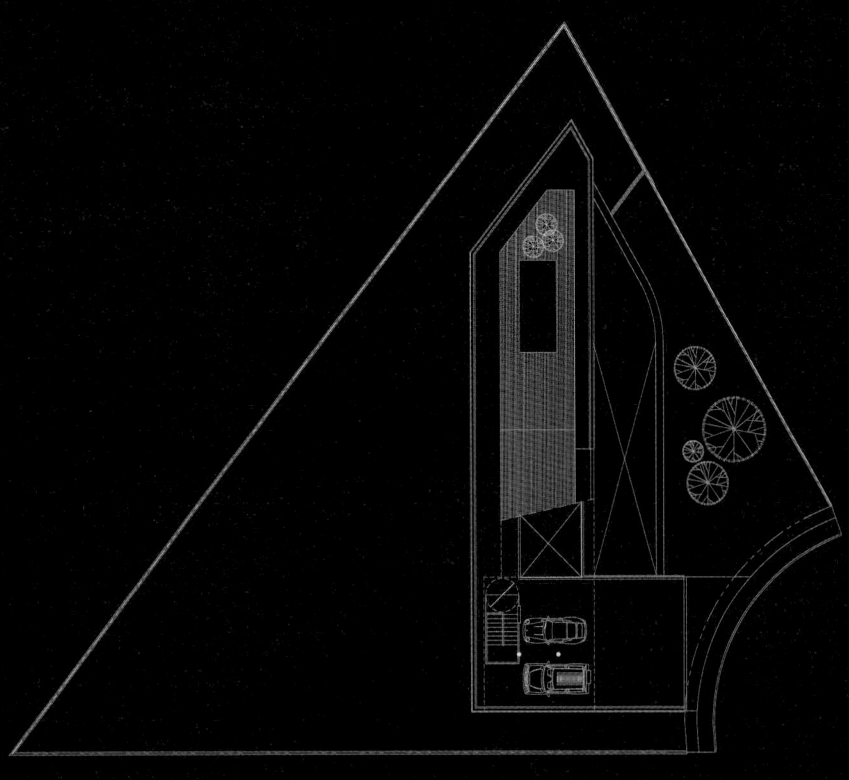

'he roof of the long, narrow house defines its ›resence in its landscape setting—with a pool and errace literally on top of the residence.

'his house is based on a concrete slab that has ›een inserted into a steep slope with savanna regetation and mountain views and ultimately ests on just two pillars. The slab defines the nain access and the garage and frames the view. .ower on the site, the slab slopes down to the site of a pool and a large wooden deck. The deck ınd the pool are all set on the roof of the house. 'he private areas are on the ground floor, while :he living and dining area is below the inclined section of the roof slab. As the architects explain: 'On one side, large glass windows allow the view of the mountains. On the opposite side, a single steel/glass gate runs through the façade, con- ıecting the room to a large grassy plateau sur- ounded by a stone retaining wall. The living room urns into a large balcony." Part of the exceptional ıature of this house is due to the fact that the ıatural setting around it is strictly protected.

Zentrales Element dieses Hauses ist eine Beton- platte, die in einen steilen Hang mit Savannen- vegetation und Bergblick eingefügt wurde und auf nur zwei Pfeilern ruht. Hauszugang sowie Garage liegen auf Ebene der Platte, die die Ausblicke einrahmt. Weiter unten auf dem Grund- stück neigt sich die Platte zu einem Pool und einem großen Holzdeck hinab. Terrasse wie auch Pool befinden sich auf dem Dach des Hauses. Die privaten Bereiche nehmen das Erdgeschoss ein, während der Wohn- und Essbereich unter dem schrägen Teil der Dachplatte liegt. „Auf der einen Seite geben große Glasfenster den Blick auf die Berge frei", schildern die Architekten. „Auf der gegenüberliegenden Seite nimmt ein einziges Stahl-Glas-Tor die Fassade ein und verbindet den Raum mit einem großen, von einer Steinmauer umgebenen Grasplateau. Das Wohnzimmer geht in einen großen Balkon über."

he volume of the house rises on one side and is upported by two thin columns over another terrace.

Der außergewöhnliche Charakter dieses Hauses st zum Teil darauf zurückzuführen, dass seine atürliche Umgebung streng geschützt ist.

.a maison est dominée par une dalle de béton qui été insérée dans une pente raide où pousse la avane avec vue sur la montagne, mais repose n fin de compte sur seulement deux piliers. La lalle délimite l'accès principal et le garage tout n encadrant la vue. Plus bas, elle descend vers ne piscine et un vaste ponton de bois, tous les leux sur le toit de la maison. Les parties privées ont situées au rez-de-chaussée, tandis que le alon et le coin repas se trouvent sous la section inclinée de la dalle de toit. Les architectes xpliquent que « d'un côté, de grandes fenêtres ont vue sur les montagnes. De l'autre, une simple alustrade d'acier et de verre traverse la façade t relie la pièce à un vaste plateau herbeux entouré d'un mur de soutènement en pierre. Le salon se transforme en un immense balcon ». Cette maison doit son caractère extraordinaire en partie au fait que le cadre naturel tout autour est strictement protégé.

A bedroom seems to be literally suspended above the mountainous landscape with the city in the distance. The angular design of the house is visible in the drawings below which make the slope of the site evident as well.

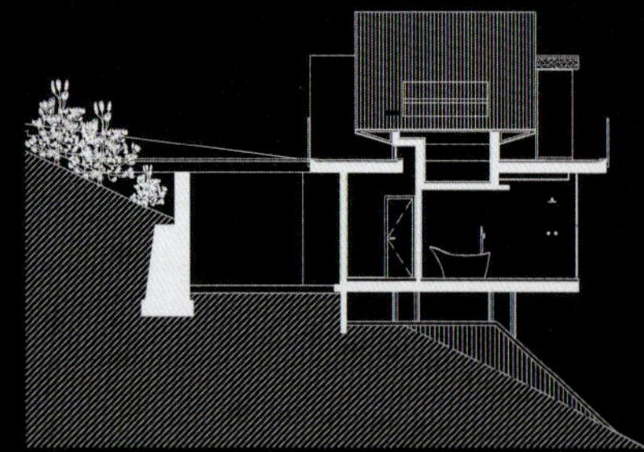

The narrowness of the house and its full glazing allow the living room to profit from the full width of the building, looking out to the sloped setting. Below: *even the bathtub has a generous view.*

SANTIAGO VALDIVIESO AND STEFANO ROLLA

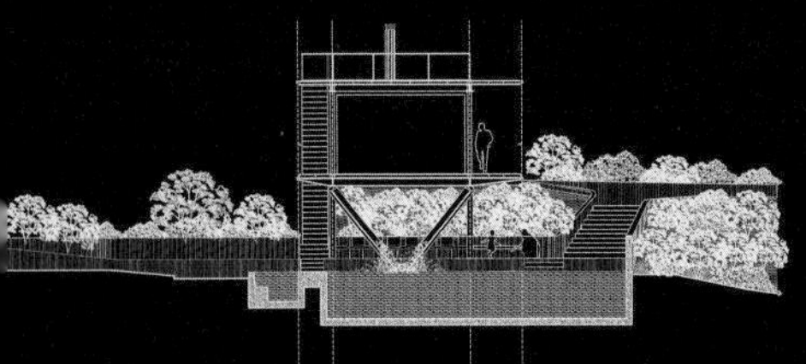

Engawa House
Punta Pite, Zapallar, Chile, 2017–19
Area: 257 m²

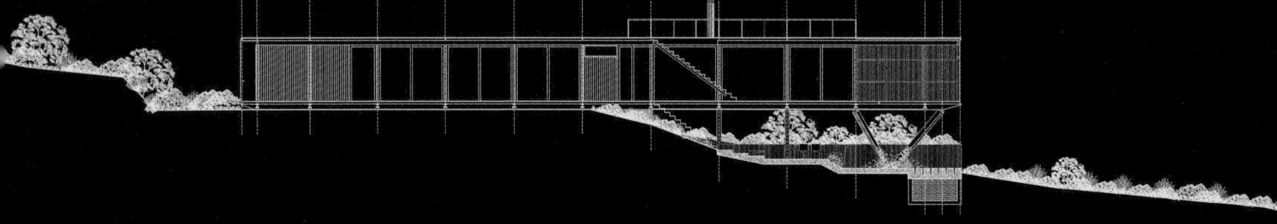

Set up off the ground, the main, rectangular volume of the house is protected from the sun by vertically arranged screens. The uppermost level offers views of the ocean in three directions.

This house was built for a cost of $380 000 on a rocky cliff at Punta Pite, 170 kilometers northwest of Santiago on the Pacific Ocean. The architects sought to combine two apparently contradictory functions—that of a refuge and a place to take in the panorama. The "intermediate condition" they imagined suggested the Japanese idea of *engawa*, a space that is neither inside nor outside, but both at once. A single-story gallery made of black steel and glass juts out over the sloping site supported by pilotis and a "quadruple diamond" support at the end. The architects explain: "The higher you are from the ground, the more public your program will be, until a public upstairs and a private downstairs are generated." Below, a series of scales, platforms, concrete walls, and river stones build the exteriors and gardens of the house; these follow the conditions of the topography, unlike the main volume.

Above, in a completely panoramic situation with three sea fronts, there is an unprotected viewpoint against the windy weather.

Dieses Haus wurde für 380 000 Dollar auf einer felsigen Klippe am Pazifik in Punta Pite errichtet 170 Kilometer nordwestlich von Santiago. Die Architekten kombinierten zwei scheinbar widersprüchliche Konzepte miteinander: einen Zufluchtsort und einen Aussichtspunkt. Der „Zwischenzustand", den sie sich vorstellten, erinnert an das japanische Konzept *engawa*: ein Raum, der weder innen noch außen, sondern beides zugleich ist. Eine eingeschossige Galerie aus schwarzem Stahl und Glas ragt, an einem Ende gestützt von Pilotis und einer „Vierfach-Diamanten"-Stütze, über das abschüssige Gelände hinaus. „Je höher man über dem Boden steht", so die Architekten, „desto öffentlicher

An angled red steel support holds up the main tructure and leaves room below for the private areas of the residence.

gestalten sich die Räume, bis ein gemeinschaft- ich genutztes Obergeschoss und ein privates Untergeschoss entstehen." Unten prägen eine Reihe von Stufen, Plattformen, Betonmauern und Flusssteinen die Außenbereiche und Gärten des Hauses, die anders als das Hauptgebäude den Gegebenheiten der Topografie folgen. Oben, in vollkommener Panoramalage mit Blick auf drei Meeresfronten, befindet sich ein dem Wind aus- gesetzter Aussichtspunkt.

La maison a été construite pour 380 000 dol- lars sur une falaise rocheuse de Punta Pite, à 170 kilomètres au nord-ouest de Santiago, au bord de l'océan Pacifique. Les architectes ont cherché à associer deux fonctions en apparence contradictoires, un refuge et un lieu où admirer le panorama. La « solution intermédiaire » qu'ils un espace ni intérieur, ni extérieur, mais les deux à la fois. Une galerie d'un étage en acier noir et verre s'avance au-dessus du terrain en pente, portée par des *pilotis* et un support en « quadruple losange » à son extrémité. Les architectes expliquent que « plus on s'élève au-dessus du sol, plus l'espace devient public, jusqu'à un escalier commun vers le haut et privé vers le bas ». En dessous, une série d'échelles, plates-formes, murs de béton et pierres de rivière forment l'extérieur et les jardins, qui épousent la topographie, à la différence du volume principal. En haut, un point de vue sans aucune protection du climat venteux bénéficie d'un panorama total sur trois fronts de mer.

Gardens and terraces are arranged below the elevated main volume. The actual living space is enclosed in glass, leaving the "in-between" or engawa *space, referred to by the architects all around, inside the vertical slat screens.*

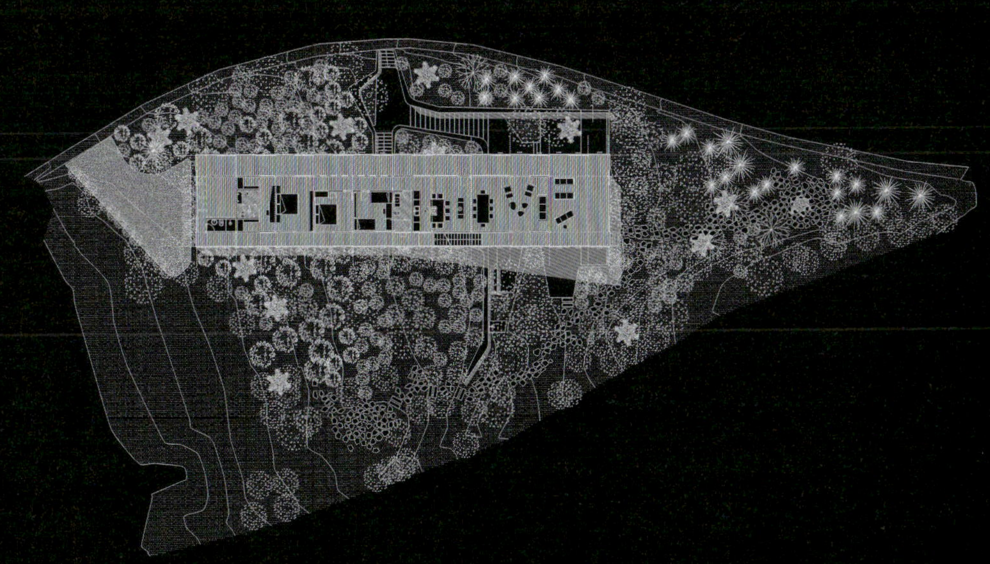

VO TRONG NGHIA

Bat Trang House
Bat Trang, Hanoi, Vietnam, 2017–18
Area: 740 m²

The open-grid structure of the house creates not only a flow of air, but also intermediary space where large plants can grow, further sheltering the interiors. Above: *the living and dining area of the house.*

This house for a family of seven was built on a 220-square-meter site in a pottery-making area, a fact that inspired the ceramic brick design of the façade. The architect explains that "the spatial arrangement of the house was based on the owner's ideal home, where nature intertwines with other functions of the house." Small gaps between the façade bricks allow air to filter through, while larger irregularly placed gaps create space for vegetation to grow. This greenery combined with the ceramic brick façade allows the house to cool in a natural way. Solar panels and rainwater collectors were also integrated into the sustainable design. Although its unusual façade does make it stand out from neighboring buildings, the Bat Trang House is quite obviously designed not only to fit into its cultural context but also to propose a responsible way to build a contemporary house in Vietnam.

Dieses Haus für eine siebenköpfige Familie wurde auf einem 220 Quadratmeter großen Grundstück in einer Gegend mit zahlreichen Keramikwerkstätten errichtet, was die Fassadengestaltung aus Keramikziegeln inspirierte. Der Architekt erklärt: „Die räumliche Anordnung des Hauses beruht auf der Vorstellung des Eigentümers von einem perfekten Zuhause, in dem die Natur mit anderen Funktionen des Hauses verflochten ist." Kleine Lücken zwischen den Fassadenziegeln lassen die Luft zirkulieren, während größere, unregelmäßig angeordnete Öffnungen Pflanzen Platz zum Wachsen bieten. Diese Begrünung sorgt zusammen mit der Keramikziegelfassade für eine natürliche Kühlung des Hauses. Solarpaneele und Regenwassersammelbecken wurden ebenfalls in das nachhaltige Design integriert. Obwohl es sich durch seine ungewöhnliche Fassade von den Nachbargebäuden abhebt,

A *bedroom inside the sheltered volume of the house which allows views of greenery and natural light to penetrate, despite the urban setting.*

Opposite: *Seen in its street setting the house does stand out but it nonetheless does not seem unreasonable in this context.* Above: *floor plans show the exterior perimeter as well as the protected inner volumes.*

wurde das Bat Trang House ganz offensichtlich nicht nur entworfen, um sich in seinen kulturellen Kontext einzufügen, sondern auch, um einen verantwortungsvollen Weg zum Bau eines modernen Hauses in Vietnam zu weisen.

Cette maison destinée à une famille de sept personnes a été construite sur un terrain de 220 mètres carrés dans un quartier de potiers qui a inspiré le motif en briques de céramique de la façade. L'architecte explique que « la disposition de la maison est basée sur la maison idéale du propriétaire, dans laquelle la nature interfère avec d'autres fonctions ». Les petits orifices entre les briques de la façade laissent filtrer l'air tandis que des orifices plus grands disposés irrégulièrement laissent à la végétation la place de grandir. Cette verdure associée à la façade en briques céramiques rafraîchit naturellement la maison. Des panneaux solaires et des capteurs d'eau de pluie ont également été intégrés au concept durable. Malgré sa façade originale qui la distingue des bâtiments voisins, la maison Bat Trang est très visiblement conçue pour s'adapter à son contexte culturel, mais aussi comme un moyen responsable de construire une maison contemporaine au Vietnam.

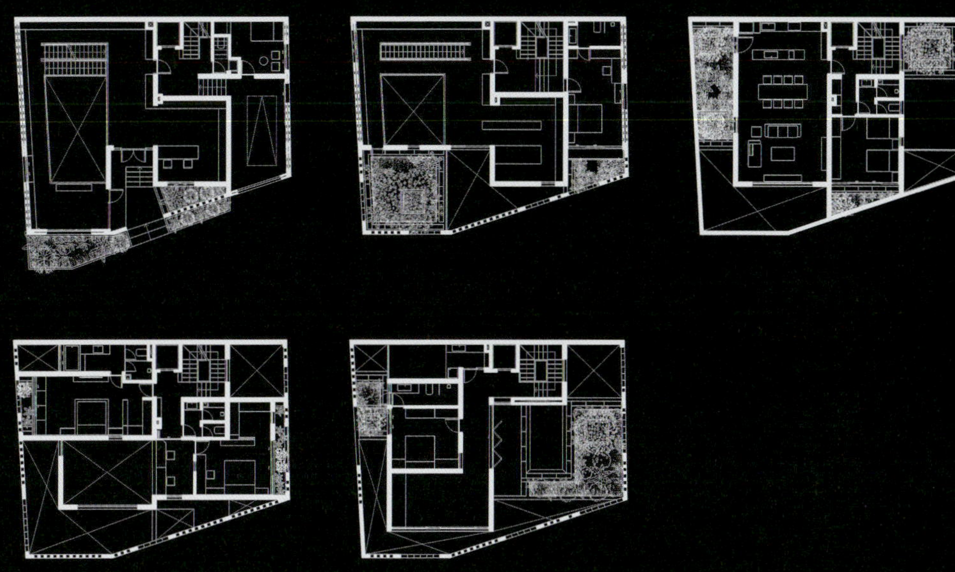

SUZUKO YAMADA

Daita2019
Tokyo, Japan, 2018–19
Area: 138 m²

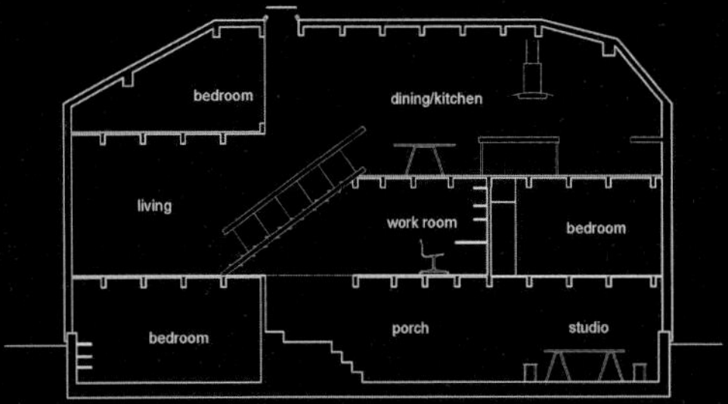

bedroom
dining/kitchen
living
work room
bedroom
bedroom
porch
studio

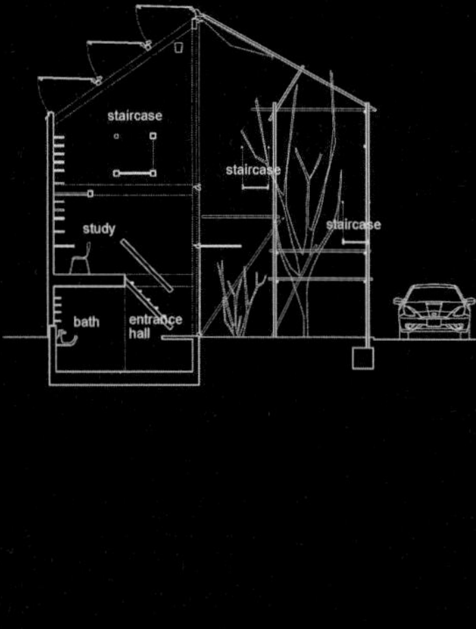

staircase
staircase
staircase
study
bath
entrance hall

Seen from the exterior the house appears to have had its construction scaffolding left in place, and yet this element is what gives it an unusual degree of flexibility and also creates ample intermediary spaces.

In an unexpected way, Suzuko Yamada compares her feeling about this house to an experience she had in a forest in Rwanda. She came on a group of wild mountain gorillas who seemed to be quite at home despite having no walls or roof to live under. She says: “This is the vernacular architecture of a gorilla forest. I wondered what it would be like to have a house like this in a small residential area of Tokyo. I wondered if it would be possible to create a house where bare life is softly enveloped by layers of wire and objects that create a variety of depths, and where the sunlight and the gazes of people passing by on the street are kept at a distance.” And so, there are no walls between this house and its garden. There are, however, “wooden lumber, steel members, single-pipe posts and beams, and braces; there are also stair risers and handrails, window sash frames, furniture, curtains, books, clothes and other miscellaneous items, potted trees and plants, bicycles, shovels, and a vast amount of books, videotapes, and DVDs.” The house has a wooden interior and a steel exterior, and it was clearly designed so that its shape could readily be changed. This may be one of the more radical contemporary houses imagined in many years, perhaps not to everyone’s taste, but certainly innovative, a fact that the architecture web site *dezeen.com* recognized in granting Daita2019 their “Urban House of the Year” award in 2020.

nside a light wooden structure confirms and amplifies the exterior complexity of the house, allowing for spaces that can be high like the one seen above, or perched between levels.

Mit Suzuko Yamadas Vergleich ihrer Empfindung für dieses Haus mit einem Erlebnis in einem ruandischen Wald rechnet man eher nicht. In Ruanda traf sie einst auf eine Gruppe wilder Berggorillas, die sich anscheinend sehr wohlfühlten, obwohl sie weder Wände noch ein Dach hatten, unter dem sie leben konnten. „Dies ist die traditionelle Architektur eines Gorillawaldes", erklärt Suzuko. „Ich fragte mich, wie es wohl wäre, ein solches Haus in einem kleinen Wohngebiet in Tokio zu haben. Ich fragte mich, ob es möglich wäre, ein Haus zu schaffen, in dem das unverhüllte Leben sanft von Schichten aus Draht und Objekten ummantelt wird, die eine Vielzahl von Tiefen schaffen, und in dem das Sonnenlicht und die Blicke der Menschen, die auf der Straße vorübergehen, auf Abstand gehalten werden." Daher trennt keine Wand dieses Haus von seinem Garten. Es gibt jedoch „Holzbalken, Stahl, Einrohrpfosten, Balken und Verstrebungen. Es gibt auch Treppenstufen und Handläufe, Möbel, Vorhänge, Bücher und diverse andere Gegenstände, Topfbäume und -pflanzen, Fahrräder, Schaufeln und eine Unmenge an Büchern, Videokassetten und DVDs." Das Haus ist innen aus Holz und außen aus Stahl, und es wurde eindeutig so konzipiert, dass sich seine Form leicht verändern lässt. Es dürfte eines der radikalsten zeitgenössischen Häuser sein, die seit vielen Jahren erdacht wurden, vielleicht nicht nach jedermanns Geschmack, aber definitiv innovativ. Dies erkannte auch die Architekturwebseite *dezeen.com* an, als sie Daita2019 2020 mit dem Preis „Urban House of the Year" auszeichnete.

Suzuko Yamada fait à propos de cette maison une comparaison inattendue entre ce qu'elle ressent à son propos et ce qu'elle a vécu dans

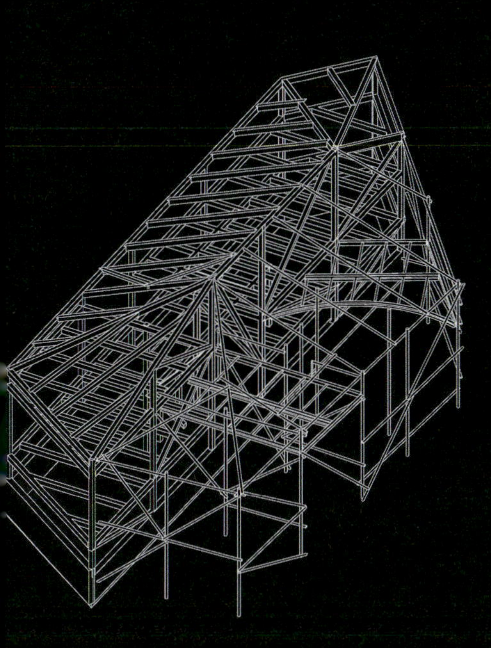

The overall complexity of the house is revealed in the drawing above.

The surprising angular design combined with elements like steel tube rails confirms the desire of the architect to redefine interior space.

une forêt au Rwanda. Elle est tombée sur un groupe de gorilles des montagnes qui semblaient être chez eux, même s'ils ne disposaient ni de murs ni de toit où s'abriter. Elle commente : « C'est l'architecture vernaculaire de la forêt des gorilles. Je me suis demandé quel effet cela ferait d'avoir une telle maison dans un quartier résidentiel de Tokyo. Je me suis demandé s'il serait possible de créer une maison où la vie serait simplement enveloppée en douceur de plusieurs couches de fil de fer et d'objets qui donneraient naissance à des profondeurs variées et où les rayons du soleil et les regards des passants seraient tenus à distance. » C'est pourquoi il n'y a pas de murs entre la maison et le jardin. Mais il y a « du bois de charpente, des éléments en acier, des poteaux à tube unique, des poutres, et des attaches. Il y a des contremarches et des rampes d'escalier, des cadres de fenêtres à guillotine, des meubles, des rideaux, des livres et d'autres objets, des arbres et des plantes en pots, des bicyclettes, des pelles et une grande quantité de livres, cassettes vidéo et DVD ». L'intérieur est en bois et l'extérieur en acier, elle a été conçue pour que sa forme puisse être facilement modifiée. C'est peut-être l'une des maisons les plus révolutionnaires imaginées depuis des années, sans doute pas du goût de tout le monde, mais innovante, un fait que le site Web *dezeen.com* a reconnu en attribuant à Daita2019 son prix de la « maison urbaine de l'année » en 2020.

YOUNG PROJECTS

Six Square House
Bridgehampton, New York, USA, 2018–20
Area: 325 m²

ʼlade up, as its name suggests, of six interconnected ;quare volumes, the sloping curving roofs of the esidence define not only its interior volumes but also he associated exterior spaces as seen in the images ›n this double page.

ʼhe Six Square House was built on a site of 3093 square meters in Bridgehampton, a town ›f about 1800 people in the South Fork area of .ong Island. It is on the same property as an 850 farmhouse which is used as a guest residence. Six square 7.3-meter gabled modules vere designed to align with each other and 'create continuity from one module to the next." 3ryan Young explains: "Starting with the simple ›ernacular typology of a barn, the hybrid roofscape of the connected squares ebbs and flows as a new dynamic figure, contemporary in its anguage but timeless in its origin." The modules are arranged around a focal point, which is a riangular courtyard near the kitchen, and each ›f the areas of the house has a different view. ʼhe garage occupies one module, while the kitchen and living room flow together. The master bedroom has its own volume, while another is occupied by a family room and guest room. A patio forms a square of its own, a counterpart across the triangular courtyard to the master bedroom. Materials used include charred, stained, and sealed Accoya rainscreen and Western red cedar rainscreen façades and ceilings, polished concrete patios, gypsum plaster walls and ceilings, white oak flooring, white oak millwork and panelling, ash millwork, and various types of marble (Calacatta Caldia, Calacatta Gold, Mountain White, Olympian White).

Das Six Square House steht auf einem 8093 Quadratmeter großen Grundstück in Bridgehampton, einer Stadt mit etwa 1800 Einwohnern in der Region South Fork auf Long Island. Es teilt sich das Grundstück mit einem als Gästehaus genutzten Bauernhaus von 1850. Sechs quadratische, 7,3 Meter hohe Giebelmodule sind aufeinander abgestimmt und „schaffen eine Kontinuität von einem Modul zum nächsten". Bryan Young erklärt: „Ausgehend von der einfachen, volkstümlichen Typologie einer Scheune, schwingt sich die hybride Dachlandschaft der miteinander verbundenen Quadrate zu einer neuen dynamischen Figur auf, zeitgemäß in ihrer Sprache, aber zeitlos in ihrem Ursprung." Die Module sind um einen zentralen Punkt herum angeordnet, einen dreieckigen Hof nahe der Küche, und jeder Bereich des Hauses bietet eine andere Aussicht. Die Garage befindet sich in einem Modul, während Küche und Wohnzimmer ineinander übergehen. Das Hauptschlafzimmer hat sein eigenes Modul, während ein anderes von einem Familien- und einem Gästezimmer eingenommen wird. Ein Patio bildet ein eigenes Quadrat als Gegenstück zum auf der anderen Seite des dreieckigen Hofs gelegenen Hauptschlafzimmer. Zu den verwendeten Materialien gehören geflammtes, gebeiztes und versiegeltes Holz (Accoya und Riesen-Lebensbaum) für die vorgehängte hinterlüftete Fassade und Decken, polierter Beton für den Patio, Gips für Wände und Decken, Weißeiche für Böden, Innenbauteile und Verkleidungen sowie Esche für Innenbauteile und verschiedene Marmorarten (Calacatta Caldia, Calacatta Gold, Mountain White, Olympian White).

.a Maison aux six carrés a été construite sur un errain de 8 093 mètres carrés à Bridgehampton, ıne ville d'environ 1 800 habitants dans le South ork (Long Island), sur la même parcelle qu'une erme de 1850 utilisée comme maison d'hôtes. Six nodules carrés à pignons de 7,3 mètres ont été onçus pour être alignés et « créer une continuité l'un module à l'autre ». Bryan Young explique son oncept comme suit : « À partir de la simple typo- ogie vernaculaire d'une grange, la toiture hybride les carrés raccordés l'un à l'autre flue et reflue elle une nouvelle figure dynamique, contempo- aine dans son langage, mais intemporelle dans on origine. » Les modules sont disposés autour l'un point central formé par une cour triangulaire côté de la cuisine et chaque partie de la maison une vue différente. Le garage occupe l'un des nodules, la cuisine et le salon sont regroupés lans un autre. La chambre principale a un volume pour elle seule, tandis qu'un autre est occupé par une pièce familiale et une chambre d'amis. Un patio forme un carré, contrepartie de la chambre principale de l'autre côté de la cour triangulaire. Les matériaux utilisés sont très divers et vont des écrans pare-pluie en bois d'accoya car-bonisé, teint et étanchéifié, et aux façades et plafonds en cèdre rouge aux patios en béton pol aux murs et aux plafonds en plâtre de gypse, aux sols, huisserie et lambris en chêne blanc, huisserie en frêne et plusieurs types de marbre (Calacatta Caldia, Calacatta Gold, Mountain White, Olympian White).

CAZÚ ZEGERS

Casa LLU
Carran, Maihue Lake, XIV Region, Chile, 2015–18
Area: 756 m^2
Collaboration: Hsü-Rudolphy
(Associated Architects)

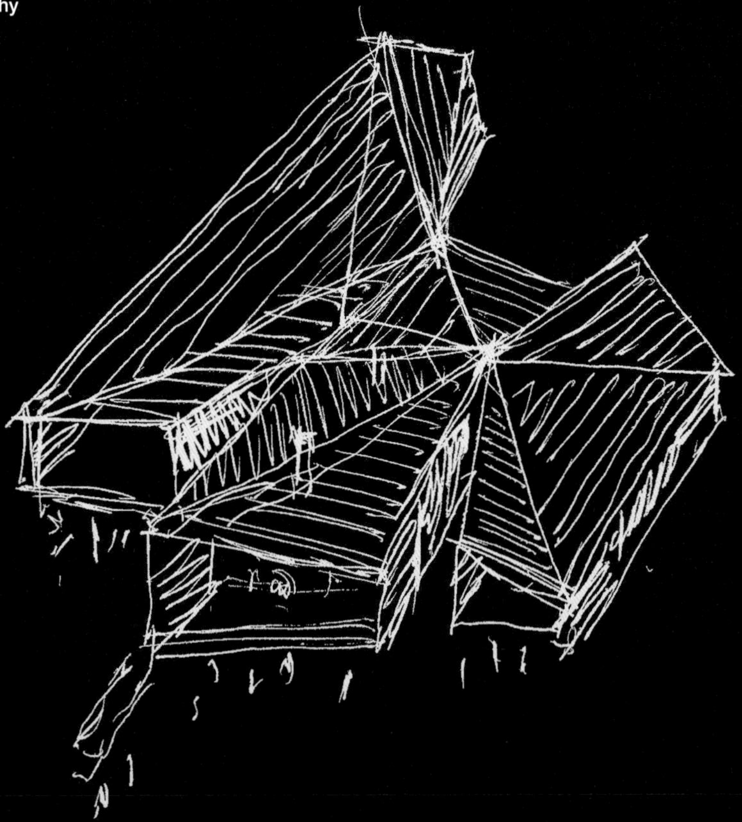

Partially lifted off the ground, the house has an unusual, essentially tri-partite form as seen in the aerial view above.

The angled, elevated volumes allow for many views o the natural setting and also serve to protect outdoor seating areas like the one visible opposite below fron the rain.

This house was built for a family of four generations, with reinforced concrete and steel on a 5000-square-meter site in the Andes of southern Chile. The windows were made on site with old oak. Interior and exterior deck floors are in rauli wood *(Nothofagus alpina)*. Interior walls are covered in local wood—roble *(Nothofagus obliqua)*, rauli, coihue *(Nothofagus dombeyi)*, and laurel *(Laurelia sempervirens)*. Exterior wall finishing is in steel plates that were worked on site. Since the region is known for its rain, the architect proposed a "rain protection mantle" composed of three elements (like H_2O). The fact that one family member had a mobility problem led the designers to create a single, interconnected level. The residence is set up on metal pillars that create the basement. The central element of the main floor includes the access zone, which is served by wood-covered steel ramps, and public areas (kitchen, living, and dining). The bedrooms are situated in the "lateral bodies that converge to the center in a smooth and fluid way." As Cazú Zegers says: "This is how, through a singular minimalist form, the work becomes a contemporary dialogue with the landscape, highlighting and enhancing its enormous beauty and magnitude."

Dieses Haus aus Stahlbeton und Stahl wurde für eine Vier-Generationen-Familie auf einem 5000 Quadratmeter großen Grundstück in den Anden des südlichen Chile errichtet. Die Fenster wurden vor Ort aus altem Eichenholz gefertigt. Die Böden der Innen- und Außendecks bestehen aus Rauli-Holz (*Nothofagus alpina*). Die Innenwände sind mit einheimischen Hölzern verkleidet, wie z. B. Buche (*Nothofagus obliqua*), Rauli, Coihue (*Nothofagus dombeyi*) und Lorbeer (*Laurelia sempervirens*). Vor Ort bearbeitete Stahlplatten verkleiden die Außenwände. Da die Region für ihren Regenreichtum bekannt ist, schlug die Architektin einen „Regenschutzmantel“ aus drei Elementen (wie H_2O) vor. Die eingeschränkte Mobilität eines Familienmitglieds veranlasste die Planer, eine einzige miteinander verbundene Ebene zu schaffen. Das Haus steht auf Metallpfeilern, die das Untergeschoss bilden.

Das zentrale Element des Hauptgeschosses umfasst den Zugangsbereich, der durch holzverkleidete Stahlrampen erschlossen wird, sowie die Gemeinschaftsbereiche (Küche, Wohn- und Essbereich). Die Schlafzimmer befinden sich in den „Seitenteilen, die fließend in die Mitte übergehen“. „Auf diese Weise wird das Werk durch eine einzigartige minimalistische Form zu einem zeitgenössischen Dialog mit der Landschaft, der ihre ungeheure Schönheit und Größe hervorhebt und verstärkt“, so Cazú.

Although the house relies on reinforced concrete and steel for its structure, its presence inside is almost entirely defined by its wood cladding on walls, floors, and the ceilings. Though very definitely architect-designed, the house exudes warmth.

La maison a été construite en béton armé et acier pour une famille de quatre générations sur un terrain de 5000 mètres carrés dans les Andes du Sud chilien. Les fenêtres ont été fabriquées sur place en chêne ancien. Les sols intérieurs et extérieurs sont en bois de rauli (*Nothofagus alpina*). Les murs sont recouverts de bois locaux – roble (*Nothofagus obliqua*), rauli, coihue (*Nothofagus dombeyi*) et laurier (*Laurelia sempervirens*). Les finitions des murs extérieurs sont des plaques d'acier qui ont été travaillées sur place. La région est connue pour ses pluies abondantes, de sorte que l'architecte a proposé un « manteau de protection contre la pluie » composé de trois éléments (similaire à H_2O). L'un des membres de la famille a des difficultés motrices, ce qui a incité les concepteurs à ne créer qu'un seul niveau interconnecté. La résidence est placée sur des piliers métalliques qui forment le sous-sol. L'élément central du niveau principal comprend la zone d'accès, desservie par des rampes en acier recouvertes de bois, et les parties communes (cuisine, salon et salle à manger). Les chambres sont dans les « corps de logis latéraux qui convergent vers le centre avec douceur et fluidité ». Pour reprendre les mots de Cazú Zegers, « c'est ainsi que par le biais d'une forme minimaliste spécifique, l'ouvrage se transforme en un dialogue contemporain avec le paysage dont il met en lumière et rehausse l'immense beauté et la majesté ».

CARLOS ZWICK

House by the Lake
Potsdam, Germany, 2016–20
Area: 610 m²

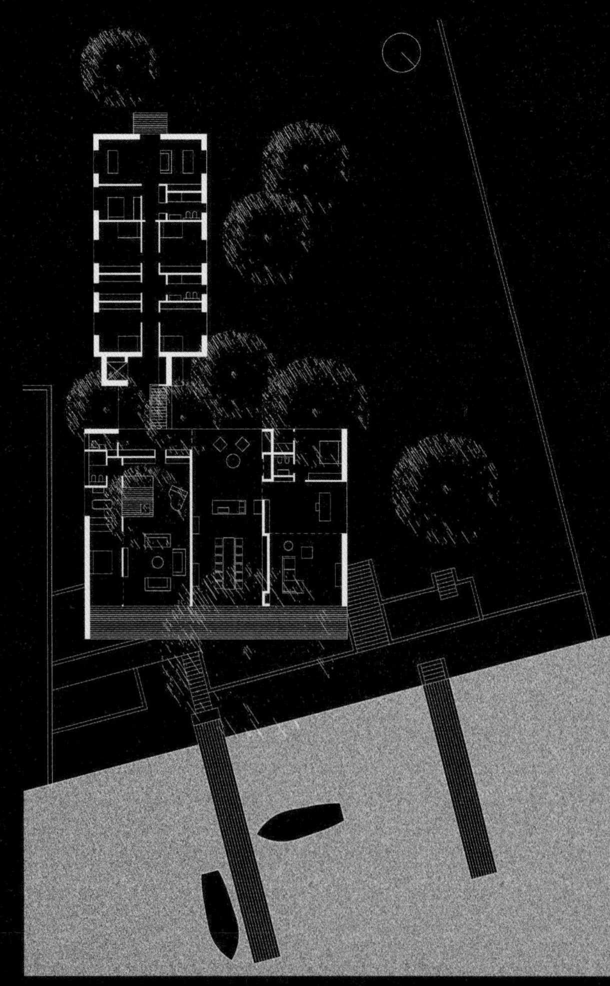

Raised off the ground in part as a response to zoning restrictions, the house also finds its spaces more pleasantly located in the setting of trees and water.

Located on a 4000-square-meter site near Lake Jungfern not far from the center of Potsdam, this house was designed and built by the architect for his own family. His inspiration came from Mies van der Rohe's Farnsworth House (Plano, Illinois, 1951). Building on 40 angled steel posts, thus raising the house three meters above the shoreline, was in part decided to ease zoning restrictions that normally required that the house should be set back 50 meters from the lakefront. The house was built without touching the old trees on the site, a fact that required that the construction be carried out using only a mobile telescopic forklift since there was no room for a more traditional anchored crane. The meeting place for the large family inside the house is a combined kitchen and dining room with a fireplace, and a 7.5-meter-long olive-wood table. A 22-meter-long loggia with a glazed railing is set eight meters above the level of the lake. The architect says that one of his major goals was to place both the interior and the exterior of the house as close to the lake as possible.

Dieses Haus wurde vom Architekten für seine eigene Familie auf einem 4000 Quadratmeter großen Grundstück in der Nähe des Jungfernsees unweit des Potsdamer Stadtzentrums entworfen und gebaut. Als Vorbild diente ihm Mies van der Rohes Farnsworth House (Plano, Illinois, 1951). Der Bau auf 40 abgewinkelten Stahlpfosten und die damit verbundene Erhöhung des Hauses um drei Meter über der Uferlinie zielten zum Teil auf eine Lockerung der Bebauungsvorschriften ab, gemäß denen das Haus eigentlich 50 Meter vom Seeufer zurückgesetzt stehen müsste. Das Haus wurde errichtet, ohne den alten Baumbestand zu berühren, weshalb der Bau nur mit einem mobile

The piers lift the house enough to allow cars to part beneath it as seen here. The rather powerful rectangular volumes seem to become weightless because of the light, angled supports.

Teleskopstapler durchgeführt werden konnte, da für einen traditionell verankerten Kran kein Platz vorhanden gewesen wäre. Treffpunkt der großen Familie im Inneren des Hauses ist der kombinierte Küchen- und Essbereich mit Kamin und einem 7,5 Meter langen Olivenholztisch. Eine 22 Meter lange Loggia mit verglastem Geländer liegt acht Meter über dem Seespiegel. Eines seiner Hauptziele war laut dem Architekten, sowohl das Innere als auch das Äußere des Hauses so nah wie möglich an den See zu rücken.

Située sur un terrain de 4000 mètres carrés au bord du lac Jungfern, non loin du centre de Potsdam, la maison a été conçue et bâtie par l'architecte pour loger sa famille. Il a puisé son inspiration dans la Farnsworth House (Plano, Illinois, 1951) de Mies van der Rohe. Il a décidé de la construire sur 40 poteaux anguleux en acier qui la surélèvent à trois mètres au-dessus de la berge, en partie pour contourner les restrictions de zonage qui exigent normalement de reculer la maison à 50 mètres du lac. Elle a été construite sans toucher aux vieux arbres présents sur le terrain, ce qui a exigé de n'utiliser qu'un chariot élévateur mobile télescopique car la place manquait pour ancrer une grue traditionnelle. L'endroit où se réunit la famille nombreuse à l'intérieur associe cuisine et salle à manger avec une cheminée et une table en bois d'olivier longue de 7,5 mètres. Une loggia de 22 mètres de long à balustrade vitrée domine le lac à huit mètres au-dessus du sol. L'architecte explique que l'un des principaux objectifs était de placer l'intérieur et l'extérieur de la maison le plus près possible du lac.

The interior volumes are rectilinear as the shape of the house might well suggest, but full height glazing gives them ample natural light and views of the trees and water.

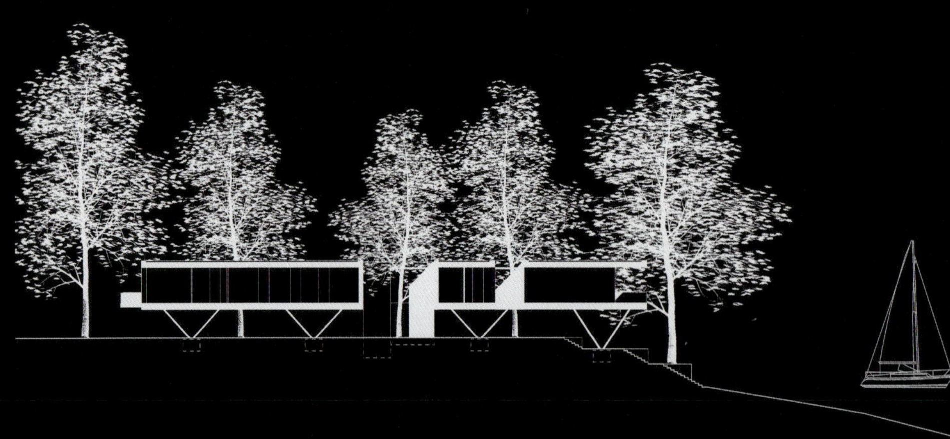

BIOGRAPHIES OF THE ARCHITECTS

93 DESIGN STUDIO
LIU JIUSAN graduated from Chongqing University with a Bachelor of Architecture degree in 2007. He received his master's in architecture from Southeast University (Nanjing, 2016). He created his own office, 93 DESIGN STUDIO in Chongqing in 2020. The architect also uses the anglicized name Lew Joeson, whence the name of the project published here, the Mountain House of Lew (Chongqing, 2017–19), a family home rebuilt with red bricks, ceramics and cement. Other work includes the Joy Between Streams house (Jiang, Ziyang, Sichuan, 2020); the Reconstruction of the former Laoshe Residence (Beibei District, Chongqing, 2020); the House of Liu (Yichang, Hubei, 2021); and the landscape design of the House of Liuhua (Bishan District, Chongqing, 2021), all in China.

GUILLERMO ACUÑA ARQUITECTOS ASOCIADOS (GAAA)
GUILLERMO ACUÑA was born in Santiago, Chile and studied architecture at the Pontificia Universidad Católica de Chile (Santiago, 1985–91). He created his own firm GAAA in 1991. He has placed a focus on traditional and vegetal materials in order "to express the possibilities of the orders of the vegetal kingdom and traditional construction in wood and fibers, which can go on to manifest the impressive geography of Chile." His work includes the Edificio Grupo Precisión (Santiago de Chile, 2011); Punta Chilen, Chiloe, 2017); Aguantao (Chiloe, 2018); Casa Malalcahuello (Malalcahuello, 2018); Riñihue (Riñihue, 2019); La Invernada (Curicó. 2019), his home on the Isla Lebe (Rilan, 2020, published here), and Casa con 4 Bóvedas (Rilán, 2024), all in Chile.
Instagram: @gaaa.arquitectos

ADJAYE ASSOCIATES
DAVID ADJAYE was born in 1966 in Dar es Salaam, Tanzania. He studied at the Royal College of Art in London (M.Arch, 1993), and worked in the offices of David Chipperfield and Eduardo Souto de Moura before creating his own firm in London in 2000. He has been recognized as one of the leading architects of his generation in the United Kingdom. Some of his key works are: a studio/home for Chris Ofili (1999); the SHADA Pavilion (2000, with artist Henna Nadeem); Siefer Penthouse (2001); Elektra House (2001); and a studio/gallery/home for Tim Noble and Sue Webster (2002), all in London. More recent work includes the Nobel Peace Center (Oslo, Norway, 2002–05) Bernie Grant Performing Arts Center (London, UK 2001–06); Stephen Lawrence Center (London, UK 2004–06); a visual arts building for the London-based organizations inIVA/Autograph at Rivington Place (London, UK, 2003–07); the Museum of Contemporary Art/Denver (Denver, Colorado US, 2004–07); and the Francis A. Gregory Library (Washington, D.C., US, 2010–12). Other work includes the National Museum of African American History and Culture (Smithsonian Institution, Washington, D.C., USA, 2016); Ruby City (San Antonio, TX, USA, 2019); the Aisht Foundation (Beirut, Lebanon, 2015); the Moscow School of Management (Moscow, Russia, 2010) the Winter Park Library & Events Center (Winte Park, CO, USA); the Abrahamic Family House (Abu Dhabi, UAE, 2023); and the dot.ateliers (Accra Ghana, 2023).
www.adjaye.com

ADND
was co-founded by Anand Menon, who studied at the Kamla Raheja Vidyanidhi Institute of Architecture and Environmental Studies (KRVIA Mumbai), and Shobhan Kothari, who is also the principal architect and partner in the Mumbai practice KDND Studio. Their team of about 30 designers is focused on "luxury architecture and high-end interiors." Significant recent projects include the Resort House (Sevasi, Vadodara

Gujarat, 2018); C'est La Vie (Alibag, 2018) and the Casa Feliz (Alibag, 2020), all in India.
www.adnd.in

AIRES MATEUS
MANUEL ROCHA DE AIRES MATEUS was born in Lisbon, Portugal, in 1963. He graduated as an architect from the Faculty of Architecture at the Technical University of Lisbon (FA-UTL; 1986). He worked with Gonçalo Byrne beginning in 1983 and with his brother Francisco Xavier Rocha de Aires Mateus beginning in 1988. FRANCISCO XAVIER ROCHA DE AIRES MATEUS was born in Lisbon in 1964. He also graduated from the FA-UTL (1987) and began working with Gonçalo Byrne in 1983, before his collaboration with his brother. Their work includes the Santa Marta Light House Museum (Cascais, 2007); a Highway Toll and Control Building (Benavente, 2007); a school complex (Vila Nova da Barquinha, 2008); EDP Headquarters, Portuguese Electric Company (Lisbon, 2009); Portugal Telecom Call Center (Santo Tirso, 2009); Parque de los Cuentos Museum (Málaga, Spain, 2009); a house in Leiria (Leiria, 2010); a house in Aroeira (Aroeira, 2010); the House in Melides II (Melides, 2015); the House in Campo de Ourique (Lisbon, 2019, Manuel Aires Mateus with Miguel Passos de Almeida), and the Elysée-mudac Museum in Lausanne (Switzerland, 2022), all in Portugal unless stated otherwise.
www.airesmateus.com

BARCLAY & CROUSSE
JEAN-PIERRE CROUSSE was born in Lima, Peru, in 1963. He was educated at the Universidad Ricardo Palma in Lima and at Milan Polytechnic in Italy, where he received a European architecture degree (1989). SANDRA BARCLAY was born in Lima in 1967 and also studied at the Universidad Ricardo Palma before getting a French architecture degree (D.P.L.G.) at the École d'Architecture de Paris-Belleville (1993). Their built work includes the reconstruction of the Musée Malraux (Le Havre, France, 1999); M House (Cañete, 2001); F House (Lima, 2010); Vedoble Houses (Cañete, 2011); Montreuil Student Apartments (Paris, France, 2011); and a 170-unit housing project (Nantes, France, 2011). More recently they completed University Facilities for the Universidad de Piura (UDEP, Piura, 2016); the Paracas Museum (Ica, 2016); Regional Government Headquarters

www.barclaycrousse.com

BAROZZI VEIGA
FABRIZIO BAROZZI born in 1976 in Rovereto, Italy, studied architecture at the Istituto Universitario di Architettura in Venice and went on to the Escuela Técnica Superior de Arquitectura de Sevilla and from there to the Ecole d'Architecture de Paris La Villette. ALBERTO VEIGA was born in 1973 in Santiago de Compostela, Spain, and studied architecture at the Escuela Técnica Superior de Arquitectura de Navarra. Barozzi Veiga was founded in Barcelona by Fabrizio Barozzi and Alberto Veiga in 2004. The pair has worked on both public and private projects and received a number of awards, including the prestigious Mies van der Rohe Award for European Architecture (2015, Szczecin Philharmonic Hall, Poland), and the RIBA Award for International Excellence (2018, Bündner Kunstmuseum Chur, Switzerland). Their other work includes the new building for the Museum of Fine Arts in Lausanne, Switzerland (2019). They are currently working on a major transformation scheme for the Chicago Art Institute (US, 2019–). For their respective apartments, they worked with their partners Cecilia Rueda (Barozzi Veiga) and Maria Diaz (MDBA).
www.barozziveiga.com

LUCIANO LERNER BASSO
was born in Brazil in 1979 and graduated in architecture from the Pontifícia Universidade Católica do Rio Grande do Sul (PUCRS, 2003). He received an M.B.A. in construction management from the Escola Superior de Propaganda e Marketing de Porto Alegre (ESPM-RS, 2005); and a master's in architectural design from UniRitter-Mackenzie (Porto Alegre, 2015). He received the Opera Prima Award (2003); his work was selected for the International Architecture Biennials of São Paulo (2005), Brasília (2007), and Buenos Aires (2018); he was invited to participate in the 10th Ibero-American Biennial of Architecture and Urbanism (2016); and he was selected by the Brazilian Institute of Architects to represent the country at the Oscar Niemeyer Award (2020). His completed work includes the Quattro Residential Building (2016); House H13 (2019) and the Fortunata House (2020; published here), all in Caxias do Sul. More recent projects are

Marau, 2023), and Ammaliato House (Encantado, 2022), all in Brazil.
www.lucianobasso.com.br

BAUMRAUM
ANDREAS WENNING was born in 1965. He studied as a cabinetmaker in Weinheim, Germany (1982–85), and as an architect at the Technical University of Bremen, where he obtained his degree in 1995. He worked in the office of José Garcia Negette in Sydney, Australia (2001), before creating his own office, baumraum, in Bremen in 2003. He has completed many tree houses and organized seminars on "The Body Language of Trees," and "Building a Tree House Without Impairing the Tree." Some of his structures include Casa Emilio (Italy, 2017); a house on stilts in the Black Forest (Oval Office, Germany, 2019); the Green Dwelling (near Hannover; published here, 2019); the Dark Room (New York, 2020); Black Crystal (New York, 2020); and the Bergchalets (Annweiler am Trifels, Germany, 2023).
www.baumraum.de

LINA BELLOVIČOVÁ
was born in 1990 in the Czech Republic. She received her degree from the Brno University of Technology, Faculty of Architecture, in 2014. She apprenticed in the offices of Tato Architects (Kobe, Japan) and StudioZurich (Zurich, Switzerland), also in 2014. She founded her own studio in Stare Mesto (Czech Republic) in 2015 and explains that her work is inspired by her stays in Japan and Switzerland. Her projects and realizations include Pappabubble Osaka (Japan, 2014, during her apprenticeship with Tato Architects); the Doctor's Nest (2016); Green Court (2016); Morava (2018); Aquarex (2018); House Lo (Chriby, 2020; published here); and Lele (2020), all in the Czech Republic.
linabellovicova.wixsite.com

THIAGO BERNARDES
was born in Rio de Janeiro in 1974. His grandfather was Sergio Bernardes, a Brazilian architect who won the Brussels International Fair's prize in 1956. His father was Claudio Bernardes, founder-Partner of Claudio Bernardes + Jacobsen Arquitetura in Rio. In 1992, he entered Santa Ursula College in Rio, but preferred to engage in a self-taught career. In 1994, he opened his first office with Miguel Pinto Guimarães, developing more than 30 residential projects between 1996 and 2001. After his father's death, he and his partner associated themselves with Paulo Jacobsen and created a new office. In 2011, Thiago Bernardes created Bernardes Arquitetura, with Camila Tariki, Marcia Santoro, Dante Furlan, and Nuno Costa Nunes. Francisco Abreu, Rafael de Oliveira, Thiago Moretti, and Antonia Bernardes have since become partners. The firm currently has a team of 130 with offices in Rio de Janeiro, São Paulo, and Lisbon. The firm's work includes the Gávea House (Rio de Janeiro, 2013); RGE House (Itacaré, Bahia, 2013); CF House (Porto Feliz, São Paulo, 2013); and the Triângulo House (São Paulo, 2016; published here). Work in 2020 includes the Lotus Building (Brasília); Casa MKM (Marngaratiba, RJ); and the Girassol and Fidalga 380 buildings in São Paulo, all in Brazil.
www.bernardesarquitetura.com.br

BOHLIN CYWINSKI JACKSON
founded in 1965, is an architecture practice of six studios across the United States focused on designing places that inspire connection and wonder. In addition to its six studios, the firm also has a Canadian affiliate, Miller Mottola Calabro, which was involved in the project published here. The firm Principals are Ray Calabro, Steven Chaitow, Thomas Kirk, Daniel Lee, William Loose, Patreese Martin, Robert Miller, Gregory Mottola, and Kent Suhrbier, with former principals Peter Bohlin and Frank Grauman serving as special consultants. The firm's six studios are in New York, Philadelphia, Pittsburgh, San Francisco, Seattle, and Wilkes-Barre. Significant work includes the Frick Environmental Center (Pittsburgh, Pennsylvania, 2016); Lauder College House, University of Pennsylvania (Philadelphia, 2016); the Bear Stand (Gooderham, Ontario, Canada, 2016); High Meadow at Fallingwater (Mill Run, Pennsylvania, 2016); CoorsTek Center for Applied Science and Engineering, Colorado School of Mines (Golden, Colorado, 2018); ANSYS Hall at Carnegie Mellon University (Pittsburgh, Pennsylvania, 2019); Reduction Residence (Pittsburgh, Pennsylvania, 2019); Boundary Point Cabin (with Miller Mottola Calabro; Christina Lake, British Columbia, Canada, 2020; published here); the Siebel Center for Design, University of Illinois Urbana-Champaign (Champaign, Illinois, 2021); and the ASU Immersive Media and eXperience Center at Arizona State University (Mesa, Arizona, 2022), in the United States unless indicated, and retail stores for Apple Inc., Blue Bottle Coffee

shops and for the San Francisco-based fashion brand Everlane in various locations in the United States and worldwide.
www.bcj.com

ALEX BRAHM AND ANTONIO POLIDURA

ALEX BRAHM received his degree in architecture from the Pontificia Universidad Católica de Chile (UC) in 1985. He was a professor at the UC School of Architecture from 1988 to 2001 and has been a LEED accredited professional since 2008. ANTONIO POLIDURA obtained his degree as an architect from the Universidad Central de Chile (2000). Between 2000 and 2001, he worked at Kohn Pedersen Fox (New York) and in 2002 he was associated with Pablo Talhouk in Polidura+Talhouk Arquitectos. Since 2016, he has been an Associate at Gubbins+Polidura Arquitectos with Pedro Gubbins. The work of Brahm and Polidura together includes the CAV Peñalolen, government municipal building (Santiago, 2013); Casa 5 Vigas (Zapallar, Valparaíso, 2018); Casa S (Punta Pite, Zapallar, 2019; published here); and Lo Recabarren office building, Inmobilaria TÁNICA (Santiago, 2020), all in Chile.
www.gubbinspolidura.cl

EDUARDO CADAVAL

was born in Mexico City in 1975. He holds a B.A. from the National University of Mexico (2000), and an M.Arch in urban design from Harvard University (2003). Before cofounding Cadaval & Solà-Morales, he worked for Abalos & Herreros in Madrid, and for Field Operations in New York. His firm with Clara Solà-Morales was created in New York City in 2003 and moved to both Barcelona and Mexico City in 2005. Cadaval has been a Visiting Professor at the University of Pennsylvania's School of Design. Their work includes Casa X (Barcelona, Spain, 2012); Tepoztlán Lounge (Tepoztlán, Morelos, Mexico, 2012); LMB Bungalows (Tepoztlán, Morelos, Mexico, 2013); Oport 1 House (Port de la Selva, Spain, 2013); Cordoba Housing Building (Mexico City, Mexico, 2013); and the San Sebastian House (Buenos Aires, Argentina, 2014). Recent work includes Casa Ombra (Monterrey, Mexico, 2020); and Noah House (Valle de Bravo, Mexico, 2023). Published here is the Theater (Barcelona, 2020), which is the home of Eduardo Cadaval and his first project with his new office Cadaval Estudio.

MINO CAGGIULA

was born in 1977 in Switzerland. He first earned a diploma as a bricklayer (1993–97) before becoming a construction site assistant (1997–2002) and then a construction site supervisor and design architect (2002–04). He earned a B.Arch degree (SUPSI, Trevano, 1998–2001) and also studied at the Mendrisio Academy of Architecture (2001–04). Caggiula worked in the office of Steven Holl while studying at the Columbia Graduate School of Architecture (New York, 2004–05) before creating his own office in Lugano in 2006. His work includes the Nizza Residence (Lugano, 2017); LECHE apartment building (Bellinzona, 2017); Eolica apartment building (Pregassona, 2018); Clouds apartment building (Biasca, 2019); Atelier Alice Trepp (Origlio, 2019; published here); the Libellula Residence (Lugano, 2021); and Blade (Canobbio, 2022), all in Switzerland.
www.minocaggiula.ch

VICTOR CAÑAS

born in San José, Costa Rica, in 1947, graduated as an architect from the Universidad Iberoamericana (Mexico City, 1973). He did postgraduate studies in urban planning at London University (1972–73) before creating his own firm in 1974. He was the cofounder of the Master of Tropical Architecture program at the Universidad de Costa Rica, where he taught architectural design for almost 30 years. Because of economic conditions at the time, he paused his career as an architect to serve as minister and consul general at the Costa Rican Embassy in London (1982–87). His work includes the EOS House (Faro Escondido, 2010); Guarumos House (Manuel Antonio Beach, 2014); Naked Indians House (Papagayo Gulf, 2014); Cocobolo House (Montezuma Beach, 2016); KaLiDa House (Alajuela, 2017); Ceibo House and Water Garden (Montezuma Beach, 2018); House for a Ceramist (The Guana-castes) (Orotina, 2019; published here); the V&A House (San José, 2019); and Three Trees (Manuel Antonio 2022), all in Costa Rica.
www.canasarquitectos.com

CARMODY GROARKE

KEVIN CARMODY was born in 1974 in Canberra, Australia. He worked in the office of David Chipperfield in London before participating in the creation of Carmody Groarke in 2006. ANDY GROARKE is also a director of the firm and was born in 1971 in Manchester (UK). He also

with Haworth Tomkinds Architects in London prior to 2006. Their completed work includes the London Festival of Architecture Skywalk (2008); 7 July Memorial, Hyde Park (London, 2009); the Architecture Foundation Headquarters (London, 2010); Regents Place Pavilion (London, 2010); and Studio East Dining (London, 2010). More recent work includes the V&A Members' Room (London 2017); the House and Studio (Lambeth, London, 2018; published here); Windermere Jetty Museum (Lake District, 2019); British Film Institute (Southbank, London, 2019); and the Hillhouse Box (Helensburgh, Scotland, 2019), all in the UK; and The Grossmarkt Theater Pavilion in Hamburg (Germany, 2020).
www.carmodygroarke.com

ARTHUR CASAS
was born in 1961 and graduated as an architect from the Mackenzie University of São Paulo, Brazil, in 1983. He has concentrated on both interiors and constructions, developing residential and commercial projects with a distinctive vocabulary of forms. In 2008, Arthur Casas won the prestigious Red Dot Design Award, in Germany, for developing creative cutlery and dinner-set lines for Riva. His completed commercial projects include the Alexandre Herchcovitch Store (Tokyo, Japan, 2007); Cidade Jardim Mall (São Paulo, 2008); Zeferino Store, Oscar Freire Street (São Paulo, 2008); C-View Bar and C-House Restaurant, Affinia Hotel (Chicago, USA, 2008); KAA Restaurant (São Paulo, 2008); Quinta da Baroneza (Bragança Paulista, São Paulo, 2009); Urca Residence (Rio de Janeiro, 2011); and the Alma Maria Restaurant (São Paulo, 2012). He also designed the Brazil Pavilion for Expo 2015 Milan (with Atelier Marko Brajovic). He built the JY House (Fazenda Boa Vista, Porto Feliz, São Paulo, 2018; published here); Brownstone House (New York, USA, 2019); JD House (São Sebastião, 2020); and R House (São Paulo, 2020). More recently, he has completed the Teená Building (Porto Alegre, 2024); and the Henrique Monteiro Square + Pulso Hotel (São Paulo, 2024) all in Brazil unless stated otherwise.
www.arthurcasas.com

BERGENDY COOKE
was born in Christchurch, New Zealand, in 1969. She studied architecture at Auckland University (1990–94) and worked in the office of Cook Hitchcock Sarginson in New Zealand (1995–97), before going to London and joining first Zaha Hadid Architects (1999–2000) and then Adjaye Associates (2002–03). Cooke worked for Peter Marino Associates (New York, 2003–05) and then lived in Barcelona (2005–06) before founding her firm BC+A in New Zealand in 2007. Since 2013, she has also been based in Barcelona. Aside from Black Quail (Central Otago, 2020; published here), she has completed the RG House renovation (Wellington, 2011); her own house the JR House (2013); Casa Familia (Queenstown, 2015), all in New Zealand; and the boutique hotel Maison Brummell Majorelle in Marrakesh (Morocco, 2023).
www.bergendycooke.com

DE KORT VAN SCHAIK
was founded in Rotterdam in 2011 by ROBERT-JAN DE KORT (born in Delft, 1979) and SANDER VAN SCHAIK (born in Horst, 1978). Both De Kort and Van Schaik received their M.Arch degrees from the TU Delft (2006). Van Schaik worked in London and Rotterdam for Skidmore, Owings & Merrill (SOM, 2008–09) and at De Zwarte Hond (2010) prior to the creation of their own firm. Their completed projects include the Moorsel Community Center (Moorsel, Belgium, 2016); Balderdorp Social Housing (Berlaar, Belgium, 2020); the House on the Raboes (Eemnes, the Netherlands, 2020; published here); and Nefkens Park (transformation of a 1960s office building into an apartment structure, Amersfoort, the Netherlands, 2020).
www.dekortvanschaik.nl

DECA ARCHITECTURE
ALEXANDROS VAITSOS was born in Lima, Peru, in 1971. He received a B.A. degree from Harvard College (1993) and an M.Arch from the University of California (Berkeley). CARLOS LOPERENA was born in Mexico City in 1970. He received a B.F.A. in Industrial Design from the University of Kansas and an M.Arch from the University of California (Berkeley). They express an interest in the "relational complexity of natural environments and material culture." Their work includes the Cliffhanger Residence (Antiparos Island, 2008); and the Aloni House (Antiparos Island, 2008). They completed The Slide (London, UK, 2018); Eurphoria (Mystras, 2019); Voronoi's Corrals (Milos, 2020); Floating Gardens (Athens, 2020); and the Hourglass Corral (Milos, Cyclades, 2020; published here), all in Greece unless otherwise indicated.
www.deca.gr

ELEMENTAL
ALEJANDRO ARAVENA graduated as an architect from the Universidad Católica de Chile (UC) in 1992. Born in 1967, he studied history and theory at the IUAV University in Venice (Italy, 1992–93). He created Alejandro Aravena Arquitectos in 1994. Between 2009 and 2015 he was a member of the Pritzker Prize Jury; in 2010 he was named International Fellow of RIBA; and in 2016 he won the Pritzker Prize. Since 2006 he has been Executive Director of ELEMENTAL whose "focus is the design and implementation of urban projects of social interest and public impact." ELEMENTAL is a group of architects that today includes Alejandro Aravena, GONZALO ARTEAGA (born in 1977), JUAN IGNACIO CERDA (born in 1980), DIEGO TORRES (born in 1979), and VÍCTOR ODDÓ (born in 1975). Aravena's architectural work includes the Mathematics (1999), Medical (2004), and Architecture (2004) Schools at UC (Santiago); Pirehueico Lake House (2004); the Siamese Towers at UC (Santiago, 2006); and facilities at St. Edward's University in Austin (Texas, USA, 2008). With ELEMENTAL he also designed the Quinta Monroy Social Housing (Iquique, 2004); Metropolitan Promenade and Children's Park for the Chilean Bicentennial (Santiago, 2012); the Anacleto Angelini Innovation Center at UC (Santiago, 2013); a building for Novartis in Shanghai (China, 2014); and the reconstruction of the city of Constitución (Chile, 2015). ELEMENTAL has completed the Ochoquebradas House (Los Vilos, 2018; published here); and the Energias de Portugal building (Lisbon, Portugal, 2022–24). The office has been involved in the design of the new headquarters for the Inter-American Development Bank (Buenos Aires, Argentina, 2018–); the Art Mill Museum and Cultural Neighborhood (Doha, Qatar, 2020–30), all in Chile unless stated otherwise.
www.elementalchile.cl

ENSAMBLE STUDIO
ANTÓN GARCÍA-ABRIL RUIZ was born in Madrid, Spain, in 1969. He graduated from the ETSA of Madrid in Architecture and Urbanism in 1995 and went on to receive a doctorate from the same institution in 2000. Another leader of the firm is DÉBORA MESA, born in 1981 in Madrid. Like García-Abril she received her master's degree from the ETSAM–UPM (2006). García-Abril worked in the office of Santiago Calatrava (1992) and in that of Alberto Campo Baeza (1990–94). He created his first firm in 1995, and his present one, Ensamble Studio, in 2000. The name of his firm is derived from a term used in architecture, "assemble," and the musical term "ensemble." His completed projects include Musical Studies Center (Santiago de Compostela, 2002); Concert Hall and Music School (Medina del Campo, 2003); Hemeroscopium House (Madrid, 2008); Liric Theater (Mexico City, Mexico, 2008); the Fleta Theater (Zaragoza, 2008); the Reader's House (Madrid, 2012); and the Cervantes Theater (Mexico City, Mexico, 2013). More recently, Ensamble has completed the Ensamble Fabrica (Madrid, 2019); the Tent (Costa da Morte, 2020); the Ca'n Terra (Menorca, 2020; published here); and the Missing Pieces sculpture at Cape Cod (Massachusetts, USA, 2023), all in Spain unless otherwise indicated.
www.ensamble.info

ESCOBEDO SOLIZ
The Escobedo Soliz studio was established in Mexico City in 2016 by National Autonomous University of Mexico (UNAM) classmates PAVEL ESCOBEDO (born in Tepic, 1988) and ANDRES SOLIZ (born in Mexico City, 1990). They were both named design studio professors at the UNAM Faculty of Architecture in 2020. According to the partners, their practice "is based on a continuous exploration of materials, structures and construction systems to find particular solutions for each situation." Escobedo Soliz was the winner of MoMA PS1's Young Architects Program in 2016, where they created an installation in Long Island City. The firm exhibited its work at the Mexican Pavilion at the 2018 Venice Architecture Biennale. They were also selected for a 2020 Emerging Voices Award (Architectural League of New York), and the Fritz Hoeger Preis in 2020. Aside from the Nakasone House (Mexico City, 2019; published here), they have completed a small Police Pavilion (Mexico City, 2017); the José María Morelos School (in collaboration with Gutierrez Architects, Santa Isabel Cholula, 2018); and the Miguel Negrete School (also in collaboration with Gutierrez Architects, San Martín Tlamapa, 2018).
www.escobedosoliz.net

STACEY FARRELL
was born in Auckland in 1972. She earned her B.Arch degree from the University of Auckland (1995). Farrell worked with Koia Architects (Auckland and Queenstown, 2004–05); Weber Consulting (Queenstown, 2008–09); 2 Architecture Studio (Arrowtown, 2005–07), and founded her own

practice in Queenstown in 2011, originally under the name Queenstown Architect. She also had a firm for outdoor furniture called Space Limited (2003–11). Her projects include Reflections (Queenstown, 2017); The Coast House (Omaui, 2018; published here); Home for a Winemaker (Arrowtown, 2019); Tilt Shift (Queenstown, 2020); and The Black House (Queenstown, 2011/2021), all in New Zealand.
www.staceyfarrell.com

FAULKNER ARCHITECTS
Formed by GREG FAULKNER in Berkeley, California, in 1998, Faulkner Architects has completed a number of homes in rural settings. Their work includes the Miner Road House (Orinda, California, 2015; published here); Burnt Cedar (Incline Village, Nevada, 2015); Creek House (Truckee, California, 2017); Big Barn (Glen Ellen, California, 2019); Tack Barn (Glen Ellen, California, 2019); and the Lookout House (Truckee, California, 2020), all in the United States.
www.faulknerarchitects.com

FORMAFATAL
Led by architect DAGMAR STEPANOVA, Formafatal is a mostly female team of architects, designers, and scenographers who focus on architecture, interior design, exhibition installation, and product design. Stepanova, born in 1975 in Dačice, Czech Republic, is a graduate in architecture from the Czech Technical University (Prague). She cofounded her previous office, Inconginto Studio, in Prague (2012–15) before creating Formafatal in 2015. Their work includes the Modry Zub Bistro (Prague, 2016); Burrito Loco fast-food restaurant (Prague, 2017); Atelier Villa (Bahia Ballena, Playa Hermosa, Costa Rica, 2019; published here); Coco Cabins (Bahia Ballena, Costa Rica, 2019); the Argentine restaurant Gran Fierro II (Prague, 2019); Autentista Wine Bar (Prague, 2019); and South Kiosk Bistro (Doha, Qatar, 2020).
www.formafatal.cz

FRANKIE PAPPAS
In a most unusual configuration, Frankie Pappas is an architectural collective that prefers to remain entirely anonymous. Simply put Frankie Pappas is not an individual but the entire office. They say that they are not a conventional architectural practice but instead a "freeform group," a "fictional persona" and a "collective pseudonym" that encourages people from various horizons such as engineers, artists, and managers to work with draftsmen and to put aside the kind of ego-driven practice so frequent in contemporary architecture. Their idea is nothing less than to "pave the way with yellow bricks and break out the pixie dust" to buildings and spaces that "people write songs about." Aside from the House of the Big Arch (Waterberg, South Africa, 2019; published here), they have also built the House of the Tall Chimneys in the same area, also in 2019. Their contact information (no street address, no phone) is also intentionally vague.
www.frankiepappas.com

WILL GAMBLE
attended Newcastle University (2008) and obtained his master's degree from Oxford Brookes University (Oxford, 2012). He completed his professional examinations at the AA (London, 2014). He worked for Farrells (London, 2012–14) and then with Francis Philips Architects (London, 2014–18). He founded Will Gamble Architects in London in 2018. His work includes The Parchment Works (Northamptonshire, 2018; published here); Burn House (Fulham, London, 2019); T-House (Clapham, London, 2020); Manor House (Clapham, London, 2021); and the House of Ash (Haringey, London, 2021), all in the UK.
www.willgamblearchitects.com

FRANK O. GEHRY
Born in Toronto, Canada, in 1929, FRANK GEHRY studied at the University of Southern California, Los Angeles (1949–51), and at Harvard (1956–57). Principal of Frank O. Gehry and Associates, Inc., Los Angeles, since 1962, he received the Pritzker Prize in 1989, the Praemium Imperiale in 1992, and the Prince of Asturias Prize in 2014. His early work in California included the redesign of his own house (Santa Monica, 1978), and the construction of a number of other houses, such as the Norton Residence (Venice, 1984) and the Schnabel Residence (Brentwood, 1989). His first foreign projects included Festival Disney (Marne-la-Vallée, France, 1992) and the Guggenheim Bilbao (Spain, 1997). Other work includes the DG Bank Headquarters (Berlin, 2001); the Fisher Center for the Performing Arts at Bard College (Annandale-on-Hudson, New York, 2003); the Walt Disney Concert Hall (Los Angeles, California, 2003); MARTa Herford (Germany, 2005); and the Hotel at the Marques de Riscal winery (Elciego, Spain, 2007). He has also completed the Louis Vuitton Foundation (Paris, 2014); the Santa Monica

House (California, 2017, published here); Luma Foundation Parc des Ateliers (Arles, France, 2021); the expansion of the Philadelphia Museum of Art (Pennsylvania, 2021); and the Youth Orchestra Los Angeles (Inglewood, USA, 2021).
www.foga.com

DAVID HERTZ
born in 1960 in Los Angeles, received his B.Arch degree from the Southern California Institute of Architecture (SCI-Arc) in 1983. He worked as an apprentice in the offices of John Lautner and Frank Gehry before founding his own firm in 1984. He was the founder and president of S.E.A. the Studio of Environmental Architecture (formerly Syndesis Inc.). His work includes the Panel House, a single-family residence made of prefabricated refrigeration panels (Venice, 2006); his own office, installed in a renovated market and restaurant using "cutting-edge green building technology" (Santa Monica, California, 2007, LEED Platinum); the 747 Wing House (Malibu, California, 2013); El Medio House (Pacific Palisades, 2014); Felix Restaurant (Venice, 2016); NRDC (Santa Monica, 2020); and the Sail House (Bequia, Saint Vincent and the Grenadines, 1999/2021; published here), all in California, USA, unless otherwise indicated.
www.davidhertzfaia.com

ROBERT HUTCHISON ARCHITECTURE & JSA ARQUITECTURA
ROBERT HUTCHINSON was born in North Carolina in 1966. He obtained undergraduate degrees in Civil and Architectural Engineering from Drexel University (1990), and an M.Arch degree from the University of Washington (1996). From 2001 to 2013 he was a partner in Seattle-based Hutchison & Maul Architecture. In 2013 he created his own firm in Seattle. Recently completed projects include Courtyard House on a River (Greenwater, Washington, 2015); Cantilever House (Seattle, Washington, 2016); Courtyard DADU (Seattle, Washington, 2019); the Rain Harvest Home (with JSa Arquitectura, Temascaltepec, Mexico, 2019; published here); and Telescope Addition (Seattle, Washington, 2024), all in the USA unless otherwise indicated. JAVIER SÁNCHEZ, born in 1969 in Mexico City, obtained an undergraduate degree in architecture from the UNAM of Mexico (1996), and a master's degree in real estate development from Columbia University (New York, 1998). From 1996 to 2006 he was a partner in Mexico City-based Higuera + Sánchez. In 2006 he established JSa. Recently completed projects include The Cape Hotel (Cabo San Lucas, 2015); Hotel Carlota (Mexico City, 2018); Museo Juan Soriano (Cuernavaca, 2018); Pedre Housing (Mexico City, 2023); and numerous housing projects in Mexico City, including Juan de la Barrera (2021), all in Mexico unless indicated otherwise.
www.robhutcharch.com
www.jsa.com.mx

PAULO AND BERNARDO JACOBSEN
PAULO JACOBSEN was born in 1954 in Rio and studied photography in London before graduating from the Bennett Methodist Institute (1979). He was a founding partner of Bernardes + Jacobsen (1980). His son, BERNARDO JACOBSEN, was born in 1980 and joined the firm in 2007 after graduating from the Federal University of Rio de Janeiro and working in the offices of Christian de Portzamparc and Shigeru Ban. Bernardes and Jacobsen split their offices in 2011, and Jacobsen Arquitetura has since completed MAR—Art Museum of Rio (with Bernardes Arquitetura, Rio de Janeiro, 2013); the SW House (Porto Feliz, São Paulo, 2013); Kalabo Business Center (Fiji, 2015); the OS House (São Paulo, 2016); RMA House (Portugal, 2016); AB House (Rio de Janeiro, 2016); GAF House (São Paulo, 2016); luxury resorts in the Caribbean (2016), and Indonesia (2017); the Marine Museum (Rio de Janeiro, 2017); ANM House (Melbourne, Australia, 2019); a beach enclave hotel and villas (Turks and Caicos, 2020); the RN House (Minas Gerais, 2020; published here); and the DRP Residency (Porto Feliz, 2024), all in Brazil unless indicated otherwise.
www.jacobsenarquitetura.com

JK-AR
JAE KYUNG KIM was born in 1977. He received a B.Sc. in Architectural Engineering from Hangyang University (South Korea, 2004) and an M.Arch degree from MIT (Cambridge, MA, 2012). JK-AR was founded in 2017 by Jae K. Kim as "a platform for design experiments." The office has focused on wood and concrete. Projects such as The House of Three Trees (Sangju, Gyeongsangbuk-do, 2018; published here) are "dedicated to studies recreating traditional East Asian timber-frame buildings with contemporary engineered woods and digital solutions." Additionally, the office investigates concrete buildings "through advanced manufacturing strategies such as 3D printers," with their project called "Solid Nature." He has

also completed a public artwork called *Semiotic Morphology* (Seoul, 2016); and a building for the Faculty of Architecture at Hanyang University (Seoul, 2017). In 2021 he completed the Hantan Observatory (Cheolwon-gun, Gyeonggi-do); in 2022 the Pavilion of Floating Lights (Jinju), all in South Korea.
www.jk-ar.com

ALBERTO KALACH
was born in 1960 in Mexico City. He studied at the Universidad Iberoamericana (Mexico City) and at Cornell (Ithaca, NY). He founded the firm Taller de Arquitectura X in 1981 and directs his firm to the present day. His work includes Casa Romany (Los Angeles, California, 2004); the Reforma 27 Tower (Mexico City, 2010); the Hacienda Tzalancab (Yucatan, 2012; published here); the José Vasconcelos Library (Mexico City, 2014); the T41 Tower (Mexico City, 2014); the Casitas by the Sea (Puerto Escondido, Oaxaca, 2015); and Escondido (Punta Pájaros, Oaxaca, 2017) all in Mexico.
www.kalach.com

PALINDA KANNANGARA
Sri Lankan architect PALINDA KANNANGARA has a background in mathematics and architecture. He was born in 1970 in the suburbs of Colombo, in Kolonnawa. He graduated with a B.Sc. in Physical Sciences (1996) with a specialization in Mathematics. He joined the study course conducted by the Sri Lanka Institute of Architects in 1994. As a student he trained under Sri Lankan Modernist architect Anura Rantavibhushana, who worked with Geoffrey Bawa for 16 years. Palinda established his own office in 2005, now located in Rajagiriya. His recent work includes an Artist's Retreat (Pittugala, 2017); Frame Holiday Structure (Imaduwa, 2018; published here); Spinal House (Mount Lavinia, 2018); Striated House (Rajagiriya, 2019); Wellness Retreat (Habarana, 2020); and The Courtyard At Bangalore (2023), all in Sri Lanka.
www.palindakannangara.com

KRADS
is an architectural studio based in Denmark and Iceland, led by architects KRISTJÁN EGGERTSSON and KRISTJÁN ÖRN KJARTANSSON. Eggertsson, born in 1973, graduated from the Aarhus School of Architecture in 2003. He worked at 3XN (Denmark, 2003–05), Aart Architects (Denmark, 2005–06), and was a founding Partner of KRADS (2006). Born in 1976, Kjartansson also received his degree in Architecture at Aarhus in 2003. He worked at SHL (Denmark, 2004–06), before cofounding KRADS. Their projects include the Langitangi Country House (Kidjaberg, 2011); Stodin Roadside Stop (Borgarnes, 2012); Showroom & Service Center (Herning, Denmark, 2014); Álalind 2 apartment building (Kópavogur, 2017); Costco Gas Station (Garðabær, 2017); Dvergur mixed-use development (Hafnafjordur, 2022); and the Holiday Home at Lake Thingvallavatn (2020; published here), all in Iceland unless indicated.
www.krads.is

MACKAY-LYONS SWEETAPPLE
BRIAN MACKAY-LYONS was born in Acadia, Nova Scotia. He received his B.Arch from the Technical University of Nova Scotia in 1978, and his Master's in architecture and urban design at UCLA (Los Angeles). After studying in China, Japan, California and Italy, working with Charles Moore, Barton Myers, and Giancarlo De Carlo, Brian returned to Nova Scotia in 1983. In 1985 he founded the firm Brian MacKay-Lyons Architecture Urban Design in Halifax. Twenty years later, it became a partnership with TALBOT SWEETAPPLE under the name MacKay-Lyons Sweetapple Architects Ltd. Talbot Sweetapple was born in St. John's, Newfoundland. He graduated with an M.Arch from Dalhousie University. He worked with Shin Takamatsu in Berlin and with KPMB in Toronto prior to the formation of MacKay-Lyons Sweetapple. Their work includes the Canadian Chancery and Official Residence (with RDHA, Dhaka, Bangladesh, India, 2005); numerous smaller structures and houses, such as the Sunset Rock House (Nova Scotia, 2011; published here); Bigwin Island Cabins (Bigwin Island, Ontario, 2018); and the Smith Residence (Upper Kingsburg, Nova Scotia, ongoing); the Shobac Campus and Ghost Architectural Laboratory (Upper Kingsburg, Nova Scotia, 2019); Horizon, Summit Powder Mountain (Eden, Utah, USA, 2019); and Queen's Marque (Halifax, Nova Scotia, 2023), all in Canada unless otherwise indicated.
www.mlsarchitects.ca

GURJIT MATHAROO
was born in Ajmer, Rajasthan, in 1966. He received his diploma in architecture (equivalent to a B.Arch.) at the Center for Environmental Planning and Technology (CEPT, Ahmedabad, 1989). He then worked for one year in the Italian-speaking Ticino region of Switzerland, first in the office of Michele

Amaboldi, an associate of Luigi Snozzi (Locarno, 1989–90), and then with Giorgio Guschetti (Airolo, 1990–91). In 1991, Matharoo established his own firm, Matharoo Associates, in Ahmedabad, and began teaching at the CEPT. Gurjit Matharoo's office deals not only with architecture, but also with structural design, interiors, product design, and landscaping. Their projects include Ashwini-kumar Crematorium (Surat, Gujarat, 2000); DRM Office (Ahmedabad, Gujarat, 2006), Religious Guest House (Pavapuri, Rajasthan, 2009); 300 Bedded ESIC Hospital (Ahmedabad, Gujarat, 2010); Fountainhead School (Surat, Gujarat, 2012); Pool (his own office, Ahmedabad, Gujarat, 2014); Urban Stitch (Delhi, 2015); a single family dwelling (Sura, Gujarat, 2018); Temple and Pilgrim Guesthouse (Ajmer, Rajasthan, 2018); and a number of houses including 150 Steps Up to the Sea (Surat, Gujarat, 2020; published here), all in India.
www.matharooassociates.com

MCFARLANE BIGGAR

MICHELLE BIGGAR is a founding Principal of the firm with which she has been working since 1997. She graduated from the Queensland University of Technology with a B.A. in Built Environment degree and has a background in interior design. STEVE MCFARLANE has practiced in Toronto, Halifax, and Vancouver, and received his M.Arch degree from the Technical University of Nova Scotia. Other firm principals are NICK FOSTER, originally from the UK and a graduate of the Bartlett School of Architecture, ROB GRANT, who has degrees in computer science and fine arts (University of Victoria, BC, Canada), and an M.Arch (University of British Columbia). Their work includes the Fort McMurray International Airport (Alberta, 2014); the Bowen Island House (Bowen Island, 2019; published here); and Victoria Airport Holdroom Expansion (Victoria, 2020). Upcoming work includes the Douglas Bay Cabins (Gambier Island, 2022); and 4533 West 2nd House (Vancouver, 2023), all in British Columbia, Canada, unless indicated otherwise.
www.officemb.ca

MCLEOD BOVELL

MATT MCLEOD and LISA BOVELL are the founders and principals of their firm, created in Vancouver in 2008. McLeod was born in 1972 in Chiliwack (BC) and received both his B.Sc. and M.Arch degrees from the University of British Columbia (1994 and 2000). Lisa Bovell, born in 1972 in Kingston, Jamaica, received a B.A. and an M.Arch also from the University of British Columbia in 1994 and 2000. Their built work includes the Four & Four House (2019); Blackcliff House (2019; published here); and the Eaves House (2021), all in West Vancouver. They have three more houses in construction in West Vancouver—the Switchback House and Westbay House, as well as the Treetop House (Vancouver), all in British Columbia, Canada.
www.officemb.ca

MAURICIO CEBALLOS X ARCHITECTS

MAURICIO CEBALLOS PRESSLER was born in 1971 and received his Architecture degree from the University Iberoamericana (Mexico City, 1997). From 2000 to 2020, he was the CEO of Fernando Romero Enterprise (FR-EE). He was a co-designer of the Museo Soumaya (Mexico City, 2011), G20 Convention Center (Los Cabos, Mexico, 2012), and the New Airport for Mexico City (NAIM, cancelled), for which FR-EE was the local architect working with Foster + Partners. He created Mauricio Ceballos x Architects in 2020. Aside from the Mague House (Malinalco, 2020; published here), other work of the firm includes offices for French firm Kering (Mexico City, 2020); Casa Bosques (Mexico City, 2021); Casa Santa Maria (Nayarit, 2021); and Casa Jesús y Ulrike (Malinalco, 2024), all in Mexico.
www.mcxa.group

MIA DESIGN STUDIO

The MIA Design Studio, created in 2003, is involved in architecture, landscape, interior design, and master planning. The firm's cofounder and lead architect NGUYEN HOANG MANH was born in 1970. He graduated from the Ho Chi Minh City University of Architecture (1997) and obtained his master's degree from the Catholic University (Leuven, Belgium, 2001). He says that his goal is to build "a separate identity for Vietnamese architecture of the 21st century in the time of integration with the world." The work of the firm includes the Naman Retreat Pure Spa (Da Nang, 2015); Naman Beachfront Villa and Naman Garden Villa (Da Nang, 2015); their own offices MIA Design Studio Office and The Straw in Ho Chi Minh City (2020); Thanh Long Bay Gallery (Ham Thuan Nam, Binh Thuan, 2020); Villa Tan Dinh, District 3 (Ho Chi Minh City, 2020; published here); and the Straw Studio (Thu Duc, 2021), all in Vietnam.
www.miadesignstudio.com

MILLER HULL
was founded in 1977 by DAVID MILLER and ROBERT HULL (1945–2014), who both studied architecture at Washington State University (Pullman, WA, 1968) and also shared a background in the Peace Corps. Today, aside from the surviving cofounder David Miller, the firm has six other partners and ten principals. Their work includes the Point Roberts Land Point of Entry (Point Roberts, WA, 1997); and the Bureau of Environmental Sciences Water Pollution Control Laboratory (Portland, OR, 1997). More recently they completed the Bullit Center (Seattle, 2013, first certified commercial Living Building, billed as the "greenest commercial building in the world"); SEATAC International Arrivals Terminal (with SOM, Seattle, 2019); the Loom House (Bainbridge Island, Washington, 2019; published here); the Kendeda Building at Georgia Tech (Atlanta, Georgia, 2020); and Waterfront Park in Seattle (with Field Operations, Washington, 2024), all in the USA. Their Emission Zero scheme launched in 2021 aims to eliminate greenhouse gases in the projects designed by the firm, adding to a long history of environmental concern and respect for equitability and equality.
www.millerhull.com

MWWORKS
was created in 2007 by STEVE MONGILLO and ERIC WALTER. Mongillo, born in 1969, received his B.Arch degree from the University of Oregon (1993). Walter received his B.A. degree from the University of Washington (1995), and a master's degree from MIT (Cambridge, MA, 1999). The two met while working in the Seattle office of Bohlin Cywinski Jackson. Their Case Inlet Retreat (Lakebay, 2016) won a 2016 National AIA Honor Award, while the firm won the 2016 Northwest and Pacific Region Emerging Firm Award from the American Institute of Architects (AIA). Their Whidbey Farm Retreat (Whidbey Island, 2019; published here) won an AIA National 2020 Housing Award. Other work includes the Helen Street House (Seattle, 2017); Ocean Drive (Miami, 2019); and the Courtyard Residence (Seattle, 2019), all in Washington, USA, unless indicated otherwise.
www.mwworks.com

NEW MATERIAL RESEARCH LABORATORY (SHINSOKEN)
HIROSHI SUGIMOTO was born in Tokyo in 1948, attended Saint Paul's University in Tokyo (1966–70), and then studied photography at the Art Center College of Design in Los Angeles receiving a B.F.A. in 1972. He moved to New York in 1974. A number of photographic series have characterized his work thus far: his pictures taken of *Dioramas* and *Wax Museums* (since 1976 and 1994); his Theaters (since 1976); the *Seascapes* (since 1980); his images of *Sanjusangendo, Hall of Thirty-Three Bays* (sculptures of the Buddhist temple Sanjusangendo, 1995); and *Architecture* (since 1997). His large, usually black-and-white photos have been presented in numerous art galleries, such as Marian Goodman Gallery, New York; Fraenkel Gallery, San Francisco; Gallery Koyanagi, Tokyo, and in one-man exhibitions in numerous major museums. Hiroshi Sugimoto has shown a consistent interest in architecture, first in his photography, but also in actual works of architecture such as his Go'o Shrine (Naoshima, 2002); Colors of Shadow (Shirogane Apartment, Tokyo, 2006); Izu Photo Museum (Mishima, Shizuoka, 2009); Glass Teahouse Mondrian (Venice, Italy, 2014); Odawara Art Foundation: Enoura Observatory (Enoura, Odawara, Kanagawa, 2017); and the Hirshhorn Museum Lobby (Washington, D.C., 2018). Sugimoto won the 2009 Praemium Imperiale Award. TOMOYUKI SAKAKIDA was born in Shiga Prefecture in 1976. He received his M.Arch degree from the Kyoto Institute of Technology in 2001 and worked for Nihon Sekkei Inc. before establishing his own practice, Tomoyuki Sakakida Architect and Associates Co., Ltd., in 2003. In parallel with running the practice, he worked for Waro Kishi + K. Associates/EX from 2003 to 2006. In 2008 Sakakida cofounded the New Material Research Laboratory (Shinsoken) with Sugimoto. He is currently teaching at Kyoto University of the Arts. Sugimoto worked with Sakakida on the project published here in the context of their Tokyo company Shinsoken.
www.shinsoken.jp/en

NO ARCHITECTURE
ANDREW HEID is the founding principal of NO Architecture (NOA). Born in Eugene, Oregon in 1980, he received a B.A. degree from Yale University (2002), before working in the offices of David Adjaye in London and Robert A. M. Stern in New York (2002–03). He received his M.Arch degree from Princeton University in 2006. From 2005 to 2008, he worked with REX and OMA in New York and Rotterdam, and then founded NO Architecture in New York in 2009. NOA has partic

pated in numerous international competitions in Germany, Switzerland, Taiwan, and Korea. Work of the office includes the Courtyard House (Aurora, Oregon, 2013); the Shed (Aurora, Oregon, 2019); Cloud Forest Qianhai New City Center (Shenzhen, China, 2019); the Flower House (Egremont, Massachusetts, 2020; published here); and the Urban Tree House (New York, 2020), all in the USA unless otherwise indicated.
www.noarchitecture.com

OLSON KUNDIG
JIM OLSON is the founding partner and owner of Olson Kundig. His work includes the Cabin at Longbranch (Longbranch, Washington, originally built in 1959 and expanded in 2014); An American Place (Seattle, Washington, 2003); The Lightcatcher at the Whatcom Museum (Bellingham, Washington, 2009); the JW Marriott Los Cabos Beach Resort (San José del Cabo, Mexico, 2016); and the Tofino Beach House (Tofino, British Columbia, Canada, 2016; published here); Water Cabin (Seattle, Washington, 2020); and the Bob Dylan Center(Tulsa, Oklahoma, 2022, both in the United States). TOM KUNDIG received his B.A. in environmental design (1977) and his M.Arch (1981) degrees from the University of Washington. He was a principal of Jochman/Kundig (1983–84), before becoming a principal of Olson Kundig Architects (1986).
www.olsonkundig.com

PATALANO ARQUITETURA AND MAREINES ARQUITETURA
RAFAEL PATALANO is the founder of Patalano Arquitetura. He graduated from the Faculty of Architecture and Urbanism and the Federal University of Rio de Janeiro (FAU UFRJ, 1997) and worked from 2001 to 2016 with Ivo Mareines (Mareines+Patalano Arquitetura). Their last collaboration was, in fact, for the Punta Cana House (Punta Cana, Dominican Republic, 2018; published here). IVO MAREINES graduated in architecture and urbanism in São Paulo in the early 1980s and added a master's in philosophy to his education in 1995 in Rio de Janeiro. In 2017, MATTHIEU VAN BENEDEN, who received his degree in architecture and urbanism in Belgium in 2011, became a partner of Mareines. Their work together includes the Leaf House (Angra dos Reis, 2009); the Mopi Primary School (Rio de Janeiro, 2009/2014); and the Wave House (Rio de Janeiro, 2016). Patalano has announced a new building for the Mopi School (2022), all in Brazil unless indicated otherwise.
www.patalanoarq.com.br
www.mareinesarquitetura.com.br

PABLO SARIC + WINCKLER ARQUITECTOS
PABLO SARIC, born in Santiago in 1971, graduated from the Universidad Central de Chile (1997), obtained an M.Arch and a doctorate from the Universitat Politècnica de Cataluña (UPC, Barcelona; 1998/2006), and a second master's in advanced architectural design from Columbia University (New York, 1999). He is currently director of the School of Design of the Universidad Adolfo Ibañez. CRISTIAN WINCKLER, born in Osorno, Chile, in 1971, received his architecture degree from the Universidad Central de Chile (1997) and an M.Arch from the UPC (1998). Pablo Saric and Cristian Winckler have collaborated on several projects, including the Sala Fajnzylber (CEPAL, Santiago, 2012); Casa Lucernas (San Bernardo, 2012); Las Quemas (Osorno, 2016); and the SS House (Huentelauquen, 2020; published here), all in Chile.
www.pablosaric.com
www.waa.cl

SAUNDERS ARCHITECTURE
TODD SAUNDERS was born in 1969 in Gander, Newfoundland (Canada). He obtained a B.A. in environmental planning from the Nova Scotia College of Art and Design (1988–92) and his M.Arch degree from McGill University (Montreal, Canada, 1993–95). He worked in Austria, Germany, Russia, and Norway (since 1996) before moving to Norway and establishing Saunders Architecture in Bergen in 1998. He is a guest professor at Cornell University and teaches part-time at the Bergen School of Architecture. His work includes the Aurland Lookout (with Tommie Wilhelmsen, Aurland, 2006); Villa Storingavika (Bergen, 2007); Villa G (Hjellestad, Bergen, 2009); Sogn og Fjordane Summer Cabin (Rysjedalsvika, 2010); Solberg Tower and Park (Sarpsborg, Østfold, 2010); and Villa S (Bergen, 2014). He realized the Fogo Island Studios (Newfoundland, 2011), and has also completed the Fogo Island Inn (2013) and the Fogo Island Shed (2018) in the same location. More recent work includes the Illusuak Cultural Center (Nain, Labrador, 2018); Villa Grieg (Bergen, 2018; published here); Villa Austevol (Austevol, 2020); and the Fedje Hotel (Fedje, in progress), all in Norway or Canada.
www.saunders.no

FRAN SILVESTRE ARQUITECTOS
was founded in Valencia by the architect FRAN SILVESTRE in 2005. Born in 1976, Silvestre graduated from the ETSA of Valencia in 2001. He then studied urban planning at the Eindhoven Technical University before working in the studio of Álvaro Siza in Porto. The architect acknowledges the influence of Siza and of the sculptor Andreu Alfaro. Fran Silvestre has built the Atrium House (Godella, Valencia, 2009); the House on the Castle Mountainside (Ayora, Valencia, 2010); Cliff House (Calpe, Alicante, 2012); and Blanc L'Antic Colonial Showroom (Villareal, 2013). More recently, he has completed the Hofmann House (Valencia, 2018); Penthouse in Costa Blanca (Alicante, 2019); Pati Blau House (Valencia, 2020); House of Silence (Cañada, 2020); the House of Sand (Valencia, 2020; published here); and the Sabater House (Alicante, 2023), all in Spain.
www.fransilvestrearquitectos.com

GEORGE SINAS
was born in Ottawa, Canada, in 1971. He received his degree as an architect from the Department of Architecture at Aristotle University (Thesalonica, 1996) and a master's from SCI-Arc (Los Angeles, 2001). He then founded Sinas Architects in 2002. His work includes the Margaritas House (Serfios, 2005); Eagle's Nest (www.waa.cl Serfios, 2010); White Spirit (Serfioos, 2018); and Xerolithi (Serfios, 2018; published here), all in Greece. As can be seen in the case of Xerolithi, he has willfully adapted his knowledge of modern architecture to the topography of Greece, and, in particular, the Cycladic island of Serfios.
www.sinasarchitects.gr

SO–IL
was founded in 2008 by Florian Idenburg and Jing Liu. FLORIAN IDENBURG was born in 1975 in Heemstede, the Netherlands. He received an M.Sc. degree in architectural engineering from the Technical University of Delft (1999), and worked with SANAA in Tokyo from 2000 to 2007. JING LIU was born in 1980 in Nanjing, China. She received her M.Arch II degree from Tulane University (2004) and worked from 2004 to 2007 with KPF in New York. The work of SO–IL includes the "Pole Dance" installation (MoMAPS1, New York, 2010); "Tri-Colonnade" (Shenzhen, China, 2011); Kukje Gallery K3 (Seoul, South Korea, 2012); Frieze Art Fair (New York, 2012); Logan offices (New York, 2012); "Passage" installation for the inaugural Chicago Architecture Biennial (Illinois, 2015); Tina Kim Gallery (New York, 2015); "Blueprint" installation at the Storefront for Art and Architecture (New York, 2015); the Manetti Shrem Museum of Art at the University of California (Davis, California, 2016); MINI LIVING—Breathe (Salone del Mobile, Milan, Italy, 2017); Duravcevic-Ben Ari House (Long Island, New York, 2019; published here); K11 Art Center (Hong Kong, PRC, 2021); Las Americas Social Housing (Léon, Mexico, 2021); Aman (Brooklyn, NY, 2021); and Site Verrier (Meisenthal, France, 2021); all in the USA unless otherwise indicated.
www.so-il.org

TETRO ARQUITETURA
was created in 2008 by Carlos Maia, Débora Mendes and Igor Macedo. CARLOS MAIA, born in 1981, earned his degree in architecture and urbanism from the Federal University of Minas Gerais (UFMG, Belo Horizonte, 2001–05). He also earned an M.B.A. degree from IBMEC (Belo Horizonte, 2014–15). DÉBORA MENDES, born in 1982, received the same architecture and urbanism degree from UFMG, also in 2005. She is the managing partner of the firm. IGOR MACEDO, born in 1981, also obtained his architecture and urbanism degree from UFMG in 2005, and went on to do postgraduate studies in interdisciplinarity (University of Itauna, UIT, 2010) and in project management (Getulio Vargas Foundation, FGV, Belo Horizonte, 2014). Aside from the Inclined Slab House (Nova Lima, 2016; published here), their work includes the Serra do Rola Moça Natural Park Visitors Center (Nova Lima, 2018); Serra do Cipo House (Santana do Riacho, 2018); Juris Headquarters (Belo Horizonte, 2019); Açucena House (Nova Lima, 2021); and a number of other private houses that are in various phases of approval or construction, all in Brazil.
Web: www.tetro.com.br

SANTIAGO VALDIVIESO & STEFANO ROLLA
Born in Santiago in 1986, SANTIAGO VALDIVIESO studied architecture at the Pontificia Universidad Católica de Chile (UC), earning his degree in 201[illegible] with the highest distinction awarded by the school. In 2018 he obtained a Master's in Landscape Architecture degree at the Universitat Politècnica de Catalunya (UPC, Barcelona, Spain). He has been running his own office in Santiago since 2014. Recently, he built Casa ALS (Chile, 2025). STEFANO ROLLA was born in La Spezia, Italy, i[illegible]

1976. He obtained his degree as an architect from Milan Polytechnic (2004) and began developing projects in Chile in 2006. Together, they worked on the Engawa House published here (Punta Pite, Zapallar, Chile, 2019).
www.santiagovaldivieso.com
www.stefanorolla.com

VO TRONG NGHIA,
the founding Partner of VTN, was born in Quang Binh Province, Vietnam, in 1976. He received a B.Arch degree from the Nagoya Institute of Technology (Japan, 2002), followed by a master's in civil engineering from the University of Tokyo (2004). The company's major works are the Vietnam Pavilion for Shanghai Expo (China, 2010); Stacking Green (Ho Chi Minh City, 2011); Binh Duong School (Binh Duong, 2011); the Stone House (Quang Ninh, 2012); Dailai Conference Hall (Vinh Phuc, 2012); Low-Cost House (Dong Nai, 2012); the House for Trees (Ho Chi Minh City, 2013); the FPT University Hanoi Administration Center (Hanoi, 2014); and the Vietnam Pavilion for the Milan Expo (Italy, 2015). More recent work includes the Bat Trang House (Bat Trang, Hanoi, 2018; published here); the Ha House (Ho Chi Minh City, 2019); the Breathing House (Ho Chi Minh City, 2019); the Castaway Island Resort (Lan Ha Gulf, Cat Ba, Hai Phong, 2019); the Grand World Reception House (Phu Quoc, 2021); and the Urban Farming Office (Ho Chi Minh City, 2022), all in Vietnam unless otherwise indicated.
www.vtnarchitects.net

SUZUKO YAMADA
was born in 1984 in Tokyo. She studied at the Department of Environmental Design, University of California (Berkeley, 2005–06), and continued with environmental studies at Keio University (Tokyo, 2007). She worked from 2007 to 2011 in the office of Sou Fujimoto (Tokyo), before founding her own firm, Suzuko Yamada Architects, in 2011. Her work includes the Air Wall Gallery (Nasu, 2011); "Pillar House" (Tokyo, 2012); Suda Port, Setouchi Triennale (Naoshima, 2013); the Waseda House (Tokyo, 2019); N House (Tokyo, 2019); and Daita2019 (Tokyo, 2019; published here), all in Japan.
www.suzukoyamada.com

YOUNG PROJECTS
Born in Los Angeles in 1975, BRYAN YOUNG received a B.A. in architecture from the University of California (Berkeley, 1997) and an M.Arch degree from the Harvard GSD (2003) before working for Allied Works Architecture (New York, 2005–10) and founding his own firm, Young Projects, in Brooklyn in 2010. His work includes the Hamptons Bungalow (Westhampton, New York, 2016); Wythe Corner House (Brooklyn, 2016); Pulled Plaster Loft (Tribeca, New York, 2016); Casa Las Olas Retreat (Dominican Republic, 2019); the Glitch House (Playa Grande, Dominican Republic, 2019); and the Six Square House (Bridgehampton, New York, 2020; published here).
www.young-projects.com

CAZÚ ZEGERS
Born in 1958, CAZÚ ZEGERS graduated in architecture from the Universidad Católica de Valparaíso (Chile, 1984). Since 1990 she has worked on architectural projects, lamp design and furniture, urban planning, and cultural and territorial management. Her industrial design, interior architecture, architecture, residential buildings, and at least 33 single-family homes "highlight the search for new architectural forms generated through the relationship between poetry and architecture." She has concentrated on low technology or Low Tech. Her work includes Casa Granero (Pucon, 2004); Casa Soplo (Lo Barnechea, Santiago, 2011); Hotel Tierra Patagonia (Torres del Paine, 2011), for which she received a 2013 Wallpaper Design Award; and Casa Esmeralda (Lo Barnechea, Santiago, 2013). More recently she completed Casa K (Santiago, 2015); Casa Ye (Valdivia, Región de los Rios, 2018); and Casa LLU (Maihue Lake, XIV Región, 2018; published here); and Casa PYR (Lake Panguipulli, 2023), all in Chile.
www.cazuzegers.cl

CARLOS ZWICK
was born in Sonthofen/Allgäu, Germany in 1951. He studied and worked as a carpenter between 1968 and 1972. He then received his diploma as an architect from the University of Applied Sciences (Munich, 1974–78), obtaining a second degree from the Technical University of Berlin (1979–83). He created his own office in Berlin in 1989. Since that time, he has completed numerous houses and larger buildings in Germany, including the Illerbogen Housing complex on the site of a former paper factory in Hegge near Kempten (2017–); and the House by the Lake (Potsdam, 2020; published here).
www.carlos-zwick.de

Photo Credits — 93–95 © Adrià Goula / **451–456, 457 top/right, bottom/left/right** © Alan Tansey / **425** © Augusto Custódio / **215–219** © Ben Ruffell / **263** © Benedikt Fahlbusch / **24, 39, 111–115, 227–231** © BoysPlayNice / **319–321** © Brenda Islas / **123, 124, 128, 129 bottom** © Bryce Duffy / **257, 259–262** © César Béjar / **45, 48, 49** © Chong Wong / **46, 47** © Chung E-Jay / **11, 13, 16, 19, 51–57, 81–87, 131–136, 193–199, 391–395, 431–437** © Cristobal Palma / **459, 461 bottom, 463** © Daniel Corvillón / **403–407** © Diego Opazo / **333–335** © Diego Padilla Magallanes / **307–311** © Dinesh Mehta / **235 right, 236–237** © Dook for Visi / **38, 59–63** © Ed Reeve / **15, 35, 317–323, 325–331** © Ema Peter / **205 bottom, 207** © Esemble Studio / **14, 105–109** © Ferdinand Graf Luckner / **153–157** © Fernando Alda Fotógrafo / **117–121, 165–171, 265–273** © Fernando Guerra / **233–234, 235 left** © Frankie Pappas / **27, 159–163** © Gilbert McCarragher / **301–305** © Greg Richardson Photography / **439–443** © Hiroyuki Oki / **397–401** © Ivar Kvaal/Hest Agentur AS / **2, 21, 23, 33, 42/43, 181–185, 201–204, 205 top, 206, 245–249, 281–285, 369–375, 417–423** © Iwan Baan / **457 top/left** © Jamie Gray / **76–78** © João Guimarães / **221–225** © Joe Fletcher Photography / **239–243** © Johan Dehlin / **426–429** © Jomar Bragança / **25, 465–471** © José Campos / **89–91** © José Hevia / **73, 74/75, 79** © Juan Rodriguez / **251–255, 347–351, 353–361** © Kevin Scott / **275–279** © Kyung Roh / **258** © Laia Rius Solá / **383–389** © Leonardo Finotti / **287–291** © Mahesh Mendis / **12, 97–103** © Manuel Sá / **460, 461 top, 462** © Marcos Zegers / **293–299** © Marino Thorlacius / **146 bottom, 147** © Mino Caggiula Architects / **377–381** © Nic Lehoux / **37, 339–345** © Oki Hiroyuki / **145, 146 top, 148–151** © Paolo Volonté / **65–71** © Photographix | Sebastian Zachariah / **8/9, 139–143, 209–213** © Sandra Pereznieto / **174–179** © Simon Devitt / **173** © Simon Wilson / **363–367** © Sugimoto Studio / **125, 126/127, 129 top** © Tamarack / **30/31, 187–191** © Yiorgis Yerolymbos / **309–415** © Yiorgos Kordakis / **22, 445–449** © Yurika Kono

Credits for Plans / Drawings / CAD Documents — 44 © Joeson&Partners Architects Ltd. / **50, 53, 56** © **GAAA / 58** © Adjaye Associates / **64** © Atelier Design N Domain / **72, 77** © Aires Mateus & Associados / **80, 84, 87** © Barclay & Crousse / **88** © Cecilia Rueda, Fabrizio Barozzi / **92** © María Díaz, Alberto Vegas / **96, 103** © Luciano Lerner Basso / **104, 109** © Andreas Wenning | baumraum / **110** © Atelier Line Bellovičová / **116, 120, 121** © Bernardes Arquitetura / **122, 125, 129** © Bohlin Cywinski Jackson / **130** © Antonio Polidura, Alex Brahm / **138** © Cadaval Estudio, collab. Clara Solà-Morales, Eduardo Alegre / **144, 151** © Mino Caggiula Architects / **152, 154** © Victor Cañas / 158 © Carmody Groarke / **164** © Arthur Casas / **172** © Bergendy Cooke / **180** © De Kort Van Schaik / **186, 191** © Deca Architecture / **192, 196, 199** © ELEMENTAL / **200, 207** © Ensamble Studio / **208** © Escobedo Soliz / **214** © Stacey Farrell / **220** © Faulkner Architects / **226** © Formafatal / **232, 236** © Frankie Pappas / **238** © Will Gamble Architects / **244** © Gehry Partners, LLP / **250, 255** © David Hertz Architect / **256, 260, 263** © Robert Hutchison Architecture & JSa Arquitectura / **264, 268, 272** © Jacobsen Arquitetura / **274** © JK-AR / **280, 284** © TAX, Susana Pantoja / **286** © Palinda Kannangara, Luka Alagiyawanna / **292, 297** © KRADS / **300, 304** © Brian MacKay-Lyons / **306, 319** © Matharoo Associates / **316, 323** © Office of McFarlane Biggar Architects + Designers / **324, 326** © McLeod Bovell / **332, 335** © Mauricio Ceballos x Architects / **338, 344** © MIA Design Studio / **346** © The Miller Hull Partnership, LLP / **352** © mwworks / **362** © New Material Research Laboratory / **368, 374** © NO ARCHITECTURE / **376, 381** © Olson Kundig / **382** © Mareines Arquitetura + Patalano Arquitetura / **390** © Saric Arquitectos / **396, 399** © Saunders Architecture / **402** © Fran Silvestre Arquitectos / **408** © Sinas Architects / **416** © SO–IL / **424, 428** © Tetro Arquitetura: Carlos Maia, Debora Mendes, Igor Macedo / **430, 437** © Santiago Valdivieso, Stefano Rolla / **438, 443** © VTN Architects / **444, 449** © Suzuko Yamada Architects / **450** © Young Projects / **458** © Casú Zegers / **464, 470** © Carlos Zwick Architekten BDA

EACH AND EVERY TASCHEN BOOK PLANTS A SEED!

Each year, we offset our annual carbon emissions with carbon credits at the Instituto Terra, a reforestation program in Minas Gerais, Brazil, founded by Lélia and Sebastião Salgado. To find out more about this ecological partnership, please check: www.taschen.com/institutoterra.
Inspiration: unlimited.
Carbon footprint: (almost) zero.

Want to see more? Visit taschen.com to view our current publications, browse our latest magazine, and subscribe to our newsletter.

Hohenzollernring 53, D–50672 Köln
www.taschen.com

Design: Andy Disl, Los Angeles
Layout: Collaborate, London
Collaboration: Harriet Graham, Turin
German translation: Barbara Thoma, Berlin
French translation: Claire Debard, Freiburg

Printed in Bosnia-Herzegovina
ISBN 978-3-8365-9956-6